Deep Feeling, Deep Healing

The Heart, Mind, and Soul
of Getting Well

Andy Bernay-Roman,
LMHC, NCC, MS, CCHT, RN, LMT

Spectrum Healing Press
Jupiter, Florida

Spectrum Healing Press
224 Colony Way West
Jupiter, Florida 33458

"....We can never be born enough. We are human beings;
for whom birth is a supremely welcome mystery,
the mystery of growing:
the mystery which happens only and whenever
we are faithful to ourselves."
                    ---e.e.cummings

∗   ∗   ∗

"Return me to the primal sanity of nature...."
                    ---Walt Whitman

Deep Feeling, Deep Healing

Dedication & Thanks

To my teacher, Maharaji, the kindest, most true-to-the-core person I know. You are my inspiration. I thank you every day.

To my sweetheart and wife, Lynne, with all your love and fire. I cherish you and our partnership.

To my mother, Nora Roman, more than a survivor: for a lifetime of love and care.

To my late father, Paul Roman. It's an honor to be your son. I still miss you dearly.

To my brother, George, who makes me laugh outloud. I still look up to you.

To my daughter, Kaia, a wise, beautiful, and life-affirming human being. I love you more than the sun and the moon!

To my son, Eli, so honorable, heartfelt, and loyal. It's been great growing up with you.

And finally, to my clients, for your relentless commitment to be real and become whole even when it hurts.

Table of Contents

How I Found Mine
Tending the Garden of Mind/Body Health
The Real and the Unreal, The Sane and the Insane
        ***Psychosemantics
Feeling and the Healing System
        ***Farmer Paul
Deep Feeling: the Good, the Bad,the Ugly
        ***Heartbreak
        ***Jens: Cracking the Shell
The Biology of Emotional Integration
Internalized Stressors: Who Needs Therapy?
Why Body-focused Therapy?

The Invisible Factors of Illness and Healing: The Body Follows What
Is In the Heart and Mind
        ***Heart #1
        ***Hearts #2 and #3
One System
        ***Clean Living
The Three Brains of Adam and Eve
The Biology of Memory
Memory and Survival: How Feelings Move or Get Stuck
Beyond Memory: The Past is Present
Our Dual Nature
Body Boundaries
The Emotional Spectrum
The Emotional Environment
Psychoneuroimmunology: the Principles of Mind/Body
Integration

"....Because to feel something is to be alive".
---e.e. cummings

✳✳✳

"All the body senses--seeing, hearing, tasting, feeling, and smelling-- are all connected to emotion. I should say emotion is connected to the senses, because the emotion is the foundation."
---Marlo Morgan
<u>Mutant Message From Forever</u>

✳✳✳

"...feelings are the essential nature of man. They are neither good nor bad, constructive nor destructive.   They are. Being natural is what is intrinsic to all of life....To block any natural process is to set in motion a force towards unification."
---Arthur Janov, Ph.D.

1

Introduction: Feeling and Healing

This Book Is For You

In <u>Deep Feeling, Deep Healing</u> I showcase my own brand of deep feeling body-focused psychotherapy, Centropic Integration, as a path to inner integration, becoming well, and staying well. So if you want to be whole, are in favor of being healthy, and like to synthesize approaches of heart, mind, and body to get there, this book is for you. If you'd like to understand your past with a new sense of finality, bust patterns of dysfunctional behavior, and find personal direction and even destiny in your life, hire me as your therapist.

How I Found My Feelings

My own personal journey into feeling began in the Sixties when I was eighteen and dragged to a weekend T-Group by friends. I assumed we'd be sipping tea and hiking in the woods (hey, anything to get out of the house for a couple of days!), but I was wrong. "T," of course, didn't stand for a beverage, but for therapy. During this unexpected marathon encounter with ten of my peers, I discovered I had feelings. Deep feelings. I cried and laughed. I came alive with a new, giddy sense of myself, and a discovered a raw desire for being intimate with others. My heart awoke from a deep sleep. I got hooked on feeling in a way that has stuck.

I studied psychology in college, but focused outside the classroom on my true passion for getting to core experiences in a wide variety of feeling-centered seminars. I worked assiduously to humanize the over-intellectual education that dominated my school, even bringing in sensitivity trainers from the Esalen Institute in California to help tip the scales more into feeling, touching, and moving. Hearing John Lennon wail out in pain and croon tenderly on his post-Primal Therapy Plastic Ono Band album, affirmed and, confirmed my own quest. I sought out Rolfing™, and discovered the magic of deep memories buried within my body triggered into consciousness through deep tissue manipulation. I immersed myself in a month of intensive inner work at the Gestalt Institute of Canada on Vancouver Island, where, in a group setting, I experienced my first Primal regression during which I relived a painful memory from my infancy. By my senior year, I had become a full-fledged feeling junkie, regularly delving deeper and deeper within myself--in private, with friends, in workshops-- feverishly seeking out some ineffable experience of my origins, my heart, my core, my truth.

After college I taught nursery school in both rural southern Georgia and then Atlanta for a total of twelve years, during which time I came to know the toddler mindset intimately, with all of its intensity, sweetness and vulnerability of heart. I also saw that most kids, by the time they reached three years of age, had already accumulated emotional "baggage". How sobering to see that nobody makes it through unscathed.

When I left daycare and entered the world of intensive care nursing, I encountered not only the other end of the age spectrum, with its complex ego games, defensiveness, isolationism, and vain attempts to control, but also on a larger scale, an entire medical system of dehumanizing trends. In the hospital I repeatedly and consistently witnessed vital human factors like touch, empathy, eye contact, and humor regularly overlooked and ignored--a habit I recognized as both wasteful and counterproductive to healing. For years I worked to integrate the high-touch wisdom I had acquired in massage school into the high-tech ICU to further prove that humanness heals.

After leaving my hospital nursing behind, acquiring a Masters Degree in psychology and setting up a private psychotherapy practice in South Florida, my thirty-three year investigation into the workings of the human heart now includes eleven years as Director of the Psychological Support Department at the Hippocrates Health Institute in West Palm Beach, Florida. At Hippocrates, the world's premiere alternative healing center, famous for its gourmet raw food cuisine, we have learned that it's not just what you eat that makes you well, but finding out "what's eating you."

Finally all aspects of my background, and everything my intuition has guided me towards, have come together into a unified approach to healing, with feelings at the hub. Psyche and soma, married at last.

Tending the Garden of Mental Health

The mind/body system, like a privately cultivated garden, displays the fruition of all the seeds ever planted in it, both wanted and unwanted. Like seeds unwittingly spilled onto the soil, our childhood experiences implant themselves deep within our neural pathways and later dictate the type of people we attract into our lives, how intimately we relate to them, our upper limits of joy and self-expression, and our beliefs about what we do and don't deserve in life.

Without careful maintenance, gardens grow helter skelter. Unpruned vines, bushes, and trees, for example, may display plush greenery but bear little fruit. Conscientious gardeners do it all: prune wild growth, weed out the unwanted, and plant the new. The same applies to therapy. The therapist's tools consist of everything from passive listening to assertive confrontation, from hand-holding to insulting -- whatever it takes to remove obstacles to genuine feelings. Here is the premise of my therapy and this book: by establishing and maintaining an inner environment of personal authenticity and the free-flow of feelings that accompanies it, the healing forces of our natural state can restore us to health. When nature is thwarted and feelings are repressed, we get sick.

Wounded Heart

It is a seed's nature to grow. When it is denied proper soil, sunshine, and water it suffers. When a child's heart is faced with no love or even conditional love, it warps. The child begins to weave unconscious indirect life strategies in order to get her needs met, and a lifestyle of struggle for acceptance and approval takes root. Survival choices and conclusions made in childhood often no longer serve us as adults, but often remain unquestioned and unchallenged deep within our own circuitry, secretly driving our adult behavior. As long we remain in the slumbering domain of a repressed heart, our present continues on as no more than an extension of a limited painful past.

Deep Feeling the Cure

Deep feeling therapy, as opposed to mainstream psychology that emphasizes superficial coping and adapting skills, reaches to the core of the person, grapples with imprinted memories from the past, and finally seeks to re-establish free choice and creativity--all based on rekindling a connectedness to Heart. The buried, forgotten heart is the door to our capacity to feel, which, when unlocked and opened, reinstates sanity and the richness of life. A repressed heart robs the system of vitality and sets the stage for physical disease. A feeling heart, on the other hand, supplies a wellspring for physical healing.

Psychoneuroimmunology and the Goal of Therapy

The thirteen principles of psychoneuroimmunology (the fancy word for "mind/body medicine") I introduce in this book describe how dysfunctional, limiting patterns get wired into our systems, and also suggest how to un-wire them. The goal of therapy, then, is to undergo the psychological equivalent of deep weeding and reseeding, i.e., to disarm the mind/body system's defenses against feeling, and by the very act of deep integrative feeling, re-establish it onto a new, life-affirming, pain-free level of being.

Psychological insight, analysis, drugs, or even emotional catharting do not guarantee freedom from pain. Even the therapies that promise "energetic release" cannot bring about lasting change, just as superficial massage cannot alter structural defects. Feelings that exist at the very core of the mind/body system must be involved in order for permanent healing to take place. This inevitably includes pain, a central topic of this book.

Homeostasis and Pain

The mind/body system operates with a homeostatic mechanism that is set to maintain and protect the status quo. It will automatically, without conscious thought or intent, split, repress, and encapsulate painful experiences in order to keep them out of consciousness. The closer a person comes to feeling pain, the more these defenses kick in to buffer the blow, and hide the pain. Fortunately, the human system also contains hard-wired directives to integrate experience. Most people know at an instinctive level that by continuing to repress those experiences that needed to be shut out of consciousness as a child, they are hindering their advancement into adulthood. They come to therapy to undo the past, only to find themselves reliving it. But this time with full feeling.

The focus of my work goes deeper than mainstream therapy's obsession with coping, adapting, or even "release". Complete integration directly requires frustrating the patient's current coping methods, forging through layers of inevitable confusion and defenses, until finally reaching a deep feeling level and draining it of stored pain. Far from the orthodox approach!

An accomplished therapist, like a double agent, brings an olive branch of loving acceptance and support in one hand, and a knife of decisive challenge in the other. He has to be willing to engage in, figuratively speaking, ruthless hand-to-hand combat with the dysfunctional aspects of the client, while at the same time helping to lay the foundation for self-acceptance and serenity. Deep feeling is the key.

Deep feeling therapy has a light side too. It focuses on the funny, the sweet, and the silly. Even though therapy is serious business, without this element of humor, it would be morbid. Interspersed throughout this book are vignettes that demonstrate the absurdities that have naturally cropped up during therapy sessions I've conducted.

Feeling Is Our Healing Destiny

I hope that reading this book makes you thirsty for inner development and discovery of your own depths, for true relationship and intimacy, and all the other good heart-infused stuff that belongs in every life. How ironic it is when we humans, with our noble lineage, end up panhandling for love in the streets. We press our noses up against the banquet hall window to drool over the majestically laid table inside, not realizing the table has been set for us, the meal prepared in our honor! And if you feel that any of the above are missing in your life, know that you at least have the raw material for fulfillment, no matter how arid your past. I believe that the heart's fulfillment is a part of the sacred inheritance of being a human being. It belongs to you, and you can have it.

I can't impress upon you enough the importance of a holistic approach to health, and that being in touch with feelings, the crux of what it is to be human, is the key to getting and staying well. Neither disease nor health occur in an impersonal vacuum, but rather are brewed in the cauldron of our personhood. Our thoughts and feelings play a decisive role in our manifest destiny. The feeling heart alone unlocks this proper destiny.

The Real And the Unreal,
The Sane and the Insane

At an international gathering of religious scholars and seekers of many denominations and sects from many countries, the question of reality was hotly debated. Some said that because of the ephemeral, impermanent nature of things, the world was essentially unreal. Some claimed that because of the abiding nature of ideas and values, and the continuity of humanity, the world was essentially real. Finally, the group turned to an elderly Zen monk who had been sitting silently.

"Do you, sir, find the world to be real?", they asked him.

"Yes," he replied.

"In what sense of the word 'real'?", they went on to ask.

"In all senses," he replied.

****

We live in two worlds: the Real and the Unreal, one that we are part of and the other we project out as an extension of our inner life, or inner world. One is Actual, the other is Virtual.

The Real World is the world of Nature. We are real when we are true to our real feeling nature. The Unreal is the world of our own inner mapping, with all its flawed conclusions, judgements, role requirements, expectations, notions of correct and incorrect behavior--in short, the arbitrary world we create and shape by our beliefs, assumptions, values, and culture. The difference between the unreality of the individual psychotic's world and the unreality of the collective unreal world is agreement, not substance or validity.

What is an "Unreal world"? Isn't that harsh language to use, if we're just talking about a little projection? Beyond benevolent projection, an unreal world is a place where needs are denied. Where the fundamental unity of life on earth and our interdependence is denied. Where the heart remains ignored or forgotten.

It is a world where striving and doing overshadow being. Where feelings and pain are guarded against and seen as weak. Where repressed needs for human contact emerge in sexual perversion and hostility. Where men and women relate in a battle mode. Where money supersedes humanity. Where in the face of an abundance of food and resources, people go hungry and unsheltered. Where substance abuse is rampant at all ages and levels of society. Where countries wage war and successfully dehumanize the enemy to do so. Where human rights violations go unchallenged. Where a legal system varies with ability to pay.

We live in an unreal world steeped in unconsciousness and repressed pain. Repression may, as Arthur Janov suggested, be necessary for personal survival through the early stages of development, but becomes the very thing that propels us towards self-destruction as adults, keeping the world unreal, and insane.

The unreal world is not unique to modern times. As long as there has been repression there has been an unreal world. Freud said we needed repression to have civilization--that without it, the raw, animal-istic, hedonistic forces of the Id would devour us. The unreal world has been with us for hundreds of years, and remains the price we pay for "civilization".

How to be real in an unreal world is a damn good question, and those who don't ask it may need the most help of all--because it means their personal Unreal Systems (the system of self-image, the sense of self based on repression of feelings) dominates their consciousness.

Repression begins as a response to a cramped psychological and feeling space, and results in inner tensions and anxieties that tend to cramp the psychological and emotional space of others. What we re-press in ourselves we tend to repress in our children. What we deem unacceptable and unlovable in ourselves, we project out onto others, either onto individuals or onto groups. Hence the chain of pain that binds humanity.

True to the Core

To be real and sane in an unreal, insane world is an act of re-sponsibility, and takes a commitment to the core Real Self. "True to the core" is an attitude and a commitment. It means being faithful to the real self, the essential being, the original simplicity and authenticity within each of us. We adore babies because there has as yet been no variance from that pure essence, no disparity between the outside tran-quil appearance and demeanor of the child and the essential peaceful nature of the child's inner experience. Children tend to be honest, because they are being true to their nature.

Because we are a part of Nature, in essence we are natural. Of all the species on the planet, only humans have the capacity to drift away from their natural selves. Historically, that Natural Self has been considered essentially one of sin--a fallen state as it were. I believe we fall from an original state of wholeness and purity, and with an attitude and commitment to be "true to the core" we can regain our wholeness.

To be aligned with nature is to be healthy. Mind/body science now tells us that an inner state of congruence, or alignment with being real, being true to the core of oneself stands central to our well-being. What keeps us from being real and sets us drifting away from a core sense of integrity or wholeness is pain. More specifically, it is our defenses against pain that shut us off from feeling, and thus from our connection to our core. Core therapy helps in the process of reclaiming our essential real nature. Reaching through our pain becomes the path of reconnecting with essence.

Our brain's tri-fold nature, a product of eons of evolution, leaves us with three brains, each with its own specific ways of organizing information, storing memory, and responding to pain. Any path towards wholeness, including therapy, must deal with this triune nature of man, otherwise the core remains untouched. This book focuses on practical methods of accessing these three-brain aspects of our being for the sake of becoming whole and true to our core once more.

"True to the core" also means righteous, like "true blue". In Buddhism, those who walk The Dharma, the path of righteousness, overcome the wheel of returning karma, or patterns of debt. Whatever unfinished business from our past we carry within recreates itself into new entanglements and struggles. By remaining true to the core and journeying to the center of our feelings we can correct past karma, and unravel ourselves from the fabric of emotional debt. Only then can we live in the moment unfettered by the chain of pain.

Real is something we're born with, our innate nature. Therefore it remains retrievable despite years and years of disconnected living. That's good news. Whatever was done can be undone, and what hasn't been done yet, can be done now.

We only need to be willing to pass through the gateway of our own repressed pain in order to reach the valley of the Real. Deep feeling therapy extends that invitation to become real and return to primal sanity.

"There is only one thing in this world that can tell you when something is real, and that is your heart...it is through feeling that the heart knows."

-----Maharaji

Psychosemantics

When I was a young man and in the enchantment of a new love, a challenging moment impressed upon me the absolute reality of how the words we use with one another can render a direct response in the physical body. When emotions run high, the effect can be dramatic.

I met long-haired, dreamy-eyed Leah at a housewarming party I was throwing to celebrate the purchase of my new home. She had tagged along to the party with a hospital co-worker friend of mine who introduced us. Leah handed me a bouquet of irises, and said in a sincere tone, " Thanks for having me at your party, and congratulations on your new home." No one had ever given me flowers before. I fell in love with her on the spot. Before the evening festivities were over I asked Leah if she'd like to get together for lunch the next day.

"Sure. Come over to my place and I'll make you pesto and hand-made buckwheat noodles." We ended up spending the day together, and the next day, too. We talked freely, laughed a lot, and melted into a comfortable fit. That weekend we went camping and set up our tent next to a waterfall an hour north of town, and that night we snuggled. The glow of our feelings kept us as warm as the fire.

As the weeks went by, Leah and I spent more and more time together, and I really felt like we were in the process of becoming an "item," but something was lacking inside me. I couldn't tell if Leah's feelings were the same as mine. Did she just like my company in a platonic way, without any desire to be in relationship?

One evening as we sat by my fireplace, Leah started getting up to go home, and I really wanted her to stay. "Leah," I said with all the passion of my desire, "I want you to know I really like you. I want us to be in a relationship. I really want something to break open at a heart level between us." Leah hugged me and mumbled something before leaving, without directly addressing my gush of feelings. I felt raw and open and yearning.

At three a.m. I awoke with dull and constant chest pains, and a layman's bout of denial. It's just indigestion, I rationalized. At 6 a.m. my pain was at a holding level of 3 on a scale of 1-10. I went to work anyway. Finally, just before lunch, when my chest pain spontaneously reached a level "5," I confided my condition to one of my fellow ICU nurses.

"Don't be a fool, Andy! You're in the ICU! What better place to be checked out." She took my hand and escorted me down to the "cath" lab to get a 12-lead EKG, and to be checked by the resident cardiologist. They took my blood to see if I had elevated cardiac enzymes, and even gave me a thallium stress test, monitoring my heart while I ran a treadmill. In the meantime, after looking over my EKG, the cardiologist called to prepare the catheterization room, and put the OR on notice. I quietly freaked out.

My enzyme test came back negative, so although my EKG showed some irregularity, they ruled out a heart attack. That's when they threw in a MUGA scan just to get a picture of my heart muscle in action. My true condition revealed itself.

"Andy, this is strange," the cardiologist said, viewing the films of my heart muscle contracting in bright red and green contrasting images before him. "Look closely at this." He pointed to a section just above the mitral valve. "See that little appendage flapping in the wind? It seems that a few strands of the tiny tendons that support your mitral valve broke loose, probably around the time you woke up in the middle of the night. Somebody been plucking at your heart strings?" he added lightheartedly.

I'm convinced my feelings of unrequited love and my declaration of "wanting something to break open at a heart level" translated from emotion to physical reality that night. The next time I saw Leah, I felt the chest pain again, elevating from a level "2" to about a "4." Leah didn't want me the way I wanted her, and that hurt--physically.

I eventually got over her, and my heart mended. Ever since, I've been very careful about how I phrase my expressions of love. I make sure there are no destructive implications. You can't be too careful when it comes to the mind/body connection!

Feeling and the Healing System

"I want you to go into my patient's room. Don't look at her chart or anything, and then tell me what body system is causing trouble." This was a colleague's challenge to me one slow evening in the Intensive Care Unit of the hospital where I worked. A good ICU nurse, just by paying attention to clues in speech and attitude for a few minutes, can pinpoint whether a patient's physical problems are gastrointestinal, cardiovascular, or neurological. No sweat.

"Let's see. This person is really really nice. She would have allowed me to do any test on her without asking what it was. She focused on me, and made me feel good. This person had cancer surgery, right?" BINGO!

ICU nurses, by raw exposure to people, know that certain personality types seem to match certain diseases, or that certain personality types tend to be associated with various body systems. Science hasn't yet narrowed it down to specifics in determining which personalities go with what system, but Louise Hay, author of You Can Heal Your Life, a pioneer in this field, has done a phenomenal job of creating a map. The link between illness and personality is a major breakthrough in how we look at disease and treatment. Can every illness have a psychosomatic component to it? Can every illness therefore benefit from a particular attitudinal treatment plan?

The field of mind/body medicine continues to grow. New books on the subject find their way into bookstores regularly, some riding the wave of the "alternative" trend (but filled with fluff), and others offering genuine practical applications for healing. One of the better books in my opinion, Remarkable Recovery, by Caryle Hirschberg and Marc Ian Barasch, highlights the phenomenon of spontaneous healings, and investigates the rare "hopeless cases" of the medical world in which the patient somehow miraculously recuperates against all the odds. The authors had the courage to ask if these healings could have come from something outside the strict medical model. (A joke: what's the medical definition of a spontaneous remission? Misdiagnosis!)

Though common threads become apparent when reading the stories of spontaneous remission, there is no single or simple formula. The path to healing unfolds as uniquely as the history that leads up to the disease. What stands out most in healing anecdotes is the part the mind and emotions play in both the development and course of the disease, and in the healing as well. Hirschberg and Barasch concluded that the patient's <u>congruence</u>, that is, alignment and attunement with her inner world of feelings and beliefs, play a central role in remarkable recoveries. The body follows what is in the heart and mind in both illness and in cure.

In my Intensive Care nursing days, I had a reputation for working well with the "wacky" or eccentric patients. I didn't mind the "extra baggage" involved in caring for these people, and in fact, relished discovering the method in their madness. I believed that if I could only "trick" them within their own framework of thinking or believing into undoing the anti-life messages that blocked recovery, healing would follow. Without those blocks, the natural and predominant impulse towards health would take over. (See next page for story about Farmer Paul)

Doctors today postulate that the body contains an inherent healing system far beyond the sole workings of the immune system. This healing blueprint uses information from every subsystem, and maintains connection and communication via the nervous system and the hormonal system--feedback mediated by the patient's feelings and inner images. What we are experiencing, including our thoughts and emotions, influences our health directly. How we construct our world experientially, i.e., how we process the information of each moment, what we make of each event and experience, directly influences the effectiveness of the healing system. If the body follows what is in the heart and the mind, then we potentially carry the most potent of medicines (and the most potent of poisons) around within us. Science affirms this. When our emotions trigger a cascade of brain endorphins, the natural pain killers that yield a sense of well-being, the end result is a calm, life-affirming one. When our emotions consistently trigger the release of stress hormones, designed to keep our system alert in times of emergency, the net result is life-negating and sets the stage for disease. Our emotional tone directly influences the sum total of all biochemical processes.

Farmer Paul

One of the "eccentrics" to come into our unit was a man named Paul, a retired farmer of 72, gaunt in face and stature and with close-cropped disheveled hair, from south Georgia, who was having a hard time being in the city, let alone in the hospital. He was in with acute pneumonia, and coughed up bloody sputum.

"I just can't take it, " he kept muttering to himself. "I just won't be well till I get home." Upon being faced with the information from the doctors that he wouldn't be going home till he was well (and none of them believed he could get well), Paul concluded he would never leave the hospital. His view that doctors knew best confirmed his doom. He sequenced his road to wellness as "home first, then well". The hospital's version was "get well first, then go home." When I went in to chat with him he was lamenting his mantra, "I just can't take it", over and over.

" Paul, don't you want to get well?" I asked him.

"Sure I do, but how'm I gonna get home?"

"Well, if it was up to you, would you go home to get well?"

"Yeah, sure."

"Well, what's your choice then? The doctors say you can't go home till you get well. They know best, right?"

"Well they are more educated than me, but I know I can't take it in here. I won't get well here."

"So what's your choice?"

"Well, I choose to get well no matter what the doctors say!" And he got pissed. His mantra changed to "I choose to get well", and he kept on chanting that for the next three days. Nurses who went to see him or even just walked by the room, rolled their eyes as they heard his new chant, and said, "Andy's been in to see old Paul," and they just sighed.

Three days later Paul transferred out of our unit to a regular hospital room, and a week later, went home. He had broken through a belief system that kept him doomed, and had tapped into inner resources that permitted his healing system to dominate unimpeded. His original beliefs could have killed him, and instead he changed his mind and changed his destiny.

Scientists have found that the physical unit of memory, the messenger molecule called the neuropeptide, harbors a biochemical code (an imprinted version of every physical, emotional, and mental response we've ever had) that is linked to a vast network of receptor sites that exist on cell walls throughout the tissue of the body. All day this network of shifting molecules tirelessly responds to electrochemical triggers via the nervous and hormonal systems, touching and mediating every single biochemical process within the body, all the while generating an inner "map" out of our impressions that is designed to help us make sense of our experience and get our needs met. When asleep, our senses are withdrawn from the outside world, and we lay immersed in virtual reality. We call that "nocturnal map" a dream. Our responses to those inner-generated images are as real as the ones to outer objects or events. What makes us think that just because our eyes are open during the day that we're not generating hologramic versions of what's occurring? We are awake and dreaming, each one of us in every moment generating our unique inner version of the world, each using the palate of sensory engagement and past memory to paint our unique version of "reality".

In the waking state we call this map the mind. Some elements of this map potentially set the stage for disruptive life-negating disease processes, and some elements help us get well. Either way, the mind, as a by-product of neuropeptide activity, directly influences the central integrity of the physical system.

So what's the formula? Are positive thinking, "good" emotions, and relaxing imagery (the holy trinity of the relaxation response) the cure? Unfortunately, it isn't that simple, because the mind, as a self-fulfilling structure within which bodily reality flows, is not changed by conscious mental effort alone. It takes immersion into deep feelings to crack open our old maps and break the hold of outdated, unhealthy systems of belief. Deep feelings, reflecting a state of whole-brain operation, serve as the integrative forces within the body that set the stage for healing. This is the foundation of deep feeling therapy.

Positive thinking and emotions, as well as relaxing imagery, naturally follow in the wake of deep feeling exploration, but without it, they do not carry the necessary life-force to overcome disease. For Farmer Paul, changing his beliefs, making a new choice, getting upset, all fueled a natural healing response in his body.

What exactly is the difference in meaning between belief and truth, and which should we work with in our efforts to further healing? You might philosophically answer that beliefs aren't necessarily true, and therefore aren't worth looking at. Or you might say that beliefs are merely a form of subjective truth and therefore not as potent as THE truth. These subtle interpretations don't exist in the body, however, for it responds to beliefs as though they are truth. Beliefs are the body's truth, which means they are crucial to the healing system. Some beliefs further and some hinder healing.

A large number of people were tested for their ability to throw basketball free- throw shots, and then they were divided into three sub-groups to be measured again in three months' time. One section practiced free-throw shooting every day for one half hour. Another had nothing to do with basketball for the entire time. The third division sat quietly each day for half an hour imagining themselves practicing free-throw shots. The results showed the two groups that either practiced in actuality or in imagination both significantly improved over the group that did nothing. In changing our inner reality we directly influence results in the outer physical world.

Deep Feeling: the Good, the Bad, the Ugly

*"And here am I, patiently squeezing four dimensional ideas
into a two-dimensional stage."*
---e.e.cummings

The feeling dimension is what makes us human. Unlike Sigmund Freud's notion that the deep recesses of the Unconscious contain a myriad of antisocial, unacceptable demons, what I have discovered beneath the layers of the persona looks more like repressed kid stuff, which, when appropriately evoked and raised into consciousness, can become the most potent of inner resources. It's good stuff. Very good stuff. Suffering is the result of not feeling.

"I'm so glad I can feel!" one of my teary-eyed clients said after a wrenching bout of sobbing. "It makes sense to me now. All my anxiety was nothing more than tears trying to surface, and now they're here. Thank God!" Feeling, even feeling "bad," affirms the aliveness of the heart. Few people realize that acknowledged "uncomfortable" or painful feelings are a gateway to a depth not otherwise easily accessed. The fight against depression, for instance, often causes it to persist, whereas a nonresistant descent into pain is the shortest path to relief.

Anger has gotten a bad rap, mainly because it is often misplaced. Anger has the potential to mobilize the system for profound change. When gasoline that has been spilled randomly is ignited, it creates a fire bomb, but gasoline sparked in the controlled environment of an internal combustion engine uses the explosive force to propel the object forward. Think of therapy as that engine.

As for pain, we expend a lot of energy avoiding it, dispelling it, squelching it, hiding it, and killing it. The human body produces its own natural endorphin painkillers, as do all vertebrates on the planet. Pain repression has endured over millennia because of its vital role to survival. Nonetheless, after years of working with critically ill people, in Intensive Care units, alternative healing centers, and hospices, I'm convinced that repressed pain lies at the root of disease. I'm also convinced that removing the blocks to feeling, and then integrating the pain, marks the most direct route to reestablishing the biological grounds for healing in the body. These so-called "invisible factors" of thought and feeling are key to influencing the physical condition.

The first rule is to stop denying that the pain exists. Stop pretending, and get real. Over and over in newly formed support groups, sessions that start out as chatty and superficial soon travel deeper towards a feeling core, delving into expressions of genuine loss, caring, and despair. The same is true of one-on-one therapy. The urge to be whole, to be real, and to feel, like a dormant seed thirsting for water, creates its own momentum, and once initiated, hopefully carries the patient into the realm of health.

When a psychologist told me years ago that "the Unconscious is dangerous, leave it alone," it sounded like demonology to me. The Unconscious contains all the information we've hidden from our awareness, not only the destructive, negative feelings, but also the more tender and vulnerable feelings of need and affection. Stuffing those feelings prevents growth. Only when repressed feelings surface do their positive aspects manifest and take their place as living parts of our psyche.

Heartbreak

Once when I worked in a hospital ICU, I had as a patient a teenage boy with severe pneumonia. His condition quickly plummeted to the point of needing mechanical ventilator support, and because each lung was infected with a different strain of bacteria, we hooked him to two respirators! He looked like the victim of a mad scientist's cruel experiment. His parents wore their despair and worry like a shroud, having lost their only other son two years earlier in a freak canoeing accident. They sat in the hospital room night and day, and as his condition worsened they became more sallow, sullen, and downcast. Finally, after weeks of medical and personal efforts on all our parts, their son died. We all felt devastated. At the funeral a few days later, I came face to face with the boy's mother. I felt awkward, knowing I couldn't possibly address the level of her anguish and loss, and that any words out of my mouth would just fall flat. Looking me deep in the eyes, she grasped my hand, and thanked me for caring for her son till the end. She then said something to me I've cherished over the years: "I don't know why this has happened to me in my life. I am so beyond tears and 'grief'... I'm hardly in this world anymore. **I think God sometimes uses heartbreak to take us to deep places inside we wouldn't go to on our own**".

The Biology of Emotional Integration

When I was two years old, I threw all my toys, one by one, off the balcony adjoining my bedroom and in that act discovered the joy of relieving myself of excess baggage. That principle has guided my life, and has also been incorporated into my therapy practice.

I frequently revert to this desire to relieve myself of burdens, to simplify my world and return to the core of my self-contained, independent heart. I see my clients do the same. We feel impelled to return to core feelings, core simplicity, core knowledge of our existence and the natural world. This is the journey to the center that deep feeling therapy facilitates.

I call my work Centropic Integration. Centropic means "natural movement towards the center". Presented with a safe atmosphere and an attentive listener who encourages self-reflection, patients naturally begin to go within, a process I call the centropic journey™. Repressed feelings emerge along the way. I discovered this healing sequence and process of inner release when working with ICU patients whose life-threatening encounters with illness shocked them into a natural regression that often facilitated a healing. I concluded that the body WANTS to integrate at the feeling level.

I learned during the process that old nonintegrated feelings dominate the feeling landscape because they NEED to be integrated. They continue to color everything in the present and influence every interaction. Repressed pain robs us of our capacity for joy. Repressed sadness and anger transform into depression or some other form of inner isolation.

Jens

Jens, a lanky, childishly blond-haired 73-year-old man of Swedish descent, found himself in my ICU after years of being a smoker and ongoing bouts with emphysema. His lungs had deteriorated in recent months, and he was so short of breath that he needed IV and respiratory support just short of being hooked to a ventilator. Jens was in shock.

"I just can't believe I'm really here. People warned me and I just never believed it could happen to me." He spiraled into a depression. One evening I entered Jen's room to find him crying. I assumed his tears were his feelings of overwhelm at the worsening of his condition finally catching up with him and surpassing his many years of successful denial. I was right, but even more than I knew.

"Poor Alex," he kept repeating with tear-filled eyes.

"Who's Alex?" I asked.

"Alex is my dog. He's my best friend." Jens cooed in a voice uninhibited and soft---like that of a young boy.

"Tell me about Alex," I said, sitting at the bedside.

"I've had Alex since he was a little puppy. I found him. Father said I couldn't keep him, but Mother said it was OK. He's my best friend." More tears.

"What's happened to Alex?" I ask.

"We're out for a walk, right by our house, and I'm watching Alex run---he's a happy dog. I see him run past the curb, into the street. I see him get hit by the car. I hear the loud bump and I hear his wild yelp of pain. I run over to him. He's twitching and blood is coming out of his nose and ears." Jen's tears are flowing over his cheeks.

"Don't die, Alex, don't die. You're my best friend." Jens moans and rocks, propped up by his pillows in bed, as if he's rocking the dog in his lap.

"I can't save him. Why can't I save him? He's my friend." Finally, Jens drifts off to sleep.

Although there's a great parallel between his helpless feelings at the death of his dog many years ago (it turns out this happened when Jens was eleven), and his current situation, his tears were not symbolic or metaphorical. He was really crying for his loss of his puppy sixty-two years ago! Jen's style as a person had been one of stoicism and denial, and it took the severity and surprise of being in the ICU to break through an iron wall of defenses to his own feelings. When he did, the feelings rushed forward into consciousness as intact as the day he first repressed them!

I began to see how the hidden dynamics of feeling memory storage directly influence life dramas in the present.

Later, Jens talked with me about his experience. "I could never feel my feelings in my house. My father just said 'good riddance' about Alex. He had no sympathy for me, and even my mother down-played my sense of loss. I think she was trying to protect me. There was no one there for me, so I've hidden it all. I guess I just can't do that any more--even if I try, it seems!"

Jens navigated the flare-up of old feelings in a positive way. He softened and opened to them and to others around him. He let his family's caring penetrate his stoic shell. Funny how allowing oneself to feel pain halts suffering.

Not everyone embraces emerging feelings in such a self-transforming way. When feelings arise initially as tension or nervousness, people tend to escalate the level of defense or distraction to match the rising tide. I have often seen patients lash out at the care giver or family as a way of coping with their fears. Dr. Elizabeth Kubler-Ross identified anger as a normal manifestation of the death and dying/grieving process. Nevertheless, it remains a defense, thus overshadowing a deeper process of integration demanding to happen.

Our first inclination as care givers may be to try to make patients feel better, to cheer them up in the face of their emerging pain, but this goes against the biology of integration. Painful memories enter consciousness in order to be integrated, to relieve the mind/body system of the burden of inner secrets. Nonintegrated experiences remain encapsulated in body tissue (my guess is somewhere near the neuropeptide receptor site intended for healthy memory storage), waiting to reveal themselves and be fully absorbed into ongoing reality. When we resist these emergent feelings, either through repression or distraction, they persist in their mounting urgency to release. Ironically, by allowing these fragments from the past to be integrated into the present, they lose their hold on us, and we no longer unconsciously act them out or attract their negativity. Repressed feelings become "shit magnets," and answer the question, "Why is this happening to me again?"

Centropic Integration is about a return to the heart, meaning both the rediscovery of the heart with the help of therapy, and a return to the heart of therapy itself. Jens experienced the biology of integration, a process compelled and directed by natural forces. Any therapy that goes against the tide of these biological currents of emergent feeling fragments from the past misses the true thrust of healing, and can even impede it. In being present for Jens therapeutically, it was also important for me to stay out of his way.

What does it mean, returning to the heart? Isn't the heart where most human problems arise, where hurt feelings are stored? Doesn't the heart manufacture the cloud of subjectivity that makes us so unhappy? Wouldn't it be easier to become more rational and learn to cope better with what we can't control? The answer is yes to all those questions. But there is more.

The heart functions as a vessel of feeling and love. It is a wellspring of caring and empathy. Without it, our mundane "objective" functioning world remains lifeless in rote activity and duty. Without heart, people focus on the empty pursuits of money, sex, power, and fame to make them feel alive. A country philosopher commented on those substitutes for love in this way: "They is what they is, but they c'aint be what they ain't." Without heart people lack meaning, purpose, or direction.

For all the irrationality that surrounds feelings, they still make sense. Rooted in the biology of need, feelings extend outward from the human heart to touch the world in a way that says "yes". Even with the most flagrantly hallucinating schizophrenics I have encountered, who spoke in seeming riddles, the feelings at the core of those deeply en-crypted expressions were completely understandable. No matter whether I am listening to the image-laden language of the schizophrenic or the crisp theoretical language of the icy intellectual, the heart re-mains simple and direct. My job is to help my patient return to that simplicity.

I have worked with an incredibly diverse group of people, in-cluding astronauts, movie stars, artists, call girls, blue collar workers, and geniuses--and what they all share is heart. At the human need level, we all stand naked. The ignored heart remains at the core of disease, and the reclaimed heart remains at the core of healing. With all the 12-step recovery programs now in effect, has anyone focused on the recov-ery of the heart?

There is a trend afoot, espoused by the rational-emotive school of therapy, with the premise that irrational thinking lies at the root of our suffering, and therefore simply by changing our thoughts we can make ourselves be happy. Even this approach can have heart, because gentler, non-crisis thinking emerges from the heart-space. Positive think-ing is the flowers, and the heart is the vase. Presenting someone with flowers calls for them to bring forth an appropriate container. Mental re-framing, although purely cognitive, can still issue an appeal to the heart to come alive and embrace life. On the other hand, positive think-ing or affirmations, done to repress painful feelings, become agents of suffering. (The story on page 251, "The Power of Positive Loving," provides an example.)

The good news is that heart as a quality transcends any particu-lar therapeutic school of thought. I have witnessed heartfelt psychoana-lysts and even heartfelt strict behaviorists in action. Conversely, I've met many clinicians with an expert ability to diagnose and explain symptoms who have perpetuated paralysis-by-analysis in the name of therapy.

How can you tell if your therapist has heart? Does it mean he or she is nice to you? Nice is not the measure of heart. Heart is honest and real. Honest enough to detect bullshit. And real enough to let you have your own pain, and move at your own pace to your destination. Heart embraces and shelters as it makes room for natural growth and development. Heart lets you be, except when you are faking. Heart invites you to be real, even if it hurts initially. Heart shows up as a fellow human, vulnerable and strong. Heart is the home for healing.

Internalized Stressors:
Who Needs Therapy?

With the introduction of the phrase "stress reduction" in the 1970s, and with the subsequent incorporation of that expression into our language by the 1980s, it has become all too apparent that reducing external stress factors in our lives is a good idea when creating strategies for better living. We generally seek out stress-free places for vacation, and we pace ourselves in job, home, relationships, childcare, and leisure, with the intention of staying out of the dreaded burnout stress zone.

Scientific studies over the past decade link lifestyle stress with diminished immune response, accelerated tumor growth, and decreased absorption of nutrients. But what about stress responses that seem to be independent of external circumstances, such as upsets and interpersonal discord that occur even when we're on vacation and at our most relaxed? And what about stress responses like panic attacks or negative "self-talk" that occur when we're alone, and seem to be self-induced?

To the body, stress is stress, whether it is externally or internally generated. As a therapist, I am more interested in the internally-generated stressors, because they pollute the inner landscape of well-being and consistently result in making the outer world a trigger for unhappiness. Outer stressors we can avoid, but we carry inner stressors wherever we go.

Based on a psychoneuroimmunology-based principle that what's out there goes in, and what's in there comes out again (that is: how learned behavior becomes a map for future interaction), internally generated stressors originate externally, and then are internalized. And just as external stressors can be eliminated by external changes, internalized stressors can be eliminated by internal changes. Deep-feeling therapy seeks to uproot these internalized sources of "poison." Good weeding requires pulling every weed, root and all.

An external event becomes an internalized or imprinted one when the body's response ingrains itself in the emotional memory of the person. From an anatomical point of view, emotions play the role of a tagging mechanism, flagging any experiences that need to be stored in memory with a high charge. Emotions associated with painful events help keep the body alert for similar threat or harm. In the case of positive experiences, emotions trigger and ingrain in memory an endorphin response to reinforce pleasurable or need-fulfilling experiences. Emotions provide a gut-level recognition of what is good and bad, what is to be avoided and what is to be sought out.

Anthony Robbins, self-help and personal transformation guru, suggests that people base their actions more on the avoidance of pain than on the pursuit of pleasure. Rather than being ruled by the Pleasure Principle of the Id, or the Reality Principle of the Ego, as Freud maintained, I believe we are ruled by the Avoidance-of-Pain Principle of the Body. Because painful experiences are tagged for self-protection by being stored with a high emotional charge in the memory system, and because pain must be avoided, conflicting forces of store it vs. stay away from it are resolved by the innate ability of the organism to do both at once The memory splits into fragments--literally. We are responding to stress in the present through fragmented memory circuits. For an incest survivor, for example, sexual encounters or even ordinary sexual feelings can trigger the emergency body-response from yesteryear and render an essentially harmless event a catastrophe. Stored pain robs us of joy.

The central approach in therapy, therefore, must be to take pain out of storage, even if it hurts. We are led to believe from recent scientific articles that emotional memory cannot be erased, only re-framed. But keeping pain in storage, that is, repressed from consciousness, keeps the re-framing process from happening. The only way to make a ceramic vase is to first put the lump of clay onto the potter's wheel. It serves no purpose sitting in the bin. Dealing with trauma only cognitively is the equivalent of discussing the theory and origins of clay without digging into the clay bin. Intellectual discussion cannot produce a real vessel. Talk therapy alone cannot heal real wounds.

Uprooting internalized pain means reversing the body's own mechanism of imprinting, by tracking down and eliciting the initial elements of trauma before they were fragmented by a survival response. Contained within pain is the magnet that draws the splintered memory bits together, and ultimately, the glue that reconnects them.

To feel childhood pain in its original format neutralizes the organismic "need" to avoid situations or persons that evoke that pain. Very simple logic, no? Feeling childhood painful experiences doesn't necessarily mean regressing to childhood, because the fact is that a non-integrated, repressed childhood memory rarely feels like something that happened long ago. It just never went away. It would more than likely feel like current reality, because it has become so deeply woven into the fabric of our adult experience that it may not even be recognizable as childhood pain any longer. But childhood pain it is, nonetheless. I haven't met anyone yet who has not carried some pain from the past into the present, and who also hasn't lost some degree of pristine enjoyment of the present because of it. Once that pain is revealed, all the associated conclusions about self and reality are loosened, and the possibility for joy reemerges.

In that regard everyone needs therapy. Like a hairy dog picking up unwanted burrs and thorns in a field of brambles, we, too, just from being in a world of human interactions, inevitably pick up and carry within our psyche inhibiting notions about what is real and true that prevent us from fully responding to the moment. Therapy serves as a thorough "comb-out" of limiting beliefs, from the superficial to those more deeply entangled in our intimate sense of self.

The knotted hair of the dog has to be cut, which will initially leave the dog's coat scraggly and irregular, but in the long run cutting out the burrs will bring out the creature's innate beauty. Hopefully, the stigma that used to be attached to therapy and counseling are gone for good, so that all of us can shine.

Why Body-Focused Psychotherapy?

Reflecting the growing mind/body interface that exists between medicine, bodywork, and psychology, body-focused psychotherapy emerges as a new approach, using the tools and wisdom of all three. Quite simply, it combines physical and psychological processes conjointly for therapeutic purposes. Although psychotherapists are technically more concerned with the wholeness of the psyche, and not the body, direct hands-on contact or body-awareness techniques often further psychological process. Despite the taboo on touching in mainstream psychology, I am convinced that appropriate and well-timed use of touch enhances the transference process, quickens inner processing, and provides corrective emotional experiences. My reasoning is based on the simple principle that because the body's physiological response is central to a person's overall response to trauma, so too must the body be involved in the therapeutic healing of such trauma---something that "talk therapy" alone cannot adequately address.

Because of the paradigm-shifting breakthrough work of psychoimmunologists like Candace Pert, Ph.D., this interdisciplinary approach to therapy has been raised a few notches above the esoteric pseudo-science realm it used to be relegated to, and directly into the rational world of clinical and experimental understanding. The psychoneuroimmunology movement, although still in its scientific infancy, has conclusively demonstrated the existence within the body of an intricate messenger molecule network that binds the nervous system, including the brain, the endocrine system, and the immune system into a single, fluid, emotion-modulated entity. The peptide molecules of emotion serve as biological mediators, not only of all the biochemical processes, but also of all human experiences. The mind, as it turns out, resides in the body, and is not localized to the brain.

Ever since Renee Descartes, the philosopher central to 17th Century Europe's scientific awakening, negotiated his turf deal with the Church to separate soul from body (he agreed that science would not challenge the notion of the Divine), these two aspects of the human being have been pushing to reunite. The same is happening in the world of psychotherapy. The movement to re-somatize, or re-embody, the mind, initially started with Wilheim Reich's psychodynamic model of the early 20th Century. Reichian therapists see the body's musculature as mirroring psychological defense mechanisms. Repeated protective muscular contractions in the face of emotional trauma freeze the body/ mind system into what Reich called "body and character armoring". His approach to healing involved direct hands-on contact with the supine client, deep breathing, and abreaction that all combine to simultaneously loosen both sets of armor. Today, this body-oriented approach finds rationale and support from within such diverse fields as neurology, acupuncture and Oriental medicine, as well as major schools of psychotherapy.

Some body-oriented psychotherapies may dispense with hands-on contact and instead may focus on reflecting the client's awareness to posture or movement in order to personalize psychological insight. All embrace the notion of internalized blocked physical energy that produces tension and anxiety, thus blocking awareness. The goal of body-oriented psychotherapy is the gradual unraveling and direct release of both physical and psychological aspects of these life-negating barriers, a healthy integration of the past into the present, and a return to the normal uninhibited state.

Examples of body-oriented psychotherapy include: Somatic Trauma Therapy™ as practiced by Babette Rothchild of Denmark, the neo-Reichian Radix™ therapy as presented by Dr. Charles Kelley, Systemic Integration™ by R. Cascone, Ron Kurtz' Hakomi™ therapy, the Pesso Boyden System Psychomotor™ (PBSP), and Centropic Integration™ of Dr. Camden Clay and me. Other modalities in this category include: Feldenkrais™ movement-oriented therapy, Rubenfeld Synergy™, Hellerwork™, the Transformational Bodywork™ of Fred and Cheryl Mitouer, and Interactive Facilitation™.

Transformation-Oriented Bodywork

Transformation-oriented bodywork stands as the counterpart of body-focused psychotherapy within the field of therapeutic touching, and includes those modalities of touch-oriented healing which deal with the whole of a person's experience, yet do not qualify as psychotherapies.

Ida Rolf's system (Rolfing™) of structural integration and realignment of body posture via a physical manipulation of the fascial sheets surrounding muscle bundles, stands as the grandmother of transformation-oriented bodywork. Rolf introduced her methods at the Esalen Institute of Big Sur, California, in the 1960s, which greatly helped somatosize the psychotherapy movement then. Fritz Perls, founder of Gestalt Therapy, became involved in Ida Rolf's early work at Esalen, and claimed her rolfing "saved my life." Unlike its psychotherapy counterparts, transformation-oriented bodywork often does not focus on the verbal or emotional content of the client's experience, but rather lets those elements naturally reintegrate in the wake of the physical realignment and dismantling of the body's armor.

Body-focused Psychotherapy and the Trance State

Body-focused psychotherapy aims to achieve wholeness of the body/mind system by facilitating physical, emotional, and mental changes. The work involves both physical contact with soft tissue and verbal emotional processing. This kind of psychotherapy capitalizes on a normal body/mind reality to evoke therapeutic change in a way that captures the directness and immediacy of experience itself. That reality is the trance state, a narrowing of focus to one thing wherein all else recedes into the background of our attention. It provides a kind of meditative relaxation, which buffers out pain and affords the body an opportunity to heal. This "hypnosis," as a direct corollary of the relaxation response itself, presents itself as an oasis in the vast world of busy experiences. Outside of therapy, humans seek it out over and over again in order to disengage from and ultimately stop the conscious mind from reporting lower levels of repressed pain.

Besides its pain-blocking function, our brain seeks out the trance state because it minimizes effort and awareness, and keeps us functioning smoothly. Running on autopilot performing familiar tasks such as driving is a good example of trance-living. Autopilot kicks in when we watch movies or TV. It helps us relax by narrowing our focus and disengaging from integrative processing. A trance state contains all the soothing elements of sleep, including the deeper brain wave rhythms. Early trance states, perhaps when we were rocked as babies, or maybe even further back when we were floating in the womb, surrounded with the oceanic sounds of blood flow and heart beat, get imprinted in the mind/body system as most desirable. Trance is the mind's version of peace. We seek it out as a return to "the good old days". When a person carries repressed painful feelings, trance-inducing mechanisms must cut off inner connectedness to achieve the desired serenity. The trance then becomes at the expense of wholeness. We veg out and live unconsciously in a trance state seemingly to enjoy peace, but organismically, to avoid pain.

In body-focused psychotherapy, the therapist introduces attention to bodily reality in the immediate moment as a way of accessing which trance state the client relies on in order to maintain her repressed status quo. Trance induction is one of the body/mind's most primitive and common defense mechanisms against pain, therefore emerging as the single most potent gateway for real change. No intellectual overlay, no amount of insight or affirmations can make for lasting change, until the trance state and the feelings hidden there are addressed. Inevitably, a trance state used as a defense against pain will simply usurp all intellectual attempts to "understand" and ameliorate it. Knowing about one's history of being unloved doesn't in itself change anything.

Ironically, the trance state serves simultaneously as a defense against pain, and also as the storage point of it, similar to an encapsulated cyst. Body-focused psychotherapy finds and engages the trance state used to buffer pain out of consciousness, with the purpose of making it conscious and therefore accessible to the patient. True mental health has more to do with easy access to inner resources (thoughts, feelings, memories, creativity, etc.) than it does with capable coping and adaptation skills. Therapy has more to do with awakening from an unconscious trance than it does with conscious learning of new behavior.

A focus on the body in psychotherapy helps to locate the experience of feelings, and the bodily sensations associated with them. Feelings located "in the head" generally are just thought-versions of emotions, and as such, cannot translate into change. That would be like saying that owning a map of Chicago automatically gets you to Chicago. The body speaks the language of feelings in its own kinesthetic way, and simply articulating with words may not be enough to access portals of new life. We are after all, embodied creatures. We are here to embody our humanity, and that means in-the-body. For many clients, even those who have been in talk-therapy for years, the body-connection finalizes the route to full integration. "Now I get it," they say, because the body gets it.

The body as transducer, or conduit of experience, stands as the true and only arena for therapy. Thoughts and feelings as the building blocks of our experience are also physical realities located in physical places within us. Our conscious mind emerges as only one expression of a feeling-centered molecular memory network embedded throughout the body. Psyche and Soma stand as reflective images of each other. The body contains our Unconscious. With the right type of reflective awareness, linking bodily sensation with thoughts and emotions, a full integration of fragmented past experiences can be accomplished. Our personal history then makes sense, and destiny opens up to welcome us.

*"Your health is bound to be affected if,
day after day, you say the opposite of what you feel,
if you grovel before what you dislike and rejoice at what brings you
nothing but misfortune. Our nervous system isn't just a function, it's
part of our physical body, and our soul exists in space and is inside us,
like the teeth in our mouth.
It can't be forever violated with impunity."*

----Boris Pasternak
<u>Doctor Shivago</u>

✳ ✳✳

*"There is no state of mind that isn't mimicked in the immune
system."*

---Dr. Candace Pert, Ph.D

✳✳✳

"When the mind is troubled, the body cries out."
---Godfather III

✳✳✳

*"I can't express anger. That is one of the problems I have. I grow a
tumor instead."*

---Woody Allen
<u>Manhattan</u>

2

Getting Sick, Getting Well: Feelings and the Mind/Body Interface

The Invisible Factors of Healing: The Body Follows What Is In the Heart and Mind

After years of counseling people who have received upsetting medical diagnoses, and after years of working in an Intensive Care Unit setting, I'm convinced that mental, emotional, and spiritual dimensions of experience influence the course of an illness and/or recovery. I believe that the body follows what is in the heart and mind, which is not to say that our thoughts, feelings, or spiritual beliefs directly cause or cure anything, but rather that they create the banks between which the river of bodily reality flows.

Over the years I have witnessed these "invisible factors" come into play in the illness/wellness process, quite often dominating and directing it, especially in the ICU, where such subtle influences can make the difference between living and dying. Why these seemingly elusive and unmeasurable aspects of experience have such a profound effect on the body I don't know, but common sense has always told us that they do, and now that theory is gaining support from scientists.

I have itemized the spiritual, mental, and emotional factors that contribute to healing into five fundamental categories, and written a section on each. They are:

1. the will to live
2. self-esteem
3. self-expression
4. support: the love of others
5. inspiration

The Will to Live

The will to live refers to a mysterious, imperceptible, unmeasurable experience, the absence of which can set the stage for a seemingly untimely and rapid physical deterioration and death. When the waters of hope spill out from the toppled vessel that is the body, the roots of life in the body dry up and wither. Microscopic pathogens, like vultures circling a dying beast, must somehow recognize the waning life force when the will to live flickers out, and move in to clean up. A man without the will to live is more than depressed; he is already dead. Let me recount a story.

Two Men, Three Hearts

Heart #1:

Charles' voice rang exceptionally chipper for someone being admitted to the Intensive Care Unit after a heart attack. He protested as his wife helped him unbutton his shirt, but willingly let me attach the monitor pads to his chest.

"I'm fine, really. They tell me I have a weak heart, but I feel fine." And in fact Charles was symptom-free. Except for an occasional irregular heartbeat that flickered on the screen above his bed, he looked fine. "What is this cardiomyopathy-thing anyway?" he asked with a mixture of curiosity and mild defiance.

"It seems that your silent heart attack has done more damage to the wall of your left ventricle than the doctor had thought."

"Yeah, that silent heart attack thing bugs me, too. How can you have a frickin' silent heart attack? I tell you I feel fine."

"Your doctor wants you here for observation. It might be nothing."

"Yeah, nothing."

But I could tell Charles wasn't really feeling as cocky as he lead me to believe. His left ventricle was so weakened that his cardiac output, that is, the volume of blood pumped by a single contraction of the heart, was very low. I knew this because we had hooked Charles up to a special catheter threaded through a central vein above his collar bone all the way through the valves of his heart in order to pick up temperature and pressure readings in the innermost chamber.

We could use the hydraulic properties of a closed circulatory system, along with simple core blood temperature readings, to determine pulmonary capillary pressure, which would tell us that Charles' heart had lost much of its oxygen-distributing efficiency. We could predict a downhill course for him just on the numbers gathered over a few hours--all before any symptoms of heart failure had occurred. So even though Charles insisted he still felt fine, he could tell we weren't resonating with his cocky mood. And with each new IV cardiac "med" we hooked up to the growing array of tubing and wiring at his bedside, the more worried he appeared.

Charles' second heart attack later that evening wasn't so silent. In fact it hurt. "God, it's like an elephant sitting on my chest, and it just won't quit." Sweat beaded around his eyebrows and nose, and his skin noticeably paled under the fluorescent lights. "Is this it? Am I going to die?"

"Not if we can help it," I said, pushing the morphine into the central IV port.

Charles' cardiologist ordered a balloon pump, which is a piece of equipment designed to reduce the workload of the heart by creating pressure differentials between aortic and ventricular spaces which makes the pumping process require less energy. The balloon pump is invasive to say the least. The doctor threads a tiny catheter through the femoral artery in the crotch area, up the aorta, and hooks it to a jukebox-size machine that pumps gas from a tank to inflate and deflate a 5-inch balloon the circumference of the aorta in synch with Charles' heartbeat. The doctor informed Charles he needed a new heart, and could now consider himself on the transplant candidate waiting list.

"I'm only 55. I just can't believe this is happening. I don't even feel that bad anymore." When his wife was present, Charles put on his cocky airs, partly to reassure her, and partly because she was falling apart, trying to fight back tears, to no avail. He tried humor, brashness, indifference, frustration with little things, self-distraction--whatever worked to keep his and his wife's thoughts focused on anything but him. He educated himself about heart transplantation, using the resources in our Education Department, and as the days went by, he more or less accepted his plight with a calm, hopeful spirit.

"I still feel pretty damn fine, except for this thing in my leg, and the fact that I can't get out of bed." Charles declared. He had to keep his leg straight, so that the plastic guide tube for the catheter in his crotch would stay straight and open. "God, what I would give to be able to scratch my own toes!"

The weeks went by, and no offers of a donor heart came in. The daily routine in the ICU became familiar to Charles. There were two long shifts, so the same two nurses were on duty during the week, and on weekends another crew came in. Charles got to be on a first-name basis with most of the nurses on the unit, and even those not assigned to him would drop by for little chats. Although he was no longer in crisis, the overall picture remained critical. How long this drug-and-machine-induced stability could last was unpredictable.

"The crazy thing is I don't feel that bad. Are you sure there's not some huge mistake here?" he repeated again. More time passed. And Charles grew weary. Somewhere along the way, his spark to continue noticeably flickered. The cardiologist called in a psychiatric consultant who put Charles on antidepressants and Valium. His wife continued to be stoic, and Charles did his best to make sure she remained so. But in private he confided in me that he didn't think he could take it much longer.

"This is no life for me. I can't stand the not-knowing everyday. I'm here wishing someone else is having a car wreck so that I can have their heart. What's happening to me? I just don't know if this is worth it anymore." The nursing staff knew he was depressed. We could all sense a marked change in him one morning almost two months after his admission date.

"I had a dream last night," he told me when his wife stepped out after breakfast. "You might think this is funny. I dreamed I was walking down a busy Manhattan street, carrying a bunch of colored party balloons. People were looking at me and laughing at the hard time I was having with the balloons in the wind. Suddenly I'm swept up off the ground holding on to these balloons for dear life. The wind carries me high up into the air, over all sorts of places like Central Park, and a church, and then a field of giraffes! Their necks are so long they're able to look me right in the face! I get real scared of them, but I'm more scared of letting go of the balloons, so I panic. That's when I woke up, still feeling the panic."

"Balloons, eh?" I remark, and he snorts in recognition of the unsubtle symbolism.

"Yeah, balloons. I'm afraid to hold on and afraid to let go. I can't take this any more. This is no life. I can't keep my family hanging on like this any more either."

"So what's your plan?" I asked.

"I don't know. I just can't do this any more".

"You know, Charles, a donor could show up any time now..."

"Yeah, I know, you've all been saying that."

That evening I could tell Charles had had a serious talk with his wife, because she no longer pretended to be fine. She wept openly in deep sobs as she floated in a daze between Charles' bedside and the family waiting room, where she had virtually camped out for months.

"He's given up," she told me, in shock. "He's said good-bye to me, and that he doesn't want to fight this any more. What can I do? He's asked me to let him go. How can I let him go?"

"What did you tell him?"

"I said I understood, but I really don't. How can he want to die?" The heaviness around her heart was evident in her voice.

Charles died that night, after a massive third heart attack, and with no warning whatsoever. I'm convinced that when he let go of his will to live, his body just followed suit. His mental suffering far out-weighed his physical discomfort. He gave up his will to live because of it.

Hearts #2 & #3:

Timothy, a 67-year old "country boy," was helicopered in all the way from rural Mississippi, unconscious and already on a breathing machine upon arrival in our unit. He had been out chopping kindling when he collapsed in his yard.

"His heart is mush," the cardiologist announced, scanning the x-rays. "Wall-to-wall mush".

"Code blue, room 234. Code blue," the loudspeaker announced, and all hell quietly and methodically broke loose. A nurse grabbed our Sears tool-carrier "crash cart" and madly wheeled it into Timothy's room. Already on a ventilator, he needed cardiac resuscitation, but CPR on a mushy heart rarely works. Somehow, with cc's of epinephrine squirted into him, and with several countershocks of the paddles against his chest wall, along with CPR, Timothy's heart kept beating. To everyone's surprise, he even woke up.

I was able to witness the look in his eyes in that moment, and I didn't really see fear, but rather wildness and anger. We tied Timothy's hands down after he had made a beeline to pull the ventilator tube out of his throat, and he was not happy about that. For someone with a mushy heart, he certainly had fire. I suspect we were lucky he couldn't speak right then, but the communication came through loud and clear in his eyes. Confusion, yes; agitation, yes; but on top of that, raw anger. How dare we do all these things to him?!

Timothy coded three times in the next hour, and each time came around--fully conscious! Finally, after a lull in the resuscitation process, the doctor came in, leaned over his bed, and spoke loudly, assuming that because of his age he must be hard of hearing.

"Timothy, I've got to be honest with you. It doesn't look good. If we had another heart to put into you, I'd say you have a chance, but this way, it just doesn't look good. I'm afraid that besides these drugs and the breathing machine, there's nothing we can do for you."

The light in Timothy's eyes faded, and a tear leaked out. I couldn't believe how callous and insensitive the doctor was, even though I knew he had spoken the truth. My self-mumblings took a back seat to Timothy's sudden jerking and straining of his tied wrists. I looked into his eyes again, and by gosh, he was pissed! I couldn't believe it! He was pissed at the doctor! And when the doctor left, Timothy stayed pissed at me! I could see the pleading in his eyes to untie him, take this foolish tube out of his mouth, and just let him get out of here. How dare I keep him against his will!?

He stabilized, and lay quietly as I monitored and adjusted his equipment. I really didn't know what to say, because the picture looked grim. An hour later, the same cardiologist who had so callously spoken the bad news before, reentered, and leaning over Timothy, spoke in his slow overly-loud voice:

"Timothy, something's come up. There's something we can do for you after all." Timothy's eyebrows shot up. "Have you ever heard of the Jarvik 7? It's an artificial heart made by a Dr. Jarvik. It just so happens it's on tour here at the hospital with a doctor who knows how to put one in. With your permission, we can do that for you. The odds are not good for long-term survival, you understand, so I don't want to get your hopes up too high."

(Thanks, thanks a lot." I'm thinking, sarcastically. No, no, mustn't lead him on at this point...)

"So what do you say?" the doctor's voice thundered.

(What's he supposed to say, you fool! And how's he supposed to say anything, you idiot!)

But communicate he does: old Timothy holds two thumbs up, as if to say, "Go for it!" Soon the entire ventilator support and cardiac machinery (including a balloon pump), like a royal entourage, accompany Timothy down to the operating room, where the visiting doctor gets a chance to show off his artificial heart transplant technique to eager surgeons.

A few hours later my colleagues and I hear that the operation was successful, and I imagine Old Timothy with the Jarvik 7 equipment emerging from his skinny chest, looking like an astronaut in a dense flight suit carrying a portable oxygen pack. I never did get to see him with the Jarvik 7 because three hours later a donor heart mysteriously came available, which matched Timothy's tissue-type perfectly. Now our surgeons got to show off their technique, and successfully transplanted the new heart into skinny Old Timothy's chest.

Three weeks later, as I was sitting and eating my lunch in the hospital cafeteria, I spotted Timothy in jeans and a hospital gown, wearing a protective surgical mask over his nose and mouth, hitting the candy bar machine when it kept his quarter. I did a double-take, and my goose bumps got goose bumps. Could it really be....? Yes, it really was!

I jumped out of my seat and went up to him. His skinny frame was taller than I'd remembered.

"Do you remember me?" I asked, after taking his hand and shaking it. He shook mine politely, but I could tell there was no recognition. "I'm one of the nurses who took care of you the night you were admitted to the hospital."

"Oh, well, thank you, young fella. Thank you for everything. Do you know how these candy machines work?"

"What a man," I thought. He seems unphased by all that has happened to him It's as if he knew all along that all they had to do was let him up and he'd be all right."

I'm convinced Timothy's anger fueled his will to live, and though his physical condition was far more wretched than Charles', it was that "invisible", unmeasurable factor that pulled him through.

Self-esteem

Self-esteem is like the keel of a boat. When it runs deep and true, a person can weather great storms and upheavals. Without it, a person flounders even in the shallow waters of small challenges. Self-esteem resides at the core as a learned sense of self-appreciation, worth, and love. Like the rest of the personality, the foundation of self-esteem is set in the first few years of life. Most issues in therapy and the progress that follows, correlate with the degree of growing self-esteem in the patient.

Self-esteem can be measured by the patient's own account and can be detected by observation. Behavior which is too loud or too quiet inevitably comes from an error in self-image or self-esteem. Bad relationships often reflect errors in self-esteem.

Self-expression and Communication Style

Self-expression and the style of communication within a family represent two invisible factors that strongly influence wellness. Honesty resides at the heart of healthy self-expression and every good communication system. "The truth shall set you free" is a stronger statement than most people realize, because speaking the truth unburdens the heart. Even criminals testify to a great sense of relief and peace after confessing their crimes. Secrets and private thoughts and feelings create isolation that breeds ill-health. Some families of patients in the ICU where I worked would purposely avoid any conversation about the reality of their feelings or the seriousness of the condition of their loved one, either to protect themselves or the patient. Often the patient in such a family system is reluctant to show anything other than cheeriness or stoicism in an effort to protect the family from pain. But in private, after the family left, those same patients would confide to me how lonely and isolated they felt, and how they wished they could share their fears and tears with loved ones. A blocked communication system relies on the forces of repression, which take their toll on the body. Conversely, I have seen families weep together openly, praise and honor each other freely, say final good-byes to each other unabashedly, and I can testify to the golden glow left in the wake of such a communication system. Whether the patient survives or not, the elements of healing are evident in the sense of peace that remains. Good communication has heart in it and that's what makes it work.

Support: the Love of Others

Closely tied to the type of communication system a person shares with family and friends is the level of support received during an illness. Group support is the equivalent of water for fish: when it's there, they thrive; without it, they gasp for life. A person without support is truly like a fish out of water, because support is part of our natural social environment. Support can be both spoken and unspoken. Group (primarily family) support feeds the emerging self-esteem of a child, sets the stage for free self-expression and good communication, and I believe is the original wellspring that nourishes our fundamental will to live. In the 1940s, a nationwide study of orphanages found that babies who were adequately fed and clothed, and yet were not held or connected with personally, mysteriously withered away and died. Why is group support so fundamental to our species? Let's go to another species.

The Tribal Gorilla

Prelude to the Gorilla story....

Why is it that there are more people in this country who would say "I'm proud to be an American" than there are those who would say "I'm proud to be a human being"? Why do we give almost fanatical loyalty to a sports team, gathering together with thousands of others in stadiums, yet feel so alienated in our own homes? How did the loss of self-esteem become an epidemic and the divorce rate come to equal the marriage rate? Something at the level of connectedness has gone haywire. We yearn to unite and identify with a larger group (such as a team or a nation), yet we've lost the capacity to connect with even one other person. What has happened to us? What's missing? The following story sheds light on this mystery:

OK, Now the gorilla story...

Once upon a time there was a baby gorilla whom hunters captured in the wilds of Rawanda and sold to a mall in the central part of the United States, where he was placed in a pit as a kind of mascot to attract customers. For years the ape lived tucked away in the recess at the center of the mall where thousands of gawking visitors came to visit. Although he had plenty of food, and a tire swing for exercise, he soon gravitated to one little corner of his hole, where he sat, making tiny circles on the wall with a forefinger. He became so inactive and nonresponsive that he was no longer fun to watch, and thus, not much of a draw.

A television magazine show heard about him, and ran the story nationally. Images of this sullen, depressed-looking monkey outraged the public, and he was soon transferred to a metropolitan zoo. Even in the new, more spacious, and natural setting, where he was in contact with other gorillas, he remained a loner and a misfit, suffering from a long history of contact-deprivation. His re-socialization was slow and difficult.

About the same time, zoos all over the world began creating a new strategy for raising gorillas. Let's put them together with each other from birth, they said. At first, after pairing them, the apes did produce some babies, and they seemed overall more content. But curiously, the mother gorillas often ended up accidentally crushing their babies, because with the absence of female role models they lacked the sensitivity skills necessary for mothering. Thus, the breeding and survival rate of zoo gorillas remained far below the rate in the wild.

Then the actions of one man, a millionaire who took it upon himself to save the great apes of the world, created a successful paradigm for raising gorillas. His approach was revolutionary: he placed entire extended families of gorillas in huge cages equipped with plush rain forest foliage and rain-simulating sprinkler systems, recreating not just their earthly natural habitat, but their social one as well. Gorillas in the wild live in tribal extended-family units, learning through a great deal of contact, interaction, and socialization, all the missing elements in the captured gorillas. The gorillas in the extended family cages thrived, and soon their breeding and survival rates far exceeded those in the wild!

Just like the gorillas, we humans plainly don't do well in isolation, and in fact, even pairing off is not enough. We, too, need our extended tribal family. We humans only really thrive in a community setting. Community carries within it the same root as communion and communication, and therein lies our connectedness as a species, which translates into our well-being as individuals.

Dr. David Spiegel's classic study of women with breast cancer who participated in a support group, as compared to a control group of women with similar diagnoses, who didn't join a group, clearly demonstrates the efficacy of group support in extending the survival time of breast cancer victims, creating speedier healing. A higher incidence of spontaneous remissions was also noted among the support group women. We need tribe for our health.

Relationship is the human arena where we experience, and life expresses through us, our innate connectedness to others. Because we are alive, we are automatically woven into the fabric of human relationships. It comes with the territory. And because relationships are as fundamental to our being human as the organic "glue" that holds our cells together, they mirror our health. The relationships we are in can either enhance our well-being, or make us sick. We need relationships that affirm life in order to remain healthy. To achieve that requires some effort, the same way a garden must be constantly tended. Healthy relationships brim over with caring, nurturing, and intimacy.

Below are some tips for creating healthy relationships:

1. First and foremost, make a commitment to have healthy relationships in your life. Be clear with your intention.

2. Next, be honest. Take the step into intimacy by letting others know what's really going on in your heart and mind. You don't have to be a saint to have good relationships, you just have to be OK.

If You Want to Live Clean, Come Clean

Clean living in all areas of life includes a wonderful and mysterious commodity: telling the truth. Which, being so basic, ought to be easy, but isn't. It takes attentiveness and courage to be honest, and maybe even more difficult, it takes innocence.

Remember the Hans Christian Anderson tale of The Emperor's New Clothes, where two fake tailors con an entire town into believing they've woven for the vain King a most beautiful suit made of cloth visible only to the wise, and invisible to fools? Of course nobody wants to admit they can't see it, so they all praise the wonders of the fabric's weave, texture, and depth of color as the monarch parades proudly down the main street in his new raiment. Only a single child's "But the King is naked!" breaks the spell of the collective lie. That kid, with a guileless heart, simply reported what her senses told her, and the King's false pride and the townspeople's folly stood exposed.

The equations underlying honesty are simple: the truth leads to trust; trust leads to intimacy; and intimacy leads to fulfillment. In light of the Emperor story, let me add another: the truth shall make you free, but not necessarily comfortable. Being honest is a challenge.

In his book Radical Honesty: How to Transform Your Life By Telling the Truth, Dr. Brad Blanton tells about three levels of telling the truth, each playing its own impactful role in establishing and maintaining quality relationships.

Level One: tell just the facts. Tell it like it is, neither under- or overstating. Even this takes practice, so start today. Notice how much you embellish or color your accounts of events. Try being totally honest with just factual things for an entire day. I think you'll be surprised at how tough this is.

Level Two: tell how you feel about the facts. This is a little tougher than the plain facts because when we're honest about our feelings we risk disapproval and/or rejection. Notice how much of your feeling-truth you hide everyday. The lessons at this level of honesty include both learning how to be tender (to get to the hurts beneath the anger, or to the love beneath the fears) and how to be tough (making appropriate boundaries and demanding respect). Try upping the ante of your feeling-sharing just a bit each day, and see the quality of your relationships move upscale.

Level Three: confession. This is the "baring-your-soul" phase of honesty, where you fess up to your shortcomings and admit your flaws. It is at once the most vulnerable and the most powerful stage of honesty. Often this level of sharing remains reserved for support groups, or therapy sessions, but why wait for those special settings?

Tickets to places or events often say "Admit One" on them. Admission of our frailty is the ticket to heartfelt living, and unlike a put-down's negative focus on our faults, carries the dignity of laying down a burdensome mind set. Not only aren't you perfect, you're completely human. Come on, admit it!

3. Learn how to identify what you want, then ask for it.
4. Vocalize what works for you and what doesn't, and take a stand, so that your relationships have healthy boundaries.
5. Affirm the people in your life with words of acknowledgment, appreciation, gratefulness, and simple kindness. Make at least a little effort each day to enhance the quality of your relationships, and watch yourself flourish!

A Systems Approach

Some psychologists emphasize a "systems" approach to mental health and therapy, implying that there is no treatment of the individual independent of their relational system. Each individual lives and functions within a larger psychological system, such as the family unit or a peer group, from which the sense of self and well-being are derived and nurtured. This, of course, is especially obvious with young children, who, with their immature sense of personal boundaries, are wide open to external influences. A system with qualities of openness, truthfulness, acceptance, and love, contributes enormously to a child's emerging self-image. Where communication in a family system is stifled or warped, the child's self-image becomes unhealthy. Besides exploring our own personal history with the intention of cleaning up unhealthy impressions we may be unconsciously carrying and acting out, there are some life-style choices we can make in our present circumstances to maintain a "clean" psychological environment:

1. Patch up resentments and unfinished business with family members. Do whatever it takes so at least you know you've tried.

2. Make room for feelings and practice honest, appropriate expression to your present family, or to others in your relationship system. A free-flow of feelings is like the healthy flow of blood in the body.

3. Focus on the love and appreciation you have for the other members of your system. This fosters an upward spiral of acceptance and ease in being together.

4. Make conscious agreements on how to handle the "negative" emotions like anger and jealousy. A good rule of thumb about those kinds of feelings is they generally don't stand alone, but overlay a deeper layer of hurt or fear. During those negative periods of time, make the choice to share the whole spectrum of truth, including the more vulnerable feelings. Let yourself be vulnerable in order to cultivate trust. Initiate the sharing of feelings in your relationship system, and stop waiting for your partner to do it for you! How often people wait for the impetus to come from the outside, and it never happens!

5. Actively respect the integrity and otherness of people in your system, and avoid the traps of right and wrong. A healthy system includes correction, not wrong-making. When you make someone in your relationship system wrong, you are literally hurting yourself.

We don't live in a psychological vacuum. In fact, we live and breathe in the psychological atmosphere of our relationships and families. Each of us has the responsibility to keep this environment clean. Positive interaction is our birthright as human beings, and, of course, our challenge when we find ourselves in a less than optimal state of health. It is within the context of our current relationship systems that corrective emotional experiences can help heal us of a painful past. Some of the therapy that transpires in a group setting can only happen in those circumstances. We need tribe to help us get well and stay well.

Inspiration

Last but not least on my list of invisible factors of healing is inspiration. As its Latin root, *inspirare*, meaning to breathe, implies, inspiration breathes life into whatever it touches. Inspiration directly feeds the will to live and coaxes us to mobilize inner life-affirming resources. With inspiration, biological functions rally and align with a fundamental yes to life. When inspiration triggers inner visions of an abiding perfection, or novel solutions to a problem, or the righting of a wrong, it infuses the organism with the excitement of positive beliefs and new possibilities, which speeds up healing.

An absence of inspiration allows for doubt, by which even the tiniest of obstacles grows beyond our capacity to cope. Without inspiration, our life force falters. Lack of inspiration keeps the status quo ordinary, uninspired, and stagnant. Its lackluster banner reads "why bother?" and at its worst becomes the breeding ground for despair.

Inspiration connects us intimately to our purpose in life. Without it we are lost. We need inspiration to be fully human.

Concluding Statement about the "Invisible Factors"

The invisible factors of our beliefs, attitudes, and feelings stand as the new frontiers of medicine today. If the simple power of suggestion can rid a person of warts or enlarge breasts (no fooling!), and the immune response can be tricked by a placebo, then surely a more thorough investigation into the deeper realms of mind and heart will uncover a veritable genie of healing. When the invisible factors of healing govern health care, a focus on wellness will predominate, hospitals will turn into hospitable healing centers, and the treatment of disease will center around eliminating both environmental and internal blocks to natural wellness.

One System

"One Blood, Mon," the Rastafarians of Jamaica say, an expression that signifies the unifying relatedness of us all. "One System, Mon" is what I say about the age-old body/mind debate. Body and mind are not separate systems, but rather two aspects of a single system, united by an ongoing seamless exchange between the level of biological electrochemical events and the level of personal experience. The bridge is a network of neuropeptide "mood altering" messenger molecules tagged with emotional charge. Feelings are not disembodied exeriences of some separate "mind", but rather, are contained in a very physical biochemistry that modulates and marks every bodily event within the human framework. If the body is in fact a machine, it's one that runs by feeling. Neurobiologist Dr. Candace Pert says, "There is no state of mind that is not mimicked by the immune system."

Although the term psychosomatic has been around since the 1920s, allopathic medicine has more recently taken large strides forward in acknowledging the connection between the "invisible" factors of heart and mind and the solely physical events of the body. Dr. Pert and her colleagues coined the term "psychosomatic network" to describe how it is no longer just the isolated physical event that can be thought of as having an emotional component, but rather the mind/body system must now be thought of as operating in an on-going feeling-driven state of being.

It was established decades ago that certain personality traits go hand in hand with specific body-system maladies. Type "A" characteristics of aggressiveness and working too hard link to the circulatory system and the heart. Type "C" personalities who don't express emotions, who deny anger, who have difficulty standing up for themselves, and who also nurture others at their own expense, seem to have a propensity toward cancer. The idea that certain emotional states, patterns of thought, and life strategies set the stage for disease in the body has recently gotten unexpected support from some pioneering insurance companies that are funding healthy lifestyle programs as a way of improving health and preventing disease.

If certain personality traits are linked with disease, are there any inner qualities of character that might bolster immune competence?

Can we go so far as to tag some personality traits as bad and good?

Studies on this subject offer mixed results. First scientists claimed it was better to express anger, because keeping it bottled up can lead to inner pressure manifesting in circulatory problems and strokes. Then opinions changed when more studies confirmed that people who gave free vent to their anger tended to show more cardiac and circulatory complications. In another area of psychology, initial evidence credited nurturing parenting as creating better adjusted children, and later studies implied that parental influence has little to do with the child's development.   In yet another area of psychosocial inquiry, some researchers are firmly convinced that congeniality and service to others contribute to health, whereas others point out the cancer-prone personality profile , as documented by Lydia Temoshok and Henry Dreher, in their book The Type C Connection: the Behavioral Links to Cancer and Your Health, leads to a "niceness" that is a detriment to health. All this suggests that a dichotomy exists among experts in this field. So what's what? Are some feelings good and some bad?

Here's my take on this issue. We may all have the capacity to experience the same feelings, but how our inner personality traits stack up inside us is what makes us unique. How we subjectively deal with thoughts and emotions, and how we reveal what we are thinking and feeling to others, determines which feeling states are good and which are bad for us. What we express and what we repress, and under what circumstances, determines what is healthy or unhealthy, all according to the dictates of our individual biology. Expressing anger, for example, is a positive action only when doing so has a life-affirming effect. And it's not good when it doesn't.

There are no formulas when it comes to feelings, except this one: judge a feeling you're having by the way your body responds. Fuming at a boss may adversely jack up one person's blood pressure, but kickstart a healthy immune response in another. Declaring some feelings universally positive and some negative misses the subjective nature of feeling, and can itself become a stumbling block in therapy.

Feelings vs. Emotion

Feeling is the state of connected emotion, thought, and body-response. Notice that emotion is only one part of the feeling state, and that the key word in this definition is connected. Feeling is natural and universal. Everyone has the potential to feel, but not everyone does.

Have you ever known someone who's very emotional, who can cry easily over a TV commercial or during a movie, but doesn't really know what he's crying about in his own life? Or someone who can easily articulate and intellectualize her beliefs and philosophies, but does so with a seeming lack of emotion or personal meaning? Or what about the person whose physical state of anxiety, tension, nervousness or sensitivity seems to dominate and rule his emotional and intellectual life? These are examples of what I mean by the term disconnected state. It's essentially a state of non-feeling. Feeling has a physical, emotional, and mental component to it. When one aspect is missing, a state of non-feeling sets in. When we're not fully feeling, we engage in quests for fulfillment. When we do feel deeply and honestly, we are fulfilled. Let's examine the biology behind this, which takes us to the most sophisticated organ of our nervous system--the brain.

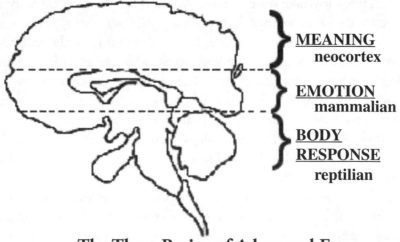

MEANING
neocortex

EMOTION
mammalian

BODY
RESPONSE
reptilian

The Three Brains of Adam and Eve

Besides having two distinct vertically-divided hemispheres, (right-brain, left-brain, with cross-wire connections located at the center called the corpus callosum), the brain also is partitioned into three horizontally divided segments, evolved over eons of time. The low-brain (often referred to as the reptilian brain: including the pons, brain stem, and cerebellum) deals with "unconscious" body functions such as breathing, blood pressure, and heart rate. The upper-brain, also called the neocortex or cerebrum, has to do with functions of thought and rationality, and is the section that projects meaning onto our experiences. The mid-brain (known as the "mammilian brain") contains the limbic system, a sophisticated electronic network that provides emotional charge to our experience; in other words, it processes our emotional response to the world. (The limbic system contains within it the hypothalamus, which controls the secretions of the pituitary gland, therefore making it director of hormonal equilibrium. It biologically links emotions and hormones!)

Every experience we have in any given moment (right this second as you are reading this, for instance!) has attached to it a physical response, an emotional response, and a mental comprehension of the meaning of it, all coming from the three separate parts of the brain
.

The Biology of Memory

Psychoneuroimmunologists have discovered the physical basis of what we call "memory." Every biological process in the body, including thoughts and emotions, contains electrochemical components which physically encode themselves into molecules called neuropeptides. Every experience generates a neuropeptide that receives information from each of the three sections of the brain. A whole-brain response keeps these information bits united. The individual neuropeptides are then sent to specific receptor sites in the body for future reference. Memory, then, does not reside just in the brain. (If it did, our heads would swell with experience!) Memory lives throughout the body. In fact, our cells contain a perfect memory of all experiences and store it. How well we access these memories is another story. Every community has a library, but not every citizen knows how to use it. Where do these receptor sites abide? In the soft tissues of the body, including the immune system! These information-carrying neuropeptides are the mind/body link , acting as transducers of semantic and emotional information at the cellular level. Our emotions play a role in every biochemical event that transpires within us, even while we sleep.

Memory and Survival:
How Feelings Move or Get Stuck

Feelings move within and throughout the mind/body system as biolgically-encoded bits of information, modulating all biological processes within us. They are designed to give us feedback about our environment at the same raw level of direct perception as our senses, and to yield insight into the motives of individuals around us. Feelings provide a cutting-edge in the mammilian game of survival by helping us be in touch.

Some feelings, by their subtlety, just like the beating heart and breathing lungs within us, live outside the realm of day-to-day consciousness. Only babies and sensitive adults feel "vibes". Other feelings, not by design, but out of a perceived sense of danger or survival, are relegated into unconsciousness. Both these subtle and the repressed feeling responses do not just go away. They circulate in the system and effect the inner landscape of mood, often warping our perceptions of ongoing reality. Feelings that were engineered to help, when rendered unconscious, hinder.

Three Communication Systems Carry Feelings

The body uses three main communication systems to handle the unrelenting traffic of prodigious amounts of moment to moment, day to day biological "information," and feelings imbibe, unify, mediate, and add a personal charge to it all.

1. The nervous system with its neurotransmitters is a rapidly moving system (think of the speed of electricity!) that involves our senses, nerves, brain, and musculature. Our emotional life mimics the qualities of nerve activity, making it subject to the laws of nerve conduction, which include flooding (overload), and gating (repression). Feelings are the barometer of our nervous system. Depression, for instance, can be viewed as impaired neurological electrical flow, and is medically treated as such.

2. The endocrine system with its hormonal messengers is a slower, cy-

clical, rhythmic system, subject to breakdown at many precursor phases, because one hormone relies on the secretion of another, which in turn depends on a different one, creating a chain of information transfer. As a communication system it links itself to emotions by the nature of its shared limbic circuitry, interweaving hypothamic stimulation of hormone production and emotional processing. Hormones mysteriously transfer and unlock emotional responses.

Here's another baffling link between hormones and emotions yet to be unraveled: Endocrinologists were surprised to discover insulin and insulin receptor sites, until now believed to be strictly involved in a pancreatic glucose-regulating function, in the brain! What's insulin doing in the brain? Could there be some overlap or shared emotional duty between hormones and neurotransmitters? Stayed tuned.

3. <u>The neuropeptide system</u> is older than the other two (pre-dating vertebrates in evolution), yet was discovered more recently. This system interfaces the electrical-chemical mode of the nervous system, and the widespread molecular-messenger style of the endocrine system. It is involved with chemical-electrical imprinting on large molecules called neuropeptides, so that information pertaining to the meaning, the emotional charge, and the body-response to an event is encoded and stored in a molecular library, to become part of a vast network of "understanding." Its content is comprised of all our myriad experiences, and its structure designed by the internal logic of the system. Information is stacked up deductively, rather than logically. This means that conclusions about reality and self established in childhood remain biologically dominant when new incoming information is processed, unless the processing circuitry itself is updated. This is to say that changing one's mind, especially at the belief level, doesn't come easily. New perceptions and understandings are generally forged out of challenge, frustration, and necessity. The mind/body system, in its innate laziness, will try to force whatever has worked in the past to continue until it just can't, and even then, might continue to make futile attempts to get the desired outcome by the familiar means that never worked in the past. Think of all the futile struggles for love in abusive relationships. Rational evidence suggests that it will not happen, but the struggle continues like a phonograph needle stuck in a groove.

Memory and Imprinting

Because atoms are constantly in flux, and, according to Dr. Deepok Chopra, are shared by every cell and being in existence, past and present, our bodies are constantly being recreated. This morning's tumor owes its continuity into this afternoon to the biology of memory, and specifically to the "unwanted" memory of repressed pain. Repressed pain taxes the entire system because it requires a stress response in order to maintain unconsciousness. Blocked memories keep unhealthy conditions pocketed in our biology.

It is at the level of the neuropeptide system where "imprints of memory" set the stage for disease. Each complete neuropeptide is composed of information from each of the triune aspects of the brain--- cortex, mid-brain, and low-brain--containing meaning, emotional charge, and body response. When one is overwhelmed, overloaded, or in pain (either emotional or physical) the mind/body's defenses against pain kick in, the imprinting process gets interrupted and the neuropeptide of that event splits into fragments, or "chips." This sets into motion the centropic impulse to allow these information "bits" to reunite. Because the external "world" is no more than a canvas upon which the artistic mind/body system imprints its reality from the palette of past experience, all non-integrated past traumatic experiences in the form of encoded, disconnected bits of information inevitably intrude into the world-creating process, infiltrating the present experience of the person. This helps to explain recurring patterns in peoples' lives, and the sense of deja vu we sometimes experience. The body has been there before! The past is present until the body is updated.

Splitting for Survival's Sake

The brain's unique capacity to split experience into fragments, both along the vertical axis of the brain (which divides the right and left hemispheres), and along the horizontal axes between the triune segments of lower (reptilian brain), mid-brain (mammilian brain), and the high brain (cerebral cortex), is evidence of the importance emotions have played in human evolution, especially when it comes to survival. Experiencing emotions that heightened electrical activity in the brain, which increased alertness in our primeval ancestors, and thus improved their chances for survival, wasn't enough. It also became necessary to form the ability to split off from an experience. A caveman walking across an open plain and encountering a saber-tooth tiger couldn't afford to have his fear response paralyze the system even for a nanosecond, or he'd be lunch. Thus a new and primitive defense was cultivated: the ability to split off, to dissociate from feeling. This enabled him to run like hell.

Psychological Defenses and Survival

The psychological defenses humans cultivated have stood them in good stead, because, to a certain extent, they work. They totally align with the body's prime directive of survival, and thus carry with them a potent biological imperative. In that way defenses are healthy. In concordance with Freud's brilliant hypothesis about psychic defense mechanisms such as projection, introjection, and reaction formation that stem from deeper biological brain structures, much of popular psychology holds defense mechanisms at the heart of ego function, and therefore at the root of mental health. I disagree.

Although defenses help to maintain survival, they also carry with them an innately disintegrative function for the self. By splitting off from our own experience in order to avoid perceived life-threatening pain, our psyche disintegrates, or our inner world becomes fragmented. Yesterday's defense mechanisms are now today's psychological problems. Defense-driven personalities, considered paragons of mental health in today's culture, are what Primal Therapy's Arthur Janov referred to as unreal systems. Although the defense mechanisms we created to offset pain, and the internal splitting that accompanied them, got us through childhood, and may even get us through current difficulties, they cost us dearly in the long run.

True Mental Health

Non-repressed experiences encoded on neuropeptide molecules rest on receptor sites (like little hammocks, I imagine), and create a vast inner library of memory. True mental health equates with the easy accessibility of this library, as well as a natural flexibility existing within this inner world.

Receptor Sites, Repression, and Disease

Neuro-biologists are also discovering that neuropeptide receptor sites that are vacant due to repression or internal splitting, pose a potential health hazard. Candace Pert wrote about receptor sites and the HIV virus:

"The AIDS virus, for example, enters the immune system through a receptor site normally used by a neuropeptide. Whether or not it can enter the cell depends on how much of this natural peptide is around, which according to psychoneuroimmunology theory, would be a function of the emotional expression the organism is in."

The Role of Therapy

When it comes to therapy, "biology is destiny". Treatment that ignores the central biological role of feelings cannot bring about lasting change. Mere intellectualizing doesn't cut it when it comes to imprinted, repressed pain.

Body Boundaries

The human body structurally demonstrates the fundamental and natural necessity for boundary-setting as a means of sustaining health, especially in two locales: the skin and the immune system. The skin as both our outermost organ and the site of physical contact with the world, marks where the self ends and the "outer" world begins. Also known as the "integument," it functions as the built-in delineator of our separateness and our integrity as individuals. When someone touches us lovingly and appropriately, we feel soothed, stimulated, "in touch", and connected. Gentle touch not only elicits a cascade of mood-altering endorphins and the relaxation response to make us feel good, it also triggers the skin to release thymopoeitan, a hormone which bolsters our immune competence by stimulating maturing immune cells. When someone touches us without our permission we feel "invaded" and "violated," and our fight-or-flight response kicks in, along with a gush of stress hormones, aborted digestion, elevated blood pressure, and increased muscle tension. Negative contact with the world is an emergency.

Even more dramatically, when we are without our skin--an example would be severe burn victims -- we inevitably fall prey to invasion by myriad bacteria, fungi, viruses, and other microscopic vultures in the world. We need our skin intact and respected.

The immune system, a sophisticated inner communication network designed to distinguish between inner and outer, between that which is me and that which isn't, serves as our second line of defense. When the skin has been penetrated by an outside particle, an army of Killer-T immune cells, mobilized through innate cellular intelligence and memory which deem that particle an invader, swiftly moves in to neutralize and/or kill it. Scientists didn't name them "negotiator cells" or "peacemaker cells", but rather killer cells, in full recognition that healthy boundary maintenance is built on natural destructive forces. Making boundaries is not "nice". The immune system is not "nice". It needs to be capable of demolishing outside forces. Without that capacity, the body falls prey to all sorts of microscpic predators, as seen clearly in the immuno-suppressed condition of AIDS patients. No boundaries, no survival.

Although we can easily acknowledge the benefit of aggressive immune cells within us, hostility that is used to maintain inter-personal (between people) integrity, however, is rarely welcomed or even recognized as a life-affirming phenomenon. As a result, anger and hate, as boundary-setting emotions, are commonly repressed. When any natural flow of neuropeptide information gets blocked, including experiences tagged with so-called "negative" emotions, the body suffers. Emotional repression often shows up in the form of weak or absent boundaries in interpersonal interactions, something more readily recognized as low self-esteem.

Feelings gauge our interpersonal place in this world, and tell us whether we stand united or isolated. They act as a feedback mechanism that helps to balance our integrity as both a separate individual and as a part of greater social units. This dual nature complicates emotional responses, inevitably triggering inner conflict in the form of boundary disputes. Sometimes our emotions don't jive with the feedback from others in our environment who say we are being "selfish" when we are taking care of ourselves; they say we are being "self-centered" when we are choosing our own path rather than theirs. To whom am I loyal, and what are my priorities? Do I take care of others first? Myself first? Family first? Do I obey the norms and demands of my family or society first, or do I follow the dictates of my own heart, my own beliefs, and my own conscience?

Everyone needs a healthy sense of boundaries that balance body biology with the greater ecology of family and group systems. When these two are at odds and cannot be reconciled, and body needs are repressed in the face of cultural norms or family pressure, the stage is set for disease.

The Emotional Spectrum

What is the role of emotions in wellness and disease? Don't they interfere with clarity? Wouldn't we be better off without them? To answer these questions, we need to return to the subject of brain anatomy. An emotional response of any kind actually increases the electrical activity in the brain, the mid-brain to be exact. In terms of evolution, according to one school of thought, emotions attached to the Tree of Life and took root because of their alertness-enhancing capacity (more electricity= heightened alertness). The more awake and in-touch individuals simply tended to survive better in a hostile environment. Emotions demonstrate a "gut" level response to the environment, one that is quicker at ascertaining what is happening than the more logical "figuring out" method, the emotional approach obviously offering an edge in the survival game. Empathy also arises out of feeling, and brings with it an innate connectedness conducive to group survival.

Even the corporate world, that bastion of social Darwinism, is coming around to the emotional approach to problems, and is infusing intuitive, creative, and humanistic methods into management--all corollaries of the emotions. Emotions can also be equated with connectedness, with team, with tribe; in otherwords, with the cohesiveness of humans interacting together, either in pairs or in families. Emotions help to create bonding, attachment, and commitment, all necessary ingredients for a family or a society that wants to remain coherent and cohesive. Loyalty and patriotism are off-shoots of emotionalism.

Emotions in their most basic function have to do with an attraction-repulsion continuum, one that is commonly also divided into the "positive" and "negative" categories. Positive emotions have to do with attraction, a pulling together, a uniting. Negative emotions have to do with a repulsion, a pushing away, a withdrawing, a separating. Humans in most cultures tend to favor positive emotions because they foster human survival, and they tend to repress the negative ones because they threaten it. Even though this cultural bias against negative emotions is universal, it still behooves each individual to make peace with the "dark side" of her emotional spectrum. Without the ability to mobilize the negative emotions, the body is at risk.

Our Emotional Environment

Childhood reflects an intense boundary-sensitive period of rapidly changing perceptions of self. Initially, an infant is considered an extension of the mother and family rather than an autonomous being, and is related to as an object. Hence: "my baby", "change the baby", "hand me the baby", "the baby has my nose".

During the toddler years, a remarkable sense of self emerges. "Me do it!" is a typical first exclamation of the self as subject rather than object. As the child enters adolescence and young adulthood, she forges her own sense of distinctiveness, and establishes boundaries and intimacy with others, while at the same time creating an emotional map marked with all sorts of attraction/repulsion, intimacy-seeking/independence-asserting landmarks.

All of these experiences with their corresponding meanings are meticulously recorded, remembered, and imprinted in the circuitry of the mind/body system and unconsciously replayed whenever we interact with others and how we feel when alone. Adults who project unmet needs of childhood onto others, continue to live within the boundary framework of an infant, forever searching for a relationship that will keep an infant's world alive. Another type of adult wrestles with Mother and Father in every contact they have with others. And there are those who become stuck in the attitude of adolescence where rebelliousness, feelings of abandonment, and non-commitment reign. An adult body does not an adult make.

We find ourselves in a complex emotional environment these days, not unlike a wildly patterned quilt stitched with patches of the projected past, all inter-mingling into undecipherable personal dramas in the present. We can perceive this emotional backdrop to our current reality as varied and rich, or extremely confusing. Because of the inner baggage we each carry forward into our present world, relationships often show up like thick jungle overgrowth, and require a great deal of attention.

The path to emotional clarity involves knowing one's own healthy sense of boundaries, and learning healthy boundary-making and assertiveness skills. In the end, each of us stands alone, responsible for filling our own emotional cup, and learning how to give to and receive from others without either of those being at our own expense. Only when we integrate our own pains from the past can we fully engage in healthy, feeling relationships in the present.

Psychoneuroimmunology: Principles of Mind/Body Integration

OK, let's recap. Biologically, we have a two-way information exchange setup that not only connects the primary internal communication systems (nervous system/brain, endocrine system, and immune system), but also links the biochemical to the experiential--all via a universal network of mood-altering molecules. Our emotional and social environment, with all its spoken and unspoken conflicts and pressures, establishes the context within which our individual organism responds. Thirteen principles govern how the translation between these levels takes place, and set the parameters for effective therapy. Here they are in a nutshell and in my own simple terms:

Principle One:

What's out there goes in, and what's in there comes out.

From the beginning, and all during the formative years of life, the nervous system is open to suggestions. It receives impressions from the environment like a passive tuning fork that vibrates from the myriad of sounds that waft by. External events thus "dominate" the nervous system, forging neural pathways which then influence all future processing. On-going exposure to a particular language, for example, imparts very specific tongue, lip, and air flow abilities, which eventually determines not just speech patterns, but how thoughts are formed, linked, and expressed. Without any conscious thought required, a map of world- and self-defining parameters is established.

Babies and toddlers naturally absorb and imitate the mannerisms of adults and siblings, manifesting those behaviors that are re-enforced by example and reward, and inhibiting behaviors deemed unacceptable by the family system.   For little children facing unrealistic demands, too much resonance with external stimuli can do the reverse of what is expected, and cause inner repression.

The second part of this principle explains how our beliefs tend to find evidence for back-up. After certain patterns of perception and interpretation are imprinted in our systems, we tend to discover those things in our environment. Someone from an abusive father who concludes that "men are insensitive" will tend to filter all further contact with men through that screen.

Principle Two:

The system responds to stress long after the source of stress is removed.

An experiment that exposed puppies to continuous electric shocks to measure their immune response in the face of on-going stress, showed the immune systems dampened long after the juice was turned off. Contact with external stressors requires recovery time even after involvement ceases. The more traumatic the contact, the more recovery time necessary.

Principle Three:

The system responds to perceived/imagined reality in the same way as it does to actual reality, and to beliefs as it does to truth.

Just the memory or reminder of a former trauma can elicit a response that is identical to the original trauma. With dreams and daydreams, our mind/body system responds to inner virtual reality exactly the same way it responds to actual external reality.

Groups coached to practice basketball only in their imagination improved as much as those who practiced in actuality, and both did better than the group that didn't practice at all.

Principle Four:

The system processes input via the laws of parsimony, or the path of least resistance, which makes the known dominate new input.

This tendency to make things "familiar," or to attempt to understand a new event based on what we already know, may bring efficiency to the system, but it also yields a built-in laziness factor, and potentially robs it of novelty. The known, or familiar, comprises what we could call the "mind": an internal map or version of the world, which may or may not have anything to do with actual reality.

Principle Five:

The system maintains a record of all experiences with a triune memory, which includes body-response, emotional charge, and personal meaning.

This holds many implications for therapy, basically requiring that the therapist deal with each of the triune factors to facilitate an integration.

Principle Six:

It takes effort to move from a trance state (where imprints from the past dominate experience and we cling to the familiar) to something new.

It requires energy to counteract the natural parsimony of the system. The familiar sits like a veil over the brand-newness of creation. The tendency to make the world familiar is hard-wired in. Unconscious automation, or the old learned "knee-jerk" responses, rule unless some effort is made to dethrone them.

Principle Seven:

The system operates on the biological imperative to avoid pain.

Avoidance of pain has more survival value, and therefore more intrinsic influence on us than Freud's Pleasure Principle. Avoidance of pain is also hard-wired into the system via a complex of neurological defense mechanisms that cause the conscious mind to dissociate from trauma and fragment feeling.

Principle Eight:

Experiences repressed out of consciousness remain imprinted in the system in their original form.

Like a cyst, or anything else the body encapsulates to deal with, certain painful experiences get tucked away into unconsciousness so we can continue functioning. Unfortunately, a built-in danger follows in the wake of this principle: the body initiates an immune response to destroy any internalized foreign matter, and may perceive the vague presence of encapsulated feelings as such. Unconsciousness is dangerous. I believe this sort of dynamic underlies the autoimmune response.

Principle Nine:

The system operates on internal deductive logic.

This is not rational logic, but rather, a more "artistic" logic based on a loose set of associations and emotional charge. Conclusions about reality are based more on things verified by our feelings than anything else.

Principle Ten

It takes energy to keep material repressed from consciousness.

That's right. Repression requires on-going vigilance to keep itself going. Defenses required to keep pain out of consciousness must be in force for the repression to be effective. When we relax or sleep, our defenses also rest. Hence the inability of repressed people to ever fully let go. Anxiety is the hallmark of slipping defenses.

Principle Eleven:

When repressed material returns to consciousness, the pain associated with it, and the energy required for the repression, does also.

This necessitates educating the client (or oneself) to make peace with pain. Learn how re-integrated pain actually forges a gateway to renewal and revitalization, so you won't resist it so much when it emerges. All the energy that went into repression gets liberated when pain is integrated. That's good news!

Principle Twelve:

Every disintegration of experience sets integrative forces into motion.

The quest for wholeness comes hard-wired in also. Things that belong whole strive to become so when split apart. In my model, the fragmented neuropeptide chips of dissociated experience begin a quest to reunite the moment they are rent asunder. The impetus to be real thus has biological fuel. This is another good news principle.

Principle Thirteen (thanks to Steve Wolinsky):

Every access is a reframe.

This makes for profoundly good news. It means that every time we consciously remember something, we change it just by accessing it. Even though the imprints of pain from age two may remain encapsulated in their original form within us, we're not two years old any more. Just by accessing the memories we alter their meaning. When we attempt reframing without full integration of feeling, however, we end up thwarting the process of fully updating our systems. Positive thinking as an overlay on top of painful feelings just becomes another neurotic strategy designed to keep us away from pain, and saps our energy from being present as much as any other neurotic thing.

Summary:

The principles of psychoneuroimmunology regulate how we process our experiences, and define "mind" as an imprinted inner mapping system that may or may not at any given moment have anything to do with as-is reality. When inner map and external circumstances fail to mesh, and inner "rules" no longer apply, a person experiences an "issue" that calls for resolution.

These psychoneuroimmunology principles also dictate what is therapeutic and what isn't, what makes for an integrative experience and what doesn't. The mind/body's healing system operates on the underlying innate movement towards wholeness, and obeys the laws of fragmentation and reintegration as mandated by the above principles.

Although many of the principles reveal our deterministic, automated, unconscious nature, just as many spotlight our capacity to enjoy consciousness, change, growth, and healing. The rudder towards freedom rests squarely in our own hands.

Let's Get Physical:
The Role of an Enzyme-Rich Diet in Emotional Integration

"...all disease must be seen in relation to feelings, for feelings
predominate and integrate human functioning."
--Arthur Janov, Ph.D.
***

"Germs hover constantly about us, but they do not set in and take root
unless the terrain is ripe. This terrain is cultivated by our thoughts,
cognitive style, feelings, and perceptions."
---Claude Bernard, biologist

All human biological processes, from sneezing to digestion to generating red blood cells, are electro-chemical in nature. So are thoughts and feelings. The ability to access and express feelings depends on the electro-chemical health of the body. An enzyme-rich diet of fresh and raw fruits and vegetables provides the main ingredient for keeping the internal environment vital: electrolytes. Electrolytes are essentially wet minerals, the result of the body's 98% water naturally unlocking the static electrical charge of inert mineral substances from our food. Electrolytes are the building blocks of proper nerve conduction and neuro-muscular functioning. Without adequate electricity at the cellular level, a person will tend to feel tired, sluggish, and even depressed. Chemical antidepressants designed to give us an emotional lift address these symptoms by keeping the gap between nerve endings flooded with neurotransmitters, thereby boosting the electrical flow. This approach misses the real source of the problem. What depletes the body of proper nerve conduction in the first place is the de-pressing of feeling, in conjunction with an electrolyte-poor diet. An enzyme and mineral-rich diet, coupled with a healthy feeling life, creates optimal health because it ensures a plentiful free-flow of electrochemical energy in the body. The life force is a physical reality you can feel.

The mind/body link-up reveals itself as a two-way mirror, where physical elements and processes are reflected in emotional and mental processes, and vice versa. The body often pantomimes the dramas of the heart and mind, and as resolution and integration find their way into the feeling aspects of our lives, so, too, does the body reflect the burgeoning health of the mind. Dealing with both aspects of the equation optimizes our chances for health.

Central to the mind/body connection is the electrical circuitry of the limbic system that dwells in the mid-brain. The limbic loop hosts the pleasure center, and is also the area central to emotion and memory. Information from this emotionally charged segment of the brain encodes itself on neuropeptide messenger molecules, which then store themselves on area-specific receptor sites throughout the soft tissues of the body.

Every physical process in the body therefore literally carries an emotional charge, as does the stored memory of each event. The mind/body system uses the level of electrical charge, or the valence of feeling (Arthur Janov's terminology), to determine what is important and what is not. Some experiences are more highly charged than others, a phenomenon that places pain and trauma (because of their high feeling valence) at the top of the biological priority list. Repressed pain thereby creates pockets of disconnected tissue that cannot receive nutrition, making them danger zones in the body, verified by MRIs and CT technology. By flushing out the physical toxins through a detoxification process that consists of eating an enzyme-rich "living foods" diet, dark spaces are brought into light--physically as well as in the consciousness of the individual.

Some levels of emotional integration are almost impossible to reach when the nutrition-depleted body cannot provide the "voltage" required for such an undertaking. Fortunately, after only a week or so of being on a regimen of fresh and raw enzyme-rich foods, inner experience shifts. Initially, you may just feel "strange." Psychological issues begin to surface, and emerging feelings signal that the body is ready for an integration. Recognize this as a good thing! A pure diet tends to make us more sensitive, and more aware of ourselves and others. Junk and heavy foods tend to buffer and blur boundary issues.

Living foods oxygenate and infuse the body with aliveness, and this initiates detoxification. Vitality equals electricity. Electricity from living foods awakens and brings to consciousness stored, emotionally charged memories that have been kept out of consciousness. Pain that has required high levels of denial and repression to cope with is released. It all comes up during detox--all the "issues" that the patient has been struggling with over time (only the pain is more direct.) It isn't easy to stuff feelings down under a regimen of raw fruits and vegetables! Pouring clean water in a dirty bucket brings dirt to the surface!

Nutrifying yourself with fresh and raw fruits, vegetables, green drinks, and wheatgrass juice, and regularly undergoing a colon cleansing, sets into motion profound transformation. Instead of the body expending energy over-taxing the large intestine, liver, and kidneys (the "eliminators") with a regular flood of junk food, it can shift into "housecleaning" mode. The toxins that your body had to contain and isolate now circulate freely on their way to being released. Introducing a good diet after years of wrong eating flushes the dirt to the surface. Fortunately, the body's innate wisdom regulates the rate of toxic release, so that although you may experience discomfort at times, it will never be too much.

As vital as living food may be to health, it takes more than what you eat or the cleanliness of your colon to yield full aliveness. Still more fundamental is consciousness, which sets the banks of bodily reality, and determines what can and cannot be healed. Food alone can never bring full life or absolute fulfillment, nor can it ever remedy undernourishment of heart and mind. A study of orphanages during the 1940s in the United States found that a large number of babies receiving adequate food and shelter still succumbed to an inexplicable wasting away and failure to thrive. In an atmosphere where they were not held, rocked, or attended to in stimulating, loving ways, food alone could not sustain them.

Beyond physical malnourishment, love-deprivation stands at the root of physical and mental disease. Love deprivation can mean anything from out-and-out abuse to the less extreme situation of growing up with a particular aspect of the natural self going through life unloved, unsupported, or neglected.

After years of witnessing thousands of people going through the physical "detox" process at Hippocrates Health Institute in West Palm Beach, Florida, I have noticed that the treatment always has accompanying vital mental and emotional components. Detoxification doesn't transpire in an impersonal vacuum, but rather, within the spe-

cific context of the individual's personhood. As cells dump accumulated toxic waste into the circulatory system for elimination, old memories, hurts, and anxieties often rear up and then are re-circulated into
consciousness. My goal is to help you understand what to expect in the
process I call emotional detox, and how to embrace it without resistance. Detox is a good thing, even when it feels bad.

Living foods and inner integrative processing go hand in hand.
As hard as changing diets may seem, it pales before the intensity of the
biological urge to integrate disconnected parts and to love and accept
the unlovable and unacceptable shadowy aspects of ourselves. Inner transformative work goes deep to the very foundation of how we put ourselves together, and challenges our deepest assumptions about what is
good or bad.

Recognize and embrace your impulses as you detoxify with living foods. Come to think of "detox" as an opportunity to unburden
your heart and mind. Often Hippocrates guests say to me: "I'm having
feelings I'd really like to get rid of."

"But," I reply, "isn't that request just like the surgical you-got-
a-problem-let's-just cut-that-part-out approach?" Rather than saying "get
rid of it," I say reintegrate! Heal by becoming whole. The word "healing" comes from the Greek word *holos* which means "wholeness." To
heal is to make whole.

Negative feelings, per se, do not damage a person; but sup-
pressing feelings does cause damage. Nature, in her unabashed simplicity, as can be seen in uninhibited children, calls for full-feeling and expression. Repression infuses an anti-life message into the body and
dampens the natural state. Repression causes the body to cut off from
certain parts, and waste energy by keeping feelings down. Reclaiming
the heart by reconnecting with feelings clears a path through the jungle
of human interactions and liberates us from the past. On-going self-
discovery and self-acceptance in a practical way stands as a banner that
lines the road to peace and health, whereas the "get-rid-of-it" approach
ends in a tragic dead end. Therefore, be gentle with yourself during the
detoxification process.

Feeling fragments re-emerging via memories into the conscious
mind make up the life-review process, a common, naturally occurring
experience for a person facing death. It's easy to understand how some-

one near the end of their life would want to reflect on their journey, and come to terms with it. However, even in the ten seconds before a mountain climber slips and falls to the end of his rope, his whole life suddenly flashes before him --and not by conscious desire. Life-review is the body's way of bringing up and integrating all unfinished business from the past, the impetus of which comes from a strong biological imperative.

Facing imminent death isn't the only path into the life-review. Detox can stir up this same integrative body function--intensively--and so, be ready for it! Centropic Integration (CI) as a form of body-focused psychotherapy, provides a way to facilitate this process without actually having to come close to death. Why wait till you're on your death bed to experience it? CI creates room for body-response, emotion, and meaning that are being carried in a fragmented form to come into consciousness and be integrated. CI is about letting these bits of unfinished business finally find each other, align, and come to rest. The process doesn't have to take a long time, either. Unlike much of conventional therapy, I say: "It's not a matter of time, but rather a matter of timing." Get ready for the life review aspect of detoxification, and meet it head-on so that these surfacing "problems" can rapidly become newly integrated positive resources for you.

The Chemistry of Tears

Once there was a man who was very emotional---that is, he wept easily, and he laughed easily. Scientists took him to a lab, and hooked him up to all sorts of measuring devices. They measured his heart rate and rhythm, temperature, blood chemistry, brain waves, etc. They got baseline values of everything, and then proceeded to show him slides, first neutral ones, and then more "emotionally charged" ones. When they showed the man slides of hungry, homeless children, he wept. And the scientists collected his tears of sorrow and spun them in their machinery, and out came a biochemical profile.

Then after more neutral slides and a return to baseline values, they showed the man another "charged" picture: a photograph of two elderly men embracing. They told him that these were two brothers separated at an early age during WWII, who were now being reunited for the first time since. The man wept tears of joy, and of course, the scientists were right there to collect those tears. These, too, they spun around in their machines and produced a biochemical read-out on them. Finally, they held up the two results for comparison, and discovered something remarkable: the chemistry of the tears of sorrow differed significantly from that of the tears of joy! Only the emotion could account for the difference! Emotions change body chemistry. Psychiatrists use the reverse of this formula: they give drugs to alter the emotions, but whichever method is used, the link abides!

Secondary Gains From Illness

Sometimes there are secondary gains for the sick person that must be addressed psychologically, otherwise the body may not release its hold on the illness. Friends or co-workers may act nicer or more considerate when they know you're sick, or when they think you might be dying. Barriers to loving relationships with spouses or family members may fall away in the wake of new vulnerabilities that come with illness . Or you might reduce your workload, or stop working altogether because of your illness, thereby removing major stressors from your life in a way you were unable to do prior to the illness. Secondary gains like this could lie imbedded in the subconscious mind, serving to reinforce illness as tenaciously and insidiously as any tumor.

Ironically, even though being sick often debilitates and demoralizes, it is not unusual for disease to heighten a sense of alertness or aliveness, putting the patient in touch with a depth of feeling and appreciation for life previously untapped. When a stunt man arranged to have himself suspended upside-down, chained in a straight-jacket, and then submerged in water until he could escape, he said he did it "because that first breath on returning to the surface totally reminds me that "I'm alive."

Disease can manifest as an unconsciously driven catastrophe to accelerate spiritual awareness. The crisis of illness can stimulate unprecedented self-examination; it frequently intensifies the search for meaning and purpose, and can bring to fruition in a short time an aliveness that might far exceed anything accomplished in all the years before the illness occurred. A young man carrying + HIV titers said, "The last few years with this disease have been the best and most meaningful of my life. Before HIV I was wandering aimlessly. Now I have more close friends, a mission in life, and do counseling work I love. I would never give this up! I don't want to be cured!"

As you detox, enjoy your new sensitivity. Enjoy this new world of a body aligned with nature! Anticipate the healthy signs of emotional detox, which include a heightened inner awareness of emotion and an increased inability to avoid it (you just cannot stuff emotion when on a clean, enzyme-rich diet), and embrace the process with faith in the greater healing it brings.

Hooray for the detox process and the way it catapults us into self-reflection with a confrontational power second only to death! Hooray for you for plunging into the health-giving stream of living foods and inner integration! May its waters refresh and renew your life!

Recommendations during your cleansing time while on an enzyme-rich diet:

1.   Cultivate an attitude of allowing in regard to your own emotions as they surface. Expect the unexpected. Find a healthy and safe outlet for the emotions, such as therapy. Know this inner work as part of your detox program, and do your best to welcome it, engage it, and participate in it.

2.   Connect with a support group wherever you go. You are not alone!

3.   Ask questions. Ask for help. It's OK to not know. And it makes sense to get the help you want.

4.   Pay attention to your thoughts and emotions as just that; remember, "you have them; don't let them have you."

5.   Pay attention to the "voices" of your body that may be reflecting inner hurts. Consciousness/attention stands out as the primary agent of change.

6.   Recognize detox as a special time for you in your life journey, and an opportunity to attend to inner realities that may otherwise go unattended.

Edith: Keep Your Colon and Your Heart Clean

When I first met Edith, I thought she was dead. Her body lay flaccid and limp on a special Intensive Care Unit air bed, while a respirator mechanically inflated her lungs. Cardiac wires and IV lines cascaded out of her neck, with only the heart monitor above her bed showing any sign of life.

Edith had received a heart transplant after having suffered as a cardiac invalid for five years. Now 56 years old, this south Georgia farmer's widow was in a vegetative state after transplant surgery, and no one could figure out why. For a patient who is in a coma and on life-support, the nurse stands as a bridge between "living death" and the return to a normal life. The nurse watches over the patient, and helps to maintain every body system-- preventing the skin from breaking down, for example, and making sure unused muscles don't enter a state of permanent contraction.

My first thought upon seeing Edith lying there so life-less was, "why are we doing this to her? We should have let her die with dignity." But I felt challenged by the case. Edith was a mess. She looked much older than her age. The anticoagulants she had taken before surgery had produced multiple deep-purple bruises all over her arms, especially where the IV needles had punctured her skin. Her hair was matted; her teeth and tongue were coated white, and her breath was foul. Her urine, flowing from catheter to bedside bag, was scant and murky.

I proceeded to clean her up, wash and comb her hair, and put crisp, clean sheets on the bed to make her as presentable as possible for her family. Her two grown sons sheepishly approached her bedside, befuddled looks on their faces, unsure about how to respond to a situation that felt overwhelming in its seriousness. They had talked their mother into having the surgery, and now, seeing her like this, their guilt had escalated into an awkward silence.

"Why doesn't she wake up?" the older son asked.

"We don't really know," I explained. "All her systems are fine. Her new heart is doing great. It's a mystery. We'll do an EEG, which is a brain wave test, later today--maybe she had a stroke."

"She really didn't want to have this surgery," the younger brother admitted. "After Dad died two years ago, Mama just lost her will to live."

"Maybe this is her way of fighting the surgery, saying she wants to go be with Dad," the elder son tried to rationalize. Their remorse hung heavy in the air.

Days passed with no change in Edith's condition. She was categorized as "stable," but she still hadn't waked up. Her EEG did not register a stroke. Her lungs were clear. Her urine output picked up, and now was within normal limits. On my twelve-hour shifts, I kept her physiologically steady by moving her, turning her, massaging her, and talking to her. I told her about the sadness and guilt her sons were experiencing, and about how it was spring in Atlanta. I talked about how lovely her farm must look. Weeks went by.

Then one day I noticed her chest X-ray on the view screen by the nurses' station. At the very base of the film I could see a huge whited-out area, which on an X-ray means infiltration or solid mass. I asked the doctor about it.

"Well, it's not her lungs. This area is below her diaphragm. You know, I'm not sure what it is." He ordered a series of abdominal pictures.

"Her colon is full of barium!" he announced after the X-rays came back. He continued, "A week before surgery, Edith had complained about abdominal pain, so we had run a barium swallow. All we found was some diverticulitis."

"Why is the barium still in there, and could that have something to do with her still being in a coma?" I inquired.

The doctor laughed at my naivete. "I hardly think being constipated is keeping her unconscious!" he said.

But it seemed worth a shot, so I asked the other doctors on Edith's case, one by one, if I could give her a high enema. Did they get a good laugh! At least one made a crude joke. I finally found one doctor, who, although he was of the opinion that my notion of a clogged colon being at the root of the coma ridiculous, finally agreed, and ordered the colon irrigation.

Five gallons of water and a basin of pasty barium later, Edith woke up. She became the talk of the hospital staff, and the subject of more jokes. Even though Edith's revival after the colonic irrigation seemed a crazy coincidence, my credibility rose many notches that day (except for the gastroenterologist on the case, who had made extremely demeaning remarks about me and the "pseudo-science" I practiced. He never looked me in the eye again!)

Edith was upset to find herself alive. I could tell by her wide eyes and agitated state. I talked to her a lot and had her sons do the same, and she finally calmed down, then slumped into depression. We weaned her off the ventilator, but she stayed silent and sullen. Taking care of her felt like I was battling her desire to die. Her sons, still overcome by guilt, came around less often, and Edith withdrew into a silent black hole.

The only time she livened up was when it was time to get out of bed. She cussed at me, and complained, and really let the venom flow.

"That hurts, you fool! Don't you know nothin'?!"

"Hey, Edith, don't blame me because you lived. I'm just treating you like you're alive, and that means you have to move and eat. This is my job. You don't have to like it, but you have to do it!"

We had a good understanding: she felt free to vent all her rage at me, and I felt free to tell it like it was. Soon the doctors ordered the wires and IV lines removed, and we increased Edith's physical therapy treatments. Her complaining increased proportionately.

"Damn you, fool. Can't you see I don't want to do this?"

"You're welcome, Edith, for everything I am doing for you," I said.

"Just leave me in bed. I don't need your help!"

"I don't think so," I said tersely. "Face it, Edith, I don't know why, but you're getting better."

After weeks of babying Edith back to life, not once did a thank-you or anything else positive come from her, and I was reaching my tolerance limit. One day, it happened. I could feel Edith's complaining voice grating against my nerves again, and when she started about how lumpy the pudding was and what kind of a damn fool would make pudding like that, I blew.

'That does it!' I thought. 'I don't care if I get fired, but someone has to tell her off!'

I walked right up to her, hunched over her bedside tray, and put my hand on her upper chest, and with a power fueled by my built-up frustration, I heard myself speak these words: "Edith, you have suffered enough!" I meant to say, "I've had enough," or, "you ungrateful bitch," but those were not the words that came out.

Just at that moment, a white dove fluttered down onto the window ledge outside the room. Edith, with startled eyes and open mouth, looked up at me and saw the fire in my face, then looked over at the dove, then back at me. And after a long silent moment, she started crying, softly at first, then in great sobs. It was then and only then that Edith received her new heart.

From that day on, Edith got well fast, with no more complaining. She had soft eyes and she started saying thank-you to everyone. Even the physical therapist went from mumbling 'bitch' to calling her "trooper" and praising her efforts. Within two weeks, Edith transferred out of the ICU into a regular room, getting around in a wheelchair.

A week after that she went home. "I just miss my front porch," she said. "I want to see and smell Spring again."

One year later I met Edith at the heart transplant patient reunion at our hospital, still sitting in a wheelchair, but looking plump and healthy. We hugged each other and reminisced about her hospital stay the year before.

"I don't remember much, but I'll never forget what you did for me. And I'll never forget that dove. It was the Holy Spirit, for sure. I'd been so bitter after my husband's death and so upset to have survived the surgery. I didn't want it, you know. I must have been very cranky. You were like an angel from God, just like that dove--sent to snap me out of my depression. I can't thank you enough. Jesus has showed me that even without my husband, and even without being able to walk, I still have a lot to live for and be grateful for."

We hugged goodbye. I never did tell Edith that doves regularly roosted on our hospital window ledges, because I'm convinced it was the religious framework she gave to that experience that reconnected her with her heart and saved her life. And her clean colon of course.

Bio-logic: the Logic of Catastrophic Thinking

The mind/body system reasons deductively, by processing evidence provided by experience in order to come to conclusions about "how things are," then creating a map for future interactions. Because deductive logic is based on internal rules that accept givens, whether they are true or not, the conclusions of this sort of primitive reasoning often end up saturated with a pathetic anti-life defeatism. Listen to these statements:

"To have a life is to have a self.
To have a self is to be separate from others.
Therefore, to unite with others, is to have no self."

Or:

"My mother loves me when I am quiet.
When I am quiet she doesn't pay attention.
I want to be what she wants so she will pay attention to me
Therefore: there is no way for me to be who I am and get what I want."

Or how about this one:

"My parents need me to be what I am not (i.e., always happy).
If I release that, then they won't need me, and then I won't exist. Therefore,
I must always be happy or die."

These are not the rantings of a madman, but words that reflect the bio-logic of a child strategizing about how to get the love she needs when it is not directly forthcoming. Unfortunately, the body takes these injunctions literally, and they become lodged in some system of the body, sometimes driving cells crazy, with no conscious awareness on the child's part.

A computer receives input, and works with it, moving from point A to Point B only within the guidelines and parameters of the program. The primitive processing that occurs in the child's mind often yields conclusions that put in motion anti-life impulses, creating an inner circuitry that sets the stage in the body for disease. Unresolved nervous energy is converted into anxiety and stress. Certain events are processed in futile, non-productive ways, creating highly anxious inner states that continually pump out more and more stress responses, all based on a primary processing system that isn't effective.

Sometimes the combinations of these unworkable seed thoughts manifest in simpler, but just as lethal, chains. Something like: "I can't but I have to," or "In order to survive this I must die." These don't make sense in terms of everyday logic, but they have their own bio-logic to them. Rational therapy claims that just by correcting false modes of thinking, healing takes place. This may be true in the more neutral realms of faulty logic, but it is not true when the skewed conclusions remain embedded within the tissue at highly charged levels of emotion. Addressing only the one-dimensional thinking level of a bio-logical imprint is equal to "healing" a pimple with makeup--i.e., healing doesn't happen. Conclusions imprinted with an emotional charge cannot be discharged or overcome by rationalizing or talking yourself out of them. That would be like saying to an anorexic: "Just eat!" No. Eating for an anorexic is such a charged event that therapeutic intervention must reach the same level of emotional charge that drives the disorder.

A bio-logical conclusion naturally seeks a way to undo itself, to remedy the painful situation that spawned it. The result is a Life Strategy. When a life strategy grows out of faulty bio-logical conclusions of catastrophic proportions, a life becomes skewed. The life strategy is then acted out to the tune of "Looking for Love in All the Wrong Places." The person's life is riddled with bad relationships, seeming self-sabotage, and a sense of futility. One can develop, then live out irrational life strategies, and never even know what they're doing. Even when they do come to recognize what they are doing, which is not uncommon for people in talk therapy, they still don't essentially change. They become what I call well-educated neurotics. Until the emotional and body components of imprinted bio-logic are addressed and uprooted, people remain stuck in the body/mind system with them--in a time long gone, in a drama with no final curtain.

Life strategies and the bio-logic that they are built upon come in a variety of packages, some more self-defeating than others. How do you like this one:

"My mother is unhappy.
I am happy. She cannot love me if she's unhappy.
If I take her unhappiness, then she can be happy and love me.
Therefore, in order to be happy I must be unhappy."

Sound like a "10" on the Richter scale of misery? It does to me.

Life strategies go hand-in-hand with struggle, because they are essentially unworkable. They are designed to meet needs and avoid pain, neither of which may be possible in actuality. Whenever love or approval are not forthcoming in a flowing manner, a child will develop a strategy to make it happen, even if it means going against her own nature and biology. Place a plant in a closet, and it will become contorted in shape in order to grow towards the sliver of light coming in through the crack at the bottom of the door. Just as plants are phototropic (grow towards the light), humans are love-tropic, and will do whatever it takes to procure it. Warped life-strategies carry built-in failure and disappointment. *"I want to be loved for who I really am, so I'll be what you want me to be in order to be loved,"* is a doomed philosophy.

Hope is what fuels life strategies. Without hope, the person must feel the total unworkable-ness of what he has developed, as well as the pain from feeling unloved.

Hope Must Die

Normally hope is a good thing. Bernie Siegel said, "There's no such thing as false hope, because hope is essentially an experience independent of evidence." Unfortunately, sometimes children put hope into an essentially hopeless situation, and even escalate it desperately as a way of offsetting the looming despair.

At a certain point in most patients' core therapy work, I say: "Let yourself have your natural response to these words: 'You will never get the love or understanding you need from your parents' (substitute "father" or "mother" where appropriate)", and inevitably the bubble of hope that has kept the struggle-based strategy going pops, and appropriate grieving can begin. Healthy grieving is far better than unhealthy despair fueled by unrealistic hope.

The bio-logic that carries unhealthy imprints and strategies of struggle, and that infuses the body with a relentless stream of internalized stress, can be "outwitted" and neutralized in therapy. Feeling is the key. Once a person connects with the pain that generated the life strategy of struggle to begin with, then the unreal system can be successfully dismantled from the inside out. The end of an unreal strategy, along with the cessation of a lifetime of struggle, feel concurrently like death and rebirth. When a person has so identified her life with the struggle for love, the end of struggle feels like the end of life itself. The raw state of vulnerability in the face of healthy surrender lays wide open the groundwork of one's being to new seeds of simple desire and fulfillment. Unreal hope must die so the seed of real hope may sprout.

My Life Is Over

"It"s over. My life is over. And I thank you. With your help, I"ve accomplished what I came to the earth to do. Now I can kill myself".

This was Laurie's announcement to me after months of therapy, culminating in an intense session dealing with her mother's suicide when Laurie was 18-months old. Laurie had worked as an ICU nurse for years, in addition to doing private duty home care nursing. She also cared for and supported her invalid brother at home. Like a true angel of mercy, on the job 60+ hours a week, she had reached the point of no return, no longer remembering how to stop. Nor did she understand what was driving her.

It became clear during our sessions that her mother's suicide had impacted her enormously. What emerged was the picture of Laurie's mother as a troubled woman who repeatedly called her little daughter "bad", and threatened to leave her. Her mother's suicide then imprinted PROOF of being bad in the mind of the child, who then became compelled to "be good" at all times. Any rest, or focus on self, opened up space for the anxiety and panic of a little girl feeling solely responsible for her mother's death.

By entering into these fears, and making the space for the anxiety to pass through all levels, which included waves of shaking, gasping, and screaming, the integration into consciousness of overwhelming pain could occur. It then became sparklingly clear to Laurie's adult mind that the 18-month-old was not in fact responsible for her mother's leaving.

To Laurie, life as she had known it was over. That circuit at the center of the switchboard had suddenly been completed, and was no longer in charge. Every action, every thought, every motivation had been based on the overwhelming guilt and anxiety of a child. Like waking from a dream, Laurie looked shocked and in a daze. With follow-up contacts and sessions, she continued to integrate the reality of her past unreal life—and became further aware of how much she had unconsciously invested in proving her goodness, how much she had to prove her goodness.

Laurie soon quit half her jobs, and went on personal leave from the others. She eventually allowed her brother to go live with another sister. The curtain had dropped on her central life-drama, and now a whole new life could begin. Yes, her life was over--the unreal life she had been living.

Pro-active vs. Victim Mentality

People who are pro-active rather than reactive in their responses are more in control of their own destiny, more in charge of their inner response to what the world hands them, and therefore tend to be healthier all around.

Imagine an experiment actually performed on two rats, both exposed to the same mild electric shocks. One rat is trained to push a lever to prevent the current from touching either of them, while the other rat can only watch. After many rounds of being shocked, and finally learning how to manipulate the lever to protect them, a blood sample from each rat was taken to determine immune function. Conclusion: the rat that was taught to stop the shocks and ultimately did so, maintained a much higher immune function in the face of stress than did the rat who was exposed to the same shocks, but did not have the capacity to ward them off. Rat number two was a passive observer--a victim, as it were.

The following is another great example of how the pro-active state is independent of circumstances, and is conducive to health. Viktor Frankl, author of <u>Man's Search for Meaning</u>, and founder of the movement of existential psychology called "Logotherapy," endured years as a prisoner in four different concentration camps during WWII. Near the end of the war, conditions worsened to the point where guards were withholding food, and many inmates perished. The soldiers who finally liberated the prisoners found most of the survivors in an emaciated and sickly state. Frankl, on the other hand, looked remarkably fit. When asked how he'd done it he said, "While everyone else was being starved to death, I was fasting!"

The Past is Present

The cerebral cortex part of our brain that symbolizes and gives meaning to our experience bases its conclusions on the past. A reactive orientation is a predominantly passive mode of relating to the world, the sina no qua of which is based in the past, meaning a person forfeits the freedom of new options when they remain attached to the hegemony of old meanings. A reactive person greets the new world with old responses. The more emotional baggage a person carries around stored in the tissue of the body, the more likely situational pressures trigger old, learned knee-jerk responses. Reactivity is largely a by-product of repressed pain.

Each one of us inhabits a space somewhere on the continuum between reactive and proactive. And everyone holds the capacity for a freedom that stands independent of circumstances, life-style, money, gender, etc. True freedom emerges from an inner experience. Freedom is fasting, when those around you consider lack of food as starving. Freedom is being able to feel in an unfeeling world.

Resistance: Escape From Freedom

Every conscious integration of old pain brings us a step closer to freedom and to the pro-active state. So why doesn't everyone rush to do some form of inner integrative work if freedom is the result? Why would anyone not partake of this, let alone resist integrative impulses? Because the act of resistance provides a form of artificial stability. Resistance to change maintains the status quo, and provides a sense of continuity and consistency to our sense of self.

Our self-image is a product of the same interpretative part of our brain that gets stuck in the past. Our mind/body system dreams up a "self" that inevitably requires effort to maintain. Fritz Perls, the Father of Gestalt Therapy, called the self "a human artifact." To keep one's familiar self-image alive, constant, and consistent requires enormous resistance to new external input and internal awareness--both of which flow as the dynamic, ever-shifting river of reality! When the mind/body works at maintaining a consistent sense of self at the expense of the new in order to "keep it together," it is struggling against reality. Our system is striving to be efficient by using familiar (and thus, old) circuitry to identify and label our present experience. Unfortunately, this frustrates and inhibits the novelty, freshness, vitality, and newness of life. Obsessive Compulsive Disorder, with ritualistic, repetitive, and restrictive rules of behavior and thought, stands as a good example of the extremes the mind/body system will go to in order to maintain a feeling status-quo, and keep pain at bay. A great price to pay for "keeping it together!"

If my "self" has no more substance than a dream image from the past, then who am I in the present? Am I anything more? Who is dreaming this dream, anyway? The irony is that one has to be awake to know. I love Alice's response to the Caterpillar in Alice in Wonderland when he asks her: "And who, who are you?" and she replies: "Well, I knew who I was this morning when I woke up, but I think I must have changed several times since then."

So how do I shift from dream state to waking state? Waking up is being aware in the moment. That subtle shift of awareness changes everything. Noticing how your eyeballs move as they shift from left to right in order to follow the words on this page. Notice that? Notice your breathing? I bet you weren't aware of your breath a few seconds ago. See how easy it is to move up the ladder of awareness? Waking up challenges the "self." Maybe even threatens it. All change does. Good therapy should.

From Self-image to Self-reflection

If I connect a video camera to a monitor, whatever I point the camera at shows up as an image on the screen. What emerges when I point the camera head-on at the screen is an infinite reflective image. Like holding two mirrors up to each other. Any self-image is like a single static image the camera can generate. In a therapy session, the "infinite reflective experience" often shows up, bursting through years of inner delusion and illusion, way beyond the boundaries of any self-image. After an especially emotion-laden integration takes place, and, as I imagine it, the reunited neuropeptide chips are resting in peace in their appropriate receptor sites, the patient experiences a uniquely tailored flood of insight into lifelong patterns of thought and behavior. Not only does he enjoy the release of tension from the body in its let-go of emotion-suppressing strategies, but frequently he enters the realm of the Core Self--that Self behind and beyond all self images. At these times, the therapy process takes on a spiritual quality, not in any dissociative sense, but rather as inner resolution and acceptance. The spiritual dimension of humanness, which is an awareness at the being level rather than the level of self-image, takes its rightful place as the vital center of the whole.

Recovery of the Self, shifting from the story-level of life, or the mind's version of what is happening, to the active and direct experience of one's own senses and depth of being is the goal of the therapy I do, and is a path that leads from illness to health.

"...no man exists who was not made by the child he once was".
---Maria Montessori

✳✳✳

"Our childhood is stored in our bodies."
---Alice Miller

3

Inner Fragmentation: Why We Need Help to Be Whole and Why We Need to Go Back to Move Forward

Pain: The Circuit-breaker System

The body handles overwhelming perceptions of pain or danger in rudimentary ways. One way is to flood an injured area with endorphins, natural endogenous pain killers, which occupy opiate receptor sites and offer a numbing calmness. In the presence of extreme physical pain, it is not uncommon for a person to pass out or lose consciousness. When endorphins alone can't handle the job, the primitive reptilian section of the human brain contains its own hard-wired circuit-breaker mechanism triggered by a primeval focus on survival and safety. When the electricity is excessive, the system shorts out and disconnects. It's a simple, direct, and time-tested solution: when it hurts too much, we go to sleep.

The same responses apply to emotional and mental pain--in fact there are far more opiate receptors in the limbic, feeling area of the brain than in any other. Unlike the direct black out response we have to excruciating physical pain, when we encounter unbearable levels of emotional and mental pain, we don't "pass out" in one fell swoop, but rather dissociate or split off from reality, thus becoming unconscious in a more subtle way. The brain buffers us from traumatic experiences by disengaging the right and left hemispheres from each other (really!), then automatically dissects intact neuropeptide molecules into fragments, with each piece carrying a bit of the whole experience (body response, emotional response, and meaning response) away from conscious perception. When feelings splinter in this way, we can't feel it. The neuropeptide "chips," or feeling-fragments, then somehow begin to free-float in the nervous system (in the form of anxiety and/or tension), seeking to eventually reunite and find rest in a receptor site.

This psychological and physiological split, in the form of a severed memory, locks certain body-responses, emotional responses, and meaning responses into our tissues, driving us to recreate situations in our lives that reflect these feeling fragments, until they reunite in their original form within us. This theory helps to explain the biological basis for dysfunctional life patterns--why, for instance, children of alcoholics tend to grow up and find addictive partners, why we keep relating to members of the opposite sex in the same way, why we manifest food addictions. The dysfunctional behaviors are our body's unconscious attempt to integrate original painful experiences that we had to split from in order to survive.

One client of mine understood this when he exclaimed, "I've needed to feel cheated by people over and over again in my life, because I already felt cheated inside. It confirmed what I already knew to be my truth."

Cognitive psychology would have us believe that how we think determines how we feel. However, although one's frame of mind influences feelings to a degree, brain physiology and evolution show that feelings come first. Our more primitive reptilian and mammalian brains dominate, and dictate to the cerebral cortex what is subsequently processed symbolically into language, dream image, or philosophy. The "thinking" brain follows the feeling and sensory brains, acquiring raw material from them, out of which it then forges story and meaning. Biologically, emotion comes first, and thinking comes second. Emotionally-charged memory, even when unconscious, dominates the inner hierarchy of what gets our system's attention. It cannot be erased--it can either be repressed, or be made conscious, and then integrated.

Unfortunately, the body/mind system, in an attempt to free itself from pain, often treats unconscious imprinted memories as it would a splinter, or any other foreign invasion: it launches an immune reaction to get rid of it, even though the "it" is actually one's own feeling response to trauma! The "get-rid-of-it" mindset of coping with pain thus has its roots in biology. I believe autoimmune responses, when the immune system attacks healthy parts of the body, are misguided self-protection attempts. Unlike the wolf who, in desperation, chews off its own trapped leg in order to survive, an autoimmune response serves no real survival function.

Inner shutdown and dissociation occur as knee-jerk responses when memories and mindsets forged and adopted long ago in our personal history are triggered by something in the present. It happens without thought or conscious intent. The mind in the grip of past trauma is so defensive and reactive that it loses the ability to access creative adult resources and options. Without any awareness whatsoever of our repressed inner state, we live hemmed in by our own limited beliefs, lost in the struggle for what we never had, and held back from growing up altogether. Yesterday's defenses and survival reactions rob us of today's possibilities.

Neonates Feel Pain

For years, surgeons operated on premature babies without anesthesia believing that even if the infants felt the pain, they wouldn't remember it. New research with rats suggests that the body does remember the pain and is forever changed.

A study using newborn rats at the National Institutes of Health (NIH) found that painful trauma mimicking medical procedures commonly performed on preemies made the lab animals much more sensitive to pain as they aged.

The reason is that pain causes the developing nervous system of the very young to grow more nerve cells that carry the sensation of pain to the brain, NIH researchers say.

The study is part of a continuing effort by medical science to understand how and when the nervous system develops and how the growth of nerve tissue is affected by stimuli like pain. Such research has a direct bearing on efforts to save and improve the lives of infants born before the normal 40-week gestation is up. Survival of babies born up to 15 weeks prematurely is now not unusual, but it takes a major medical effort and many painful procedures, including countless needle sticks, breathing tubes, and even surgery.

Other studies have shown that premature babies tend to report more pain in their childhood years, and their parents report that these children's pain response is greater than their siblings'.
(Reprinted with permission from Nursing Spectrum August 21, 2000 Vol. 10, No. 17, page 27)

Four Worlds, Three Brains

Our Brain Creates a World

Every living organism with a brain creates a separate world with its brain, and then proceeds to live within the parameters of that world. Kittens raised from birth in a special environment consisting exclusively of polka dots and curved surfaces, and then placed in a room with squares and straight edges, stumbled all over themselves, fell down stairs, and bumped into walls. Their internal map no longer matched the terrain.

When this mismatch of inner map and external reality takes place in humans, they often seek help. Old ways of thinking, and old behaviors inevitably fall short in providing adequate solutions in new, unfamiliar circumstances. Some people simply "try harder" with old strategies formed in their developing years, and end up banging their heads against what shows up as more and more undoable. Those clients seek out therapy primarily to make the discomfort of difficult transitions "go away". They focus on reducing the tension inherent in encountering new things, and thereby deeper entrench themselves in the rut of old habits. When they continue to refuse or avoid the challenge of change, the therapist may actually try to intensify the Unworkable, to frustrate the old map-maker brain even more, and hopefully coax the patient to eventually birth herself into a new-world grid of possibilities. Sometimes things need to get worse before they can get better.

On the other hand, some people seek change head on. The stress of encountering the Unworkable moves them to learn new ways to engage their problems. Struggling harder to change others or the environment as a way to make things better is no longer good enough. The shift they seek lies not necessarily in the outer world, but rather within their own internal map, or even more deeply, their map-making style.

Lazy Brain Syndrome

Unfortunately, the brain prefers familiar, old maps, even in people who actively want to change, and so the "known" is given precedence. If you follow the same route to work every day for many years you will naturally gravitate to the interior automatic pilot of familiarity. The narrowed, parsimonious focus of that type of "brain-efficient" behavior is the trance people fall into. Repetition, and thus, familiarity, invokes a trance state that requires minimal alertness. The reticular activating system (RAS) at the base of the brain somehow determines the degree of alertness required in any given situation, (unexpected situations require more alertness, familiar ones require less) then channels it to the appropriate areas of the brain, where coping mechanisms kick in. The brain prefers the path of least effort, and delegates more and more of a person's routine involvements into the lower levels of alertness. Automatic pilot is the brain's modus operendus of choice.

"Alertness" or "consciousness" beefs up electrical brain activity. So does pain. Pain boosts alertness at a time when we may need it, but then, because it hurts, don't want it. Emotions, because they increase electrical activity in the brain just as pain does, also "up" the alertness factor. Depression is the hallmark of low electrical brain activity, not because of sad feelings, but because of the depression of feelings. Depression, because of its numbing effect, is not a feeling state, but rather is a defense against pain.

Feelings are a mixed blessing. They keep us in touch with the subtleties of human interaction and foster bonding, but also bring a heightened awareness of pain. We need to have feelings in order to be alert enough to survive danger, and yet we need to be able to repress them so we won't suffer. It is this evolutionarily hard-wired dilemma that makes change so hard.

The ever-efficient, lazy brain leans towards the familiar, thus resisting change. Because of that, the circuitry responsible for creating a new inner-world map is reserved exclusively for emergencies. Only in the face of the Unworkable, the Unknown, and the Uncomfortable does the brain scream out for a new world and move beyond its self-imposed trancelike limitations. Nothing screams louder for change than pain. When pain is repressed, the scream doesn't go away, it just gets muffled. In extreme cases, this cry will manifest as a suicidal tendency. The person experiences a deeply felt understanding that something needs to radically change in order to be free from the damned-if-I-do, damned-if-I-don't, unworkable scenario and its pain. What is obvious to the therapist, but not to the client, is that the body doesn't have to die in order to get past the pain.

Map Making

Reality map-making begins before birth. Even in the womb, the developing brain, in response to its environment via simple kinesthetic and sensory feedback loops, along with emotional input from the Mother-host, lays into its own neural circuitry a map of "how it is." The descriptive map of "how it is" soon turns into a prescriptive mapping process in the form of assumptions, predictions, and rules. Have you ever navigated a car, found yourself at a dead-end, gazed unbelievingly at your map, and said, "We can't be here!", as though the map was dominant over reality? In the same way, birth into this reality from the "wombal" world is a transition that cannot be computed by the brain circuitry set within the womb. Our subjective interpretation of our birth experience comes from the old circuitry. (This applies to all understanding: it's based on old information.) Because each new experience is the end of the old, birth easily gets construed as a death. Birth dramatically terminates an essentially tranquil world, and its accompanying body and emotional response of terror becomes imprinted and generalized to include any sense of impending change as a threat.

Transitions like birth, with all the overwhelmingly incomprehensible new input, knock the world-creating nature of the brain for a loop. Disorientation and confusion ensue. Think of the culture-shock and heightened mindfulness that occur when traveling in a foreign land. Every billboard, plant, facial expression, and smell comes at us with a sense of novelty lost to us in our home turf where we take everything for granted. Encountering newness makes us more vigilant, because we need extra awareness to help us through the initial phases of disorientation and confusion.

"Total immersion" into a new environment induces the most dramatic learning, but also the most disorientation and confusion. Although they make us uncomfortable, frustration, confusion, and the tension of not-knowing may be necessary ingredients for change, as well as vital ingredients in productive therapy. Therapy either accesses this level of brain functioning by frustrating old mind-sets, and encountering confusion, or it merely offers band-aid treatments. Sometimes good therapy feels threatening, and it is--to the part within us that clings to the status quo!

The Four Map-making Grids

The human brain evolves through four basic developmental stages on our journey to adulthood--think of passing through different lands on a journey--each with its unique set of assumptions and customs. I call these four map-making modalities of the brain: wombal, primal, adolescent (outer-directed adaptive), and adult (inner-directed relational). Although consciousness proceeds primarily in one direction on the way to maturity, most human growth unfolds in a nonlinear manner--a few steps forward, a few steps back. Nothing in nature moves in straight lines. Rivers meander on their way to the sea. Transitioning from one stage to the next has its own "problem areas," sometimes referred to as "developmental tasks". Social psychologist, Erik Erikson, postulated that as toddlers we must first learn to trust others before we can move on to fully become autonomous. Whenever we opt to repress feelings to make it through painful times, and thereby miss learning the age-appropriate developmental skills, maps or mind-sets from the skipped period of development get locked in, dominate our psyche, and inevitably get us into trouble. It would be like using a map drawn in the 18th century to navigate in the modern world. Old maps inevitably lead us astray.

No Two Maps Alike

The brain is responsible for creating an entire world. And though all humans share a common form and chemistry, no two brains process or route experiences the same way. The meanings we attribute to any given situation arise from a backdrop of our unique history that led up to that moment. Put me in a little hat and tight vest and pants, and place me in an arena with a red cape where I will face a wild bull, and I will have a markedly different experience from the bullfighter wearing the same clothes who was trained to fight bulls. Where his brain exalts, "Come at me, Toro!" my brain chants the great American mantra-in-the-face-of-death: "Oh, shit!" The trained bullfighter and I are using different internal maps to orient ourselves to the same situation, thereby we will have completely varied body-responses. Where I would break into a panicky sweat with knocking knees, his heart would race with exhilaration.

If that sort of total brain subjectivity weren't enough to make being an individual in a world with billions of other individuals a totally awesome mystery, the fact that some brain circuitry is neither learned or individually acquired, but is universal, certainly does. Core neural pathways common to all human brains: archetypes--are a-historical, instinctual, and have a compelling, almost irresistible quality to them. Although we encounter them subjectively, they belong to the race collectively. The plot, as it were, when it comes to living within the confines of the virtual reality of the mind, thickens. (See later section on Archetypes).

What It Takes to Change

1. Self-awareness : In order to counter the trancelike automation of living in the familiar, we need consciousness. Noticing, witnessing, and self-remembering create a foundation for the awakening experience. (Learning to shift into a witnessing state of mind, which is nothing more than a once-removed place from the actual event, so that you notice your response to the event.) Similar to the dissociation used by defense mechanisms, witnessing serves to help separate your identity from your problem, resulting in a sense of control. In other words, you learn: "I have my feelings, they don't have me. I have my thoughts, they don't have me," etc.)

2. New behavior :Take a different approach. Taking new action replaces the old circuitry with the new. Doing something different counters the brain's tendency to "just try harder" with old behavior when faced with problems.

3. Self-expression : Closing the time gap between having feelings and expressing them prevents buildup, and maintains a state of empowerment. Immediacy works best.

4. Self-affirmation--in word and deed : "I am worthy of good relationships." "I have the right to express my feelings and concerns." These are important and healthy assumptions from which we can reach out and touch the world and others in new, more satisfying ways.

5. Self-assertion : Asserting your own needs and desires and values means a more accessible world.

6. Self-disengagement : Practice letting go. It's the deathbed perspective. The solitary confinement perspective. How well a person can disengage at any moment from any situation is a marker of how inner or outer-directed they are. Inner-directed people have healthier systems, and healthier relationships.

Making a Case for Healthy Regression

I've seen clients' lips and nostrils turn blue as they gasp for oxygen on my office floor. I've heard them cry for Mommy and Daddy in a toddler's voice. I've seen forcep marks reappear on a forehead in the reliving of a birth. I've witnessed clients shake and sweat as memories of early childhood abuse erupted into their consciousness . I've heard full-grown adults wail like babies in ways they could not do on purpose. So when I write about regression in therapy, I'm not only bias, I'm an extremist. I've had to stretch my therapeutic perspective to include what might seem like a bizarre cosmology. I'm convinced that a healthy, orderly regression to the incompleted early stages of one's own development is essential for deep healing to take place.

According to myth, when Buddha was born he strode out of the womb, enlightened, and able to speak. Except for him, nobody starts off fully mature. On the road from birth to adulthood, we develop physically, emotionally, cognitively, and morally in incremental stages documented by the giants in the fields of individual, social, and cognitive psychology—Sigmund Freud, Erik Erikson, and Jean Piaget, to name a few. Transpersonal psychologist and former LSD researcher, Dr. Stan Grof, maintains that these developmental "bands of consciousness" that go all the way back to perinatal days remain within us as the foundation of our current experience. As Swiss Psychoanalyst, Alice Miller, said, "Our childhood is stored in our bodies." Our conscious mind, like the flower of a plant, grows out of the stem of our biologically-encoded history.

The origin of our identity goes even farther back than childhood. From the time we begin life as a single cell, we individually recreate the evolution of all animals on earth, transforming morphologically from amoeba to fish to salamander to mammal to primate to human. Our brain follows that same evolution, as does our growing consciousness as individual human beings. We start off primitive, vegetative and small, unaware of anything but our immediate surroundings, cultivate the ability to emotionally and socially bond, and progress all the way up to possess a sophisticated analytical, symbol-making neocortex, by which you are now reading and understanding this book. Unbeknownst to the conscious mind, we carry within us the collective memory of every prior stage of evolution. And every earlier stage of our own brain's development.

I believe that in this development, the brain creates and traverses four basic world-creating modalities--Wombal, Primal, Adolescent, Adult-- or "grids," each reflecting the world view according to the section of brain that is developmentally dominant at the time, and each having its own set of rules about what is and what is not, and what can and what cannot be. Random experiences are organized into a grid when an entire set of generalities seem to apply consistently to events. Until exceptions show up, grids work. A grid is modified to accommodate new experiences until it can no longer do so in the face of an event that "just doesn't fit", and then a new grid, with new assumptions and internal rules, sprouts forth. The brain resorts to grid formation because it's an efficient way to handle and organize data. World grids represent the bold strokes of the brain's map-making artistry.

New world grids also form according to a preordained genetic timetable of our brain's maturation. We all roughly grow up according to the same blueprint, and go through the same phases. These developmental changes do not take place in a vacuum, but rather in an atmosphere of need. Without parental love, nurturing, and sensitivity at every stage, normal, let alone optimal, growth is disrupted, and a grid stays active long after it is naturally due to go dormant. When needs are not met, the views, beliefs, and feelings of childhood linger.

When feelings become fragmented in the response to pain at any early stage in life (and I'm maintaining that this is a sure bet), development is either arrested or prematurely accelerated, and a smooth transition from one grid to the next is impaired. Integration of a feeling repressed in an earlier grid of development requires regression back to that same grid when a patient enters therapy. The same map-making part of the brain involved in the split must be involved in its renewed wholeness. Repressed feelings from age 5 must be accessed and integrated from within the original mind-grid within the client. The same holds true for splits that occur even earlier, as far back as the womb. Those integrations will look very different from each other because how a five-year-old experiences pain is very different from how a fetus does. Any therapeutic intervention short of regression to the grid within which the split took place is symbolic, and leaves the disruptive effects of that

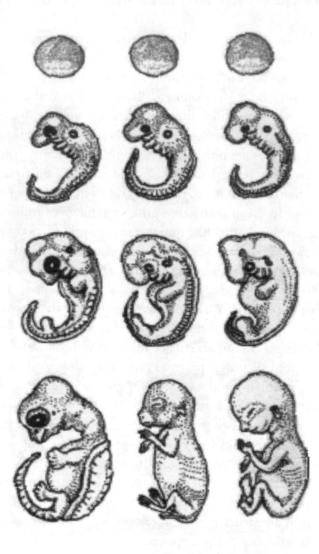

From Lizard to Mammal to Human

repression intact. That's why cognitive therapy alone may help us know about our pains without necessarily changing the dysfunctional patterns that result from that pain. The adult mind-grid can compensate for but cannot integrate childhood pains.

By the nature of their narrow scope, mind-grids are limited in their ability to handle discordant events, and so inner conflict is inevitable. As in the card game, War, inner world grids clash, to the point where the struggling person experiences anxiety and an "issue." Without integration, the issue is handled by having one world-grid dominate another.

Here's an example: one of my adult clients actually complained, "If I go to a place and I'm hot, I have to open the windows, and if I'm cold I have to put my jacket on." She whined about how she had to be responsible for her own comfort wherever she went. Imagine that! To cling to the Wombal world, with its unspoken credo of "everything is done for me with no effort on my part," as the dominant reality in her life was this woman's mission. Can you imagine a world so out of whack as to require her to be responsible for her own comfort? This particular patient was a "reformer," and an "educator," intent on designing an outer world to fit a Wombal model. (This is not meant to imply that there is no room for reform or education, but from the way this client was carrying out her mission, it was doomed from the start!) She experienced the world as a hostile place, and maintained a high level of frustration and defeatism. Eventually her antagonism manifested in her body in the form of numerous severe allergies. This is what can happen when we refuse to be in the world with rules that go beyond the womb! Even at age 40, this same woman lived via a strong financial umbilical connection to her parents. Her helpless, dependant behavior, aberrant thinking, and misplaced affect all added up to severe "mental illness". Drugs didn't help her. What did was regression back to the earliest of visceral pains that she experienced when her wombal needs were thwarted. Her repressed pain had been fueling a whole life of insanity and misery.

Different parts of the brain coincide with the different world grids I am proposing. The Wombal World grid is associated with the primitive, reptilian brainstem, the Primal and Adolescent World Grids, with the mammalian midbrain, and the Adult World Grid, with the neocortex.

Dr. Ernest Rossi, confirming this theory in his 1986 book, <u>The Psychobiology of Mind/Body Healing</u>, asserted that the limbic system, at the core of midbrain activity, serves as the "transducer" between the semantic and mechanical. The same circuitry that is involved in processing emotions translates verbal (or semantic) information into a mechanical (or body) response, linking a body response with a verbal conclusion about reality. Feelings thus reside at the core of real therapy and real change, not just by decree of a humanistic school of psychology, but as proven by the study of human biology.

When Inner Worlds Collide: "From Tissue to Issue"

Many problems, concerns, or conflicts experienced via the neocortex, thinking part of the brain reflect repressed pain from lower levels. When we don't feel emotional or visceral pain directly, we channel it into a more conscious level of experience where it takes the form of an "issue." We rationally "work out" the pain we refuse to feel, don't go the full distance to integrating it, and end up dragging out and postponing that integration. The issue continues, and finds new forms. When pain is fully integrated at a feeling level, issues dissolve.

The urgency of a need disappears as the need is met. Thirst disappears when we quench it, and intensifies the longer it goes unquenched. The incompleteness and unresolvedness of a need unmet, or repressed, at any level of development, then reshapes into a higher function mode such as philosophy, beliefs, theology, etc. You can learn a great deal about someone's level of feeling or repression based on his life philosophy. Pessimism as a mental outlook naturally emerges from a painful history of mismatched needs and fulfillments. A self-avowed racist, as another example, has corralled his personal pain into a cortical philosophy of hate and separatism. His ideas scream out loud the pain his brain is silencing.

Lets return for a moment to the definition of a trance, which was explained earlier. Whenever there is a narrowing of focus, combined with relaxing repetition, the body enters a state similar to the early stages of REM sleep, where the brain disengages from the outer senses, emits slower brain waves, and tunes in to its own internal map of reality. In a trance we are more influenced by inner already-assimilated (and hence, past) impressions than by any new external contacts. Dreams, as the interior pictures painted by the brain, completely independent of sensory involvement with the external world, are truly the "royal road to the Unconscious" as Freud said, and are also the deepest of trance states. They contain symbolic versions of feeling fragments seeking integration.

Humans seek out trance states because of the relaxation and the fact that in a trance the conscious thinking mind stops, nothing feels urgent, nothing is compelling. A trance fills the mind with familiar images and the body with soothing sensations. (Television facilitates a passive, trancelike state, which explains its popularity.)

A trance state for a baby is easily elicited by rocking, and repetitive cooing and patting. The trance state for a fetus is filled with oceanic surround-sounds of blood flow and heartbeat in a world of total free-floatation. These may very well be the trance states humans seek to emulate the most.

Trance states that have the most emotional charge are the most potent over time, that is, they linger the longest, strongly influencing future engagements and experiences. The minute the first Christmas decorations start going up, I am instantly transported into my "Christmas trance," which includes body and emotional responses that reach all the way back to my first encounter with Santa Claus. The emotional charge of an event is the body-mind's way of tagging it with a gradient of importance to survival. Trances further survival by keeping us calm. Depression is a form of trance that calms us by numbing out pain. If you don't feel it, it won't hurt. Unconsciousness, as the ultimate trance, has found a central role in human life because of its survival value. Unconsciousness helps us keep going.

As each world-grid created by the brain has an investment in numerous trance states because they maintain the status quo of a familiar map, and because change and the possibility of a new outcome often depends on the death of an old way of looking at things, the therapist has the daunting task of helping the client snap out of trance living. As a therapist, I find myself in the business of awakening. Because unconsciousness keeps us comfortable and away from pain, waking up is hard to do.

Each of the four grids exists as a segmented area of the brain's mapping abilities, as well as a substratum of the individual's consciousness. How we experienced the world as babies, for instance, lives within us as a sub-grouping of our total map-making abilities, and when conditions are "right," we might revert to that baby-world as our primary mode of engagement or interaction. In face of stress, as seen especially in the case of a severe trauma like a plane crash or a rape, people regress to a more basic, primitive form of being-in-the-world, confirming that a substratum of infantile circuitry secretly coexists with more mature mind-sets, in a seemingly adult framework. Stroke patients, too, are known to revert to earlier modes of map-making and relating when the more adult features of their brain physiology are incapacitated.

I am also suggesting that fragmentation of feeling into repressed pieces of experience outside our conscious awareness exerts an on-going regressive tendency in the psyche that we often fight with our more rational, adult frames of mind. Therapy based on a natural integrative rather than on a "get-rid-of-it" model makes the space for regression to happen, recognizing it as central to the healing of old feelings. What often keeps a person "intimacy-impaired" as an adult are the hurts and conclusions of childhood. True updating, beyond mere behavioral changes, requires regressing to the original feeling state.

If you lose your wallet on the way to your destination, you must backtrack in order to retrieve it. Instead of unconsciously staying in the area where you lost your wallet and never moving on, therapy in this context is about backtracking in order to move forward. A good therapist knows the difference between healthy regression to the past and wallowing in the past.

The child within us lives as a trance-identity in many varied forms. The level of influence old world-grids have on our current reality varies for each of us. The core essentials remain similar enough for me to generalize about what it is to be stuck within each grid. Let's start with babies.

The Catastrophic World of Infancy

Babies are like little mystics in that each moment holds everything. Unfortunately, at the same time, they have no sense of the big picture, so a gas pain becomes eternal torture. The immediate and the eternal intertwine, with the immediate dominating. A true mystical experience goes the other way--the immediate moment reveals itself saturated with the eternal; the mortal and the immortal meet at the crossroads of time and space and a gas pain is just a gas pain.

Because everything an infant experiences goes into building the lifelong foundation of world-perception, a whole strata of catastrophic consciousness, a personal Underworld of eternal damnation abides inside each of us. Think about it--for a newborn, emergence into the world terminates an eternity of blissful floating and undisturbed Unity. Gravity poses insurmountable obstacles. Being a prisoner in a body one cannot move or control is everyone's nightmare, and a baby's reality. At regular intervals, a horrible gnawing emptiness settles in like fog in a valley--a fog that is amorphous and unpleasant. It's hunger! And when tears of protest don't yield an instant response, how easy to conclude : "No one knows what I need!" To be embodied in these conditions is like prison.

Time itself appears as an oppressor, in the form of gaps between when we feel a need and when it gets fulfilled. Waiting, when it comes to infant needs, is intolerable. Besides delayed gratification, time also highlights unfulfilled desires, because when desires are fulfilled, we stand outside time.

Next there is the ignobility and humiliation of being an object-in-the-world, "THE baby." "See if the baby is wet." "Hand me the baby." The baby's unarticulated conclusion: "I am merely an object in the world," thus begins a victim-consciousness that we all have a common capacity for, and which depressives tap into regularly. Helplessly floating down the river of a constantly changing world with no self to hang onto, and no ability to effect anything. The victim's credo remains etched into our unconscious from our earliest days. One client of mine, whose mother died when he was only a year old, lived in a world constantly flooded with catastrophic consciousness—a situation he was only beginning to extricate himself from fifty years later! His mother's death followed him daily in thousands of little deaths, in an on-going encounter with changes, conflicts and losses, all tinged with his noninte-grated cataclysmic feeling fragments of a single horrific event long ago.

The constant state of being overwhelmed also needs to be mentioned. Babies sleep a lot because their immature nervous system can handle only so much input before it needs to withdraw and regroup. Babies, wanting it all now, can only take a little at a time. Toddlers easily get "wired" and "overtired" and cranky when their capacity for stimulation is overextended. Both disengagement from the world (as in being alone without stimulation), and over-engagement in the world can be a personal hell. To navigate the waters of human infancy comfortably, with its extremes of pleasure and pain, isolation and over-stimulation, may be a challenge few can actually meet. The tendency to perceive the catastrophic seems to come naturally to humans, regardless of upbringing.

And yet, infants truly are little mystics in the positive sense. Their universal experience of the world and other people transcends purely individual perceptions. "Mother" isn't just Sadie Jones, a 25-year old white female who grew up in Tulsa, Oklahoma, and who loves to go dancing, but rather someone who carries the Archetypal Female and the Universal Mother, and whose breasts belong to Mother Earth.

Babies are also like little mystics in their immediacy, independent of concepts like "shoulds", and in the direct way they need and feel love. For a baby there is no difference between biology and theology, for they are imbibed with the spirit of aliveness, and the aliveness of spirit. Inner peace comes easily to babies, as do smiles. (And not because they've heard a good joke.) They smile from sheer being.

We adore babies the way Christians worship the Christ child. We recognize and resonate with the infant's inherent peace more readily than we acknowledge its terrors and impotence. What is more endearing than watching a baby sleep, with its little chest rising and falling with each breath, its tiny body tension- and carefree? We could watch for hours, and sometimes we do.

I started this section with the premise that "being a baby is hell," and now I find myself in adoration of the blessed state of infancy. It is both heaven and hell. And the hellish aspects that get carried into childhood and beyond continue asking to be integrated into the bigger picture of what it means to be a complete human being.

The Primal World of Childhood

The Wombal and Primal world grids established by the brain lay the foundation of personality, because all subsequent development in the human is influenced by, and forged out of, the meanings and associations from those earlier days. When a toddler learns to call Rover a "bow-wow," everything with four legs is called a "bow-wow" until a new category is introduced and assimilated. The past remains present, because the present has to go through past circuitry already established.

Early childhood meanings and associations stand as the broad-based assumptions upon which new information is processed. By the time a child is five or six years old, general mappings, or suppositions, about safety, movement, gender and gender roles, family roles, emotional and social parameters, and all other facets of human concern, govern new input by channeling raw incoming data into old associative categories. Like the kittens who, raised in a rounded, curvilinear environment, manifested complete bewilderment when exposed to a straight, right-angled world, our Primal notions of reality often render us incompetent or dysfunctional in the advanced world of adult relationships and interactions.

Conclusions from early childhood are especially disabling when they no longer align with organismic capability or well-being. (See section on Bio-logic.) These anti-life conclusions about reality become internalized stressors which show up in distinct arenas of experience:

1. Responsibility--Kids often take on false responsibility, for example, the problems between mother and father, even going so far as to find the solution to their parents' problems. Because of a primarily self-centered, Wombal view of their position in the universe, coupled with their dependence on parents or adults, the absorption of outside problems happens automatically. The principle of Psychoneuroimmunology--"What's out there goes in, and what's in there comes out"--reflects this reality. Adult clients who cling to the Primal World Grid, living in a state of too much responsibility, need to have their very identities dislodged from that grid which keeps imposing outdated and warped requirements on them. Without inner change, the act of altering external circumstances alone will only serve to perpetuate the Primal world.

2. <u>Worth or Value</u>--- Children live by injunctions to "be good," which can mean anything from obedience to academic achievement; the point is to somehow meet the needs or expectations of their parents. A sense of self-valuing then occurs that depends on the imposed expectation of "goodness," too often outer-directed, and inevitably at the expense of biological realities.

The Primal World Grid has two main functions: upholding Wombal conditions of stability, and assimilating the outside world in the process. Because the first years of life mark a period of dramatic and rapid change within a context of total dependence, toddlers seek out repetition and ritual to accomplish these goals.

The Primal World Grid of the child's mind seeks to absorb the world in a way that best buffers the ongoing insults to the omnipotence of its Wombal past. To resolve the problem of having once been All, and now suddenly being small, the mind resorts to a strange and awesome strategy: it swallows whole and assimilates parents and the entire family into its individual psyche.

The Outer-directed World Grid of Youth

This mind grid works with a world beyond the scope of the family as a way to define and adapt the self to its surroundings. Whereas a toddler, adjusting to the mores of the family system, may repress parts of the self to get security from adults, the young adolescent throws caution to the wind when it comes to pleasing the family, and works to secure acceptance and approval within the social structure of his peers. This inevitably jeopardizes or at least stretches the limits of acceptance from the family, and exerts inner pressure on the passive acceptance aspects of the Wombal and Primal grids. Conflicts between the safety and stability of childhood, and the emerging sense of a sexual self in a larger world, often take on cataclysmic proportions of confusion and extremism. Puberty exerts itself as an intense time of transition.

Unlike the toddler's proclivity towards repetition and ritual for a sense of security and order in a rapidly changing world, teens naturally seek out chaos, destruction, sensory indulgence, and nihilism to handle the flood of change. Every generation of teens has its own form of sex, drugs, and rock-n'-roll.

An adolescent's growing sense of power and capability in the world often show up as rejection. He seeks to return the slap in the face his essentially omnipotent wombal identity received as a toddler. Having once swallowed all the rules as a way to get love, and get by, the teen now expels them to find his own way.

Although the world grid of adolescence seems to run solely on peer pressure, it is more deeply a time of inner isolation, where the self for the first time, encounters the Void of standing alone in the universe. Teen poetry often expresses a bleak existential loneliness, reflecting a dramatic leap forward on the path of individuation. The desperate need for peer acceptance ultimately stands as a smokescreen to the teen's true yearning for an individual identity, and his natural grief at the loss of childhood and the security of outer regulation of the self.

The Inner-directed, Relational World Grid of Maturity

Hallmarked by relativity, and a sense of boundaries between individuals, this world grid includes "otherness," which sets it apart from the other grids. "I am other than you, and you are other than I. We don't need to be one, or the same, to be together." This world grid is rooted in the ground of healthy aloneness. Separateness is OK. Personal integrity and wholeness come first, before acceptance and adapting. A person within this grid fulfills Wombal and Primal requirements with a sense of self-responsibility. Accountability replaces blame. Tension or conflict with others serves to strengthen the integrity of self, not diminish or threaten it, as in the other grids.

Four Polar Processing Styles:
A Second Axis of Repression

Life involves duality. Coins have heads and tails. Every yin has its yang. We all encounter opposites in life, and must come to terms with them. Most experiences carry both pleasure and pain, gain and loss. From our early formative years of development, there grows within us a neural "reconciliation system," a method of processing opposites that keeps conflicting impulses and aspects of experience apart. Sometimes we simply let one aspect consistently dominate over the other without visible struggle. Sometimes conflict's the thing, propelling a person to become a malcontent or a seeker. Such reconciliation strategies follow the prime directive of the mind/body system to avoid pain, but unfortunately, because pain is inherent in dualistic structures, the reconciliation system can unwittingly become the purveyor of suffering.

Dualities within the psyche of the client consistently show up in therapy as a form of confusion or conflict. Whenever a client says something like: "Part of me wants to stay to talk things over calmly, and part of me wants to yell and run out of the room", we know a duality is emerging to be reconciled. Common conflicting dualities involve qualities like strong and weak, good and bad, brave and cowardly, thinking and feeling, masculine and feminine, selfish and selfless. Fritz Perls, father of Gestalt Therapy, coined the term Topdog/Underdog to describe a common form of inner conflict he found in his clients. The Topdog speaks the condemnations and "should's", and the Underdog, groveling and subservient, agrees--a very dysfunctional set of dualities, indeed!

Some reconciliation strategies work more in alignment with biology than others. Others are rigid, stress-filled and disease-producing. Part of the therapist's job in assessing the client's world view focuses on identifying the dualities the client is wrestling with, the polarity reconciliation system they are using, and ultimately helping the client dismantle the repressive aspects of it. A feeling person naturally makes room for the paradox of coexisting opposites, but the avoidance of pain warps the mind/body's natural integrative stance towards opposites and robs the individual of a full repertoire of being.

The extremely skewed reconciliation system is one that leads a person to carry aspects of her own psyche around as unlovable, unacceptable, and when in a full state of denial: "not even part of me at all." These become the dangerous pockets of encapsulated unconsciousness that help set the stage for disease.

I have named four basic Polarity Reconciliation Systems. Which one do you see yourself in?

1. The Pulverizer: Polarize and Repress --This system creates the "dark side" of a personality, that is, all the unacceptable aspects that must be put out of consciousness because they appear to threaten the incoming love so necessary for survival. "They love me when I'm good and when I'm smart" inevitably creates the "bad" and the "stupid." This kind of thinking forms the "dangerous" part of the psyche, and requires repression to keep them at bay. And what better way to keep these demons away than to project them onto someone else in the family, or if that is not acceptable, onto someone of a different race, or sect, etc.

A good example of this reconciliation style is found in the so-called cancer personality. "Nice" is good, and to have or express needs is "selfish," and therefore bad. These are people who give and give, expecting the same to come back to them. They rarely take a stand for themselves or ask for what they want, because that part of them is considered "selfish."

Hand-in-hand with this sort of reconciliation style comes the "get-rid-of-it" surgical approach to feelings and inner life. "If only the bad part of me wasn't here, I would be OK." That kind of thinking, to me, is a pseudo, or actual, death-wish in the making.

2. The Minimizer: Polarize and Buffer--This style involves never having opposites face, or heaven forbid, confront each other. This is the "peace-maker" style that tries to soften the clash of opposites by being in the middle. These are the people who are forever in the midst of family dramas, working hard to keep friction from manifesting. These are the people who primarily live a neither-here-nor-there limbo existence with great difficulty making decisions, taking a stand, or making a commitment.

3. <u>The Maximizer</u>: Polarize and Take Sides --This style resolves some of the tension inherent in the former two, by accepting the polarities and siding up with one against the other. A child will categorize one parent as "good," and the other as "bad," sometimes going so far as to generalize judgment into "women are good, men are bad," or vice versa. These are people who find their niche in life by opposing others or certain beliefs or lifestyles. Unlike the previous two styles, the Maximizer does take a stand when it comes to dualities. The pathology of this reconciliation style is in the antagonistic nature of the stand.

4. <u>The Harmonizer</u>: Polarize and Accept---This style is the "mature" reconciliation mechanism of a feeling system. It makes room for opposites to coexist, and interact freely. It allows the tension naturally created by polarities to bring new levels of understanding, harmony, and creativity into the system.

Remember, these reconciliation styles indicate generalized methods whereby the nervous system processes information, both inside and outside. What the person does externally with opposites is what they do inside, and what the person does internally with opposites is what they do outside. A person who has polarized good and evil in the religious schema of God vs the Devil, does so in both inner and outer realms. For the Pulverizer, the Devil is banished from the system, and then constant vigilance must be maintained to keep it out. For the Minimizer, conflicting impulses are to be avoided altogether. Go to church, pray, and stay away from temptation. For the Maximizer, the forces of the Devil are both inner and outer enemies to wage war against. For the Harmonizer, the Devil or dark side contains a potency that is to be integrated into an effective and empowered whole.

When I say the Harmonizing style is the most mature method of processing opposites, it still doesn't mean that it's the system for all times, especially in the therapy context. Some people who have matured in the realm of processing opposites, but who are severely lacking in other realms of development, may need to "dip down" temporarily into a more primitive mode of dealing with polarities in their effort to resolve ambiguities or confusions held in the system since childhood. Many "good" children, for instance, feel "bad" about their hostile or negative emotions, and the childlike system of polarizing must be accessed in its original form, and then accept new input at that level in order to totally integrate the emotion as an adult. I call this "updating" the system. Rather than bullying someone into being mature (the way many people treat themselves), the therapist can help access the more primitive and historically younger aspect of the nervous system and provide new input at that level. The truly mature embrace the immature, rather than repress it. Harmonizing opposites is held up as an ideal in therapy, not a prescription.

The body itself is governed by two binary, polarized structures: we have a right brain and a left brain. We have a central nervous system with a sympathetic branch and a parasympathetic branch. Just as you can see only one side of a double-sided coin at a time, only one of these polar aspects can be dominant at a time. You can't do math and poetry at the same time. You can't do karate and digest your food at the same time. It is possible when opposites are not reconciled well in consciousness, to end up with a person at odds with an entire half of his or her own psyche, whether it has been repressed, avoided, or is still in conflict. A man can be so macho and homophobic, for instance, in order to completely disown his sensitive, feeling side. I strongly suspect autoimmune diseases pantomime this kind of inner struggle. I strongly suspect cancer is the manifestation of unsuccessfully trying to encapsulate something "unacceptable," (sexual or aggressive feelings, for example). Treatment must then involve making the unacceptable acceptable; the bad, good; the unlovable, lovable. Therapy must engage a person's ability to perceive and regard both polarities as part of the whole. Remember, even though we can only see one side of a coin at a time, we can feel both simultaneously. Feeling carries out the integrative function of the body and brings the hope of ultimate inner reconciliation. Both inner and outer reconciliation of opposite forces and a healthy tolerance of dichotomies are the victory trophies on the mantle of inner work, and naturally follow in the wake of deep feeling integration.

Tension: Bane or Boon?
Backwards or Forwards?

"The neurotic seeks to reduce tension by going backwards.
The artist seeks to resolve tension by creating."
---Arthur Janov

Let's talk about tension. Physiological tension manifests as bodily tightness that accompanies a restrained, inexpressive state of being. The muscular armoring of a tense system reflects a defensive stance in life, and has anxiety coursing through it as its shadowy companion, an anxiety that free-floats in the form of loose, unsuccessfully repressed feeling-fragments. A person can be either predominantly anxious or predominantly tense. Both conditions stem from feeling fragmentation.

Psychological tension could be called mental uptightness--a rigidity of thought, along with a limited range (if any) of emotion. Psychological tension, too, remains rooted in the mind's defense against feeling. People who look to release tension or relieve anxiety through sensory or mental distraction, sexual release, drugs, or alcohol, never completely resolve the discomfort, but merely reduce it temporarily.

Structural tension, the brainchild of Robert Fritz, composer and teacher, refers to a healthy form of tension that propels creativity. In his book, The Path of Least Resistance, Fritz refers to structural tension as the inherent tension in changing systems that fuels the change process. When someone wants to move from point A to point B, that desire creates a tension--a forward-propelling pressure. As long as she remains true to that vision of Point B, the accompanying tension aids her movement in that direction. Think of stretching a rubber band between two hands--the hand that lets go automatically launches the rubber band towards the other hand. Releasing the rubber band without the tautness or tension is completely ineffective. Release without tension renders the action ineffective.

Robert Fritz's model looks like this:

structural tension

POINT A	POINT B
(current reality)	(desired outcome)

He rightfully advises us to "keep psychological and physiological tension out of it!" in order for the creative process to fully benefit from structural tension, and as a result, come to full fruition. His advice includes educating ourselves to easily recognize the difference between unhealthy and healthy tensions, and to ignore the unhealthy ones.

Below is my revision of Fritz's model, the premise of which maintains that the process of projecting into the future and manifesting a desired outcome must take into account the emotional level at both Point A and Point B stages, otherwise it remains one-dimensional, cerebral, and impotent.

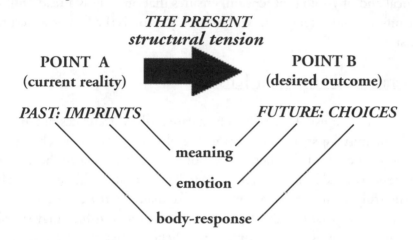

Point A and Point B each have their own energy. Point B energy carries the excitement of a fulfilled dream, and Point A energy contains a paralyzing inertia, the blocks to forward movement in the form of fear, doubts, or limiting beliefs. I firmly believe we must recognize that what we call the "current reality" of Point A has deep roots in the past. What I now have in my life is a direct result of what I believe possible and desirable. Beliefs like that stem from the past. The only way to keep psychological and physiological tension from interfering with Fritz's elegant model of manifestation is not to ignore or attempt to bypass those tensions, but rather to consciously attend to, and tap into, those elements for empowerment.

Too frequently, by mistaking structural tension for psychological and physiological tension, we attempt to reduce the discomfort produced when those tensions arise. When we seek to relieve tension, and not resolve it, we sell a potentially creative process short, and live with our cups empty, dependent on others, or upon serendipitous circumstances, to fill us. Robert Fritz calls that placid way of being the "Reactive Orientation." The results of this approach to life hardly satisfy us. We use others to remove our pain, all in order to make ourselves feel better. When people learn to "relate" in this way, they want their cup to be filled by others, to have others alleviate their loneliness, or take care of them. This kind of behavior establishes a blueprint for resentment and frustration, and yet, ironically, it is often considered normal. Working with structural tension, as opposed to attempting to reduce psychological and physiological tension, ensures that our cup is already full at the onset of our interactions with others. Passion is the fuel of structural tension.

Therapy and Structural Tension

A therapist also needs to be aware of the differences in tension, and not mistake structural tension for physiological or psychological tension. The job of the therapist is not only to help relieve the anxiety or stress involved in Point A, but also to help the client discover what he or she truly wants (Point B), which can actually increase the tension in the system. A person with a history of abusive relationships may simply give up wanting a good one, or not even believe a healthy relationship is possible, because it seems that the desire for one has been at the root of the pain. A person who has been battling a disease may no longer wish to feel hope, for fear of having it dashed again. Someone else carrying a lifelong thought pattern of undeserving-ness, or less-than, may never at all have set her sights on true fulfillment! Because desire fuels creativity and manifestation, part of my job as a therapist is to help a client rekindle that flame. A system fraught with psychological and physiological tension still may need a healthy infusion of passion to get it moving, even though that passion makes all the tensions rise.

True fulfillment is full-feeling, where I feel my current reality with no resistance or defense. My heart is free to manifest structural tension with which to creatively propel myself forward, according to my own desires. As I release my hold on current reality by letting it be, with no resistance whatsoever, the body/mind system releases the hold the past has had on me and opens me up to receive the future.

How many people try to use the present to heal the past! Some therapies focus on providing "corrective emotional experiences" to help neutralize past traumas. This happens through both a loving, attentive therapist, or a supportive family-like group. Hear this: the present cannot heal the past. As good as having loving people in the present may be, they cannot fill the broken cup of the past. Only feeling can mend that. Although we cannot heal the past by filling the present, we can fill the present by healing the past. The past is constantly present as body tension, and will remain so until that tension is resolved. Only then can we generate a healthy structural tension within us that will enable us to proceed into our own future, open to receive what we truly want.

*"...remember one thing only: that it's you---nobody else---
who determine your destiny and decide your fate. Nobody else can be
alive for you, nor can you be alive for anybody else."*
----e.e.cummings

***

*"...the possibility cannot be dismissed that the entire human organism
is alive with thought."*
---Larry Dossey, M.D.

***

*"We as humans are here to experience emotion and to use our bodies
as vehicles to achieve emotional wisdom."*
----Marlo Morgan

Life Issues: the Universal Backdrop for Therapy

Suffering: One For All

All psychological and physical issues remain rooted in deeper underlying matters of existence itself. To think otherwise is to suffer the same reductionistic disconnectedness that is so prevalent in Western medicine, which treats symptoms and not cause, parts and not wholes. When treatment for mental and physical illness is based on a view of man as an unfeeling machine, or as a body with a disembodied mind, the medicine itself inevitably promotes further fragmentation, and exacerbates the suffering. Physical and psychological ailments occur within the context of the whole person within a social network within a natural world, and leave their mark in every aspect of a person's life. Likewise, every facet of our connectedness contains a potential for a cure, and that includes our loving relationships, purposeful work, and contact with nature as in having pets or growing a garden.

Questions of separateness, suffering, pain, and loss are inevitable in every healing process, and are to be embraced, not avoided. Human suffering stems from an unconscious mistake about the fundamental unity of all things. The unified interrelatedness of things is not the mistake, nor is our dependence on it, but a self-sacrifice

factor that creeps in, is. The Gaia Hypothesis--the notion that the entire planet functions as a single organism--casts a problematic light on
individuality. The Gaia Hypothesis pushes the theorizing used by family systems therapists to its limits. In family therapy, one looks at the
entire family in terms of structure and function in order to get to the
root of the individual patient's problems.

The individual is inevitably not only acting out intrapsychic
conflicts, but also enacting inter-psychic conflicts of his family drama,
easily falling into roles such as Scapegoat, Black Sheep, Loser, or Peace-
maker. It is not uncommon, for example, to see a child adopt problem
behavior as a way to get otherwise argumentative or distant parents
together. There is no artifice when the child does this. It just happens.
In a sense, we humans are unconscious slaves to the Gaia Principle of
Unity, and during our formative years, before the onset of a definite
separate self, we absorb the reality (or unreality) of our surroundings.
What's out there goes in, and then comes out again. Our self-image
itself is rooted in distant family-of-origin theatrics. For better or for
worse, we tend to become whatever role we played to ensure our family's
unity and to get the love we needed.

The Principle of Unity works against us when we end up ignor-
ing our individual biology because of it. From a child's point of view,
the error sounds like this: "What is good for the unity of the family is
good for me. If I fulfill the needs of the family, then the family will
fulfill my needs." Sacrifice of the smaller body for the Greater Body
provides the impetus and the fuel for personal life-strategies that are
filled with dismal and disappointing struggle. "If I'm good enough, or
obedient enough, or _____ enough, then I'll get what I need from
my family." The logic of this kind of thinking, which is tied in to the
Gaia Principle, seduces the soul of the individual into derailing itself
from personal well-being for the sake of the greater unity of the family.
The fundamental dilemma underlying all childhood struggle strategies
goes something like this: "How can I be real and still have the love and
acceptance I want from others?" This is a question that reaches far beyond the constraints of youth and into the heart of mature relationships. How often do we "put on our best behavior" so that we'll be liked
and accepted? How often do we hide the darker sides of our experience
from others for the same reason?

Freud said this disparity between the inner and outer worlds was inevitable and even necessary. The "natural" impulses of the id, so raw and hedonistic, must be controlled in order for civilization to exist. Without external controls and internal repression, chaos would reign. Not a very optimistic or life-affirming view. I think Freud was wrong, and based on the primacy of biology that he himself postulated, the reverse is true: it is because of external control and internal repression that chaos reigns. Call me a humanist. And if you agree, call yourself one.

Am I suggesting that our natural link with the Underlying Unity of All Things (isn't that another term for "God"?) generates human suffering? No. What I am saying is that our built-in capacity to negate or minimize our self while living within a greater family-unity context, is the culprit. Buddha said that attachment to the transitory nature of things lies at the root of suffering. When we mistakenly look to a temporary source for a permanent solution, we're set up for let down. Because parents stand as the source of love (and so they should) for their children, and because children have a limited perspective on things, it's not uncommon for a child to engage in struggle for love when love is not directly forthcoming. A child wrongly concludes: "If I can't get the love I want from them, surely I will never get it. Therefore, I must do whatever it takes to win their approval and love." The Gaia Principle skewed through the mind and heart of a child.

The goal of therapy is to pop the bubbles of the little-systems-of-unity which the client has swallowed and to which he remains attached; inotherwords, to extract the sense of self from years of warped, repressive roles and self-definitions, and from deeply ingrained habits of struggling for approval, so the person can rediscover an identity within the simple capacity to feel. From the client's point of view, the process inevitably feels like a psychological earthquake, shaking the very ground he has been walking on. It is a call to reject not only the dysfunctional aspects of the past, but also old habits of unity, which we strangely hold sacred, no matter how much trouble they get us into.

John Lennon said, "God is a concept by which we measure our pain," for we often project onto the Underlying Unity, or God, all our unfulfilled childhood needs and the failed strategies for getting those needs met. It is only our projected sense of the greater unity, and our attachment to it, that causes suffering. God and Mother Gaia remain innocent. Furthermore, our link-up with the Unity we crave remains possible, first as an inner commitment to be true to the core of our feeling self, and second, to reveal ourselves honestly to each other. Thank God!

The Difference Between Suffering and Pain

Pain hurts. Suffering is being in a continual state of pain without the hurt. When pain is repressed it doesn't just go away. It goes in. You can leave your feelings but they don't leave you. A person carrying unfelt pain inevitably suffers.

So what hurts? When a need goes unmet, it hurts. Our needs change, of course, throughout our development. Whenever a need goes unmet, and we repress the pain of it, we stop growing. Children can't bring themselves up, either physically or psychically. We need food, shelter, and parenting. When those needs aren't met, they remain frozen in time and space, embedded in the tissue of our body and in the memory of the cells. Every reminder that occurs in the present that is vaguely reminiscent of the original precipitating painful event will elicit suffering. Pain cries out to be integrated.

We perpetually recreate unfinished inner situations from the past where pain sits at the core precisely because we're not finished with that pain. Each day we either successfully repress the pain all over again, or we succeed in feeling it and moving forward. Pain that is not allowed to be felt follows us like a shadow of suffering. How paradoxical that our method of protecting ourselves from pain (repression) actually perpetuates it. How paradoxical that the path of feeling one's pain leads to the healing of the suffering heart.

To Be Or Not To Be--- Is That Really the Question?

Sooner or later we each must face the moment of our own death. We may expend a lot of time and energy fighting, avoiding, and denying that fact, but at some point, it will get us. Until then we remain compelled to seek meaning in our experiences on this earth. Themes of Unity versus. Separateness, Innocence versus Worldliness, Good versus Evil, the question of Suffering, the reality of Death and Non-being, the encounter with the Void or Nothingness, the quest for true happiness--are some of the universal "existential elements" in our lives that lurk like specters in the shadows, urging resolution.

Some people seek answers in religion or philosophy, or in a code of ethics, while others do their best to focus on anything but the meaning of life, spinning their wheels in superficial dilemmas, and going about their business in ways designed to prevent the deeper issues from intruding into consciousness. People who fill their time with doing or thinking, lose sight of human being. The "being-ness" of those people waits patiently for them to come around, knowing it will have its moment in their final breath. Sometimes life-challenges, such as illness, natural disasters, or personal losses, burst through the veil of "doing", and provide a key that unlocks the door to the world of "being." For some people, coming face-to-face with one's own being is anxiety provoking, for others, revelatory, and for the majority, both.

An existential dilemma occurs when a person realizes that his current focus in life contains unworkable, unacceptable, and unavoidable elements or tenets. Anxiety is the hallmark of unresolved issues and inauthentic living. Suddenly, unworkable contradictions leap into the foreground of experience, stare us in the face, and short-circuit our rational minds. To face and feel the paradox in conclusions such as-- "loving hurts, and not loving hurts," or "I'll be what others want so I will be liked for who I am"--and not come up with easy solutions, can feel chaotic.

Existentialists say that because life-and-death issues cannot ever be resolved, we must make peace with the ongoing uncertainty of them, and accept the normal existential anxiety they bring. Existential anxiety, according to them, is healthy, and prods us into deeper levels of authentic, meaningful living. Existential anxiety comes in the wake of questions like: "what is my life's work?" or "do I have the quality relationships I want?"

Some inner conclusions about reality, however, remain unresolved and anxiety-producing, not because of any real underlying dilemmas about existence, but only because they are formatted within the body/mind system, usually during childhood, with the primitive deductive reasoning of childhood, with all the convoluted, confusing patterns that eventually make life unworkable. Like this one: "My parents need me to be what I'm not. If I release that, my parents won't need me, and then I won't exist." Strange, no? Generally, the earlier the childhood trauma, the more a person's issues take on an existential flavor.

Deep-feeling therapy digs up these root strategies of avoidance and denial, and challenges them head on, often using the tools of larger existential dilemmas as the wedge to pry patients loose from self-absorption and erroneous conclusions. We can change such a formula set as a child, by feeling the original crisis or occurrence that caused the formula to be set. By facilitating a full resolution at the child level of feeling, therapy reduces anxiety, even though the patient is being confronted with the larger existential realities of life, which by nature are anxiety producing. The disempowering, paralyzing uncertainty of "to be or not to be" established in a repressive survival mode, transforms with feeling into the empowered uncertainty of an awakened heart, with the new motto, "I am, and I can handle whatever comes my way."

We can perceive ourselves in existential terms as "thrown into this world" with "no exit" from the human condition, a condition riddled with paradox and uncertainty, or we can come to understand that we have the uncanny ability to feel our pain and continue living more positively and powerfully than ever. Those moments of feeling and integrating pain become pivotal moments of choice and inner freedom, when we can say, "Let the specter of Death hover over us like an angel and sing to us a constant reminder of the precious and passing nature of life itself. Let the largeness of life prevail over the finiteness of my problems."

Worse than any existential Void is the Avoid, when we stand in denial of our true human condition. Avoidance as a tactic to keep pain (or even death) at bay also prevents us from feeling deeply and authentically. Real fulfillment is full-feeling. The kind of therapy I espouse stands as a reminder that even though our problems may not be matters of Life and Death, living life is just that. The two should not be confused. To be or not to be is only a question when repressing feeling is an option. To feel, and continue feeling--that is the challenge.

Lust, Evolution, and Individuation

"A sea was storming inside of me
Baby I think I'm capsizing
The waves are rising and rising
And when I get that feeling
I want Sexual Healing
Sexual Healing is good for me
Makes me feel so fine, it's such a rush
Helps to relieve the mind..."
---Marvin Gaye

"I miss the warmth and closeness of erotic touching and or-gasm, and I want it back!" complained my 93-year-old client. "Our daughter who is five, spends time every evening masturbating herself to sleep. Should we be worried about her?" According to the Centers for Disease Control and Prevention (1995), 2/3 of all high school seniors in the USA have had sex. According to a survey taken by <u>Modern Ma-turity</u> magazine, 26% of men and 24% of women over the age of 75 have sex one time a week or more. Sex spans the life-span. If the subject did not come up in therapy, I'd be concerned. It is a topic that spills over into therapy in both positive and negative ways.

Freud attributed all human motivation from infancy on (refer-ring to the eroticism of babies as, get this, polymorphous perverse !), to the libidinal impulse, and many theorists today basically still agree with him. Sex rules.

Sex is introduced socially early in life as we begin to base our sense of self in the world through gender identity. Boys and girls are treated differently, and from an early age are conditioned to perform in the way society perceives them. Our sexual identity eventually extends beyond gender roles into the realm of personal relationships. Orgasm feels good, so good in fact that it is easy to convince ourselves that it is enough of a bond with another. Heart also experiences the urge to unite by knowing and being known, by loving and being loved. Herein lies a problem: sexual urges and heart urges become misaligned, and imbal-ance and suffering occur. What we won't do for sex! What we won't do for love! But what do we do to bond the two?

Let's back up a bit and look at sexual energy from the body's point of view. Just what is it? The nervous system runs on bio-electro-chemical energy (a fancy euphemism for libido?), which contains all the dynamic energy properties of electrolytes in a fluid system, such as buildup, polarization, and depolarization wave (these describe how nerve impulses get generated at a cellular level, and how they move through the body) all of which gets sexualized at puberty. The prepubescent version of this energy experience--excitement--is a measure of aliveness. We can respond to excitement either by embracing it, and riding the wave of creativity and intimacy that comes with it, or we can stifle it. As kids we quickly learn what level of excitement is acceptable, both at home and at school, and generally we are taught to keep excitement levels down. As teens we are collectively compelled by dramatic changes in our own physiology to cut loose and reject the inhibitions imposed on us. Every generation has its "rock-n'-roll" to help the process along.

Besides all the wonderfulness about sex, people also commonly use it as a major tool to mask pain. With the endorphin rush that comes with orgasm, sex is like a drug that can be abused. (Remember, endorphins are primarily painkillers). In addition, orgasm triggers hormone responses that induce sleep, reinforcing sexual release as a form of self-medication. Because the nervous system is like a battery that discharges with nerve conduction and then needs to recharge at regular intervals, the body cycles between contact and retreat modes to keep proper balance. The mind, active and engaged for hours at a time, also seeks stillness. We depend on sleep to help us to gather strength and reorganize. Babies, whose systems lack sophisticated filtering mechanisms for the raw voltage of experience, must sleep a large portion of the time in order not to become overtaxed. Sleep is vital to the body's well-being and survival. Why is orgasm so closely linked to sleep and endorphin release? Sexual release and the ensuing sleep it induces serve to help keep high voltage levels of pain buried, so the body can continue functioning without having to deal with awareness of pain. After aeons of evolution sex has been wired into us, and reinforced with bliss, not only to reproduce offspring, but as a protection against overload, against pain, and unfortunately, against consciousness. Unconsciousness has great survival value, and thus whatever reinforces it also makes it through the selectivity gates of evolution. The compelling and abiding force of sex rests not just in its ability to carry on our genetic material or in providing a built-in source of pleasure, but because of its painkilling, sleep-inducing properties. This is where sex gets abused.

The endorphin high from orgasm is sought out again and again by the sex addict to keep from feeling pain. "Compulsive sexuality means being motivated to engage in sexual activity time and time again in hopes of finding some sort of fulfillment," explains Al Cooper, PhD, clinical director of the San Jose Marital and Sexuality Centre in San Jose, California. People treated for compulsive sexual behavior often have difficulties with genuine intimacy and use sex as a means of dealing with other problems: loneliness, depression, anxiety, or daily stresses. "They compulsively use sex as a form of physical and psychological release," Dr. Cooper says.

Pornography also serves as a quick fix to soothe unexpressed disappointments in real relationships, and is used to self-medicate against feelings of anger, disappointment, boredom, or sadness. Such mood altering strategies keep individuals from developing healthier ways of managing emotions, and keep them emotionally immature. I personally and professionally have come to believe that beyond just the category of compulsive sex, what our culture considers a "normal" sex drive, is more addictive and pain-driven than we'd like to admit.

Individuation

Individuation, a word coined by C.G. Jung, the father of Depth Psychology, to describe the lifelong process of development from an undifferentiated conglomerate of cells into a unique, autonomous, separate, interdependent, aware individual, is strongly influenced by sexuality. Lust mobilizes the integrative forces that move us either forward or backward in consciousness. We know when we are moving backward when sleep, lethargy, sameness, and rigidity of thought and action prevail, and we know we are moving forward when we change and grow in alignment with our inner sense of excitement, fulfillment, and destiny. Homeostasis, or the self-regulatory, stability-seeking mechanism that helps us keep an even keel from moment to moment, is flexible in this case, which leaves the rudder of this ship in the hands of free will. Forward or backward, conscious or unconscious is up to you.

Those who have learned to successfully integrate the challenges of life with awareness tend to resolve tension through creativity. They embrace change, and navigate forward. But people who engage the world resisting change, resolve tension through discharge and distraction (yes, this means sex, drugs and rock and roll) eventually discovering that their coping methods push them backwards in terms of their individual growth. The manner in which we resolve our tension reveals a lot about who we are, because we are either using our inner resources to grow and develop, or we are resisting what is new, thus maintaining the status quo. Forward motion along the path of individuation, is far more life-affirming and dynamic than a mere discharge-oriented self-maintenance.

The need to Individuate drives us relentlessly because it is a built-in possibility. It beckons us all. Unlike the involuntary expression of evolution, an adaptive process over many generations of trial and error, mutation, and selectivity, human individuation happens by choice alone. The context of a person's family and community can either enhance or inhibit the urge to individuate, but they do not create it. True heroes individuate no matter what their circumstances.

A structural tension exists within us between a sense of our-selves as a separate person, and a sense of ourselves as part of a unity constantly interacting with others. That unresolved conflict sometimes causes us to link with others sexually, for resolution and completion. Depending on our deeper life orientation, whether we on one hand choose the path of individuation, or on the other hand, as philosopher, Frederick Nietzche said, the path of "blending with the herd", we either seek out partners who help us feel better through unconsciousness or those who subconsciously match our inner yearnings to be whole. Sex is very different in these two orientations-- one based on the innate electrical imperative that comes from protoplasmic excitability, and the other based an innate archetypal imperative to grow and become.

Sex Mask

Because our emotions sometimes add an unpleasant "charge" to our life experiences, and sex offers a discharge, people often use sex to mask uncomfortable feelings. Sexual stimulation, which provides touch, excitement, a sense of safety and pleasure, is often purposefully introduced into painful feeling situations for the sake of making the pain go away by somehow overriding it. It isn't too farfetched, either, to think it possible to balance or neutralize pain by adding pleasure. People who use this strategy in the face of emotional pain are too often disappointed, because in fact one does not cancel out the other.

Sex inevitably masks some aspects of the individuation process. By using sex to diminish tension, without achieving some resolution or integration of pain, we veil a deeper inner reality by engaging sexually rather than holistically, and end up camouflaging avoidance. Using sexual anesthesia as a way to buffer the inevitable discomforts and confrontations of relationships keeps a person immature and intimacy-impaired.

More than any other sexual experience, childhood sexual abuse sets in dysfunctional patterns which hugely influence one's sexuality for life, often freezing into space and time the child's confusion about pleasure ("feeling good is bad"), embodiment ("to survive I must leave my body"), gender ("bad things happen because I have breasts"). Where the body played such a central role in the early trauma, a focus on bodily-reality in the healing emerges as paramount. To think intellectual insight or understanding alone can heal sexual trauma, without accessing the body's response, is delusional.

Richard: Am I a Pervert?

Richard, a 37-year- old married man with a three-month-old daughter, came to me for help for pedophilia. He had sexually molested children in his past, had served time in jail for it, and now with a daughter of his own, he wanted help.

"I get this uncontrollable urge to touch children's genitals and butts," he said. "I don't understand it. It turns me on sexually. I don't really mean to hurt the kids. I am not a bad person---- or maybe I am the monster they say I am--- I don't know anymore." His face was contorted with confusion and self-loathing. He wrung his hands while speaking. Somehow, in the arena of the mind wrestling between impulse and conscience, sexual urges win. What can it be that compels Richard to touch children in ways he himself abhors, despite his conscious resolutions to "be good"? Is Richard simply weak-willed? After months of therapy probing at the myriad levels of feeling involved, at the infant level of his own repressed consciousness, emerged his own history of being molested, with all the confusions of "good" and "bad," pleasure mixed with wrongdoing, and the skin hungry for loving touch mixed with inappropriate sexual contact.

According to his own inner circuitry of experience, sexual contact with a child had been distilled as the only means of keeping his deep pain at bay. What compelled him to repeat the abuse was the survival need to repress his own rage and fear over being violated. By reexperiencing the original feelings according to how they were still encrypted in his adult body, Richard overcame the need to repress his pain, and therefore his need to keep repeating it externally for the sake of integrating it. He worked hard for months and months to override his defenses against his own pain. When he could fully feel the wrongness of being sexually molested as he'd been carrying it within his own body, he could finally align with the wrongness of his own abusive acts. He successfully neutralized his urges from the inside. Finally it was his love for his daughter that fueled his healing
.

Sexualizing Non-Sexual Experiences

Sexual feelings often get linked to other feelings and "issues." What are often perceived as sexual issues are not sexual at all, but simply represent the sexualization of deeper pain or unmet needs that are emerging. A woman for whom sexual intercourse with her husband was painful, finally opened up a Pandora's Box of feeling when she admitted to feeling used, unloved, and unappreciated in her marriage. Her honesty initially led to massive discomfort, but eventually opened a deepening of communication with her husband and a reconnection at a feeling level. Enjoyable sex followed naturally.

Sexuality has been referred to as a microcosm of our relationship life, and cannot be treated as separate. Although sex therapy can correct mechanical sexual dysfunction, it does not necessarily address, or even claim to address, the bigger picture of feeling. Conversely, addressing the big picture of feeling, and integrating repressed pain, often translates directly into sexual healing as well. Arthur Janov reported that many of his primal therapy patients had greatly reduced sex-drives after therapy, along with a deeper experience and appreciation of sexual enjoyment. A significant number of his patients reported the erasure of premature ejaculation, frigidity, adhedonia (non-enjoyment of sex), and some even reported a reversal of homosexuality. That's how intimately deep feelings and sexuality get interwoven.

Brian: Do It Now!

Brian, an athletic 34-year-old with years of history as a sex-a-holic, frequent visits to adult book stores, masturbating, and one-night-stands, sat in my office after months of therapy, and a hard-fought week of the sexual abstinence I had recommended.

"I am so jittery, and uncomfortable! I did what you asked--no sex for a whole week, and I can't stand it any more! I've got to get some release!"

He lies down on the sofa in my office, as he's gotten accustomed to doing in the course of getting in touch with feelings and body sensations in therapy.

"I've got to have an orgasm! I really want to cum!" he shouted, writhing and squirming. "I can't stand feeling this way any more!"

"Say that again!" I urged.

"I can't stand feeling this way any more! I want this feeling out of me!"

"What feeling, Brian?"

"I feel so....bad."

"Feel it. Sink into the feeling. Let it happen this time. You've whacked this one off enough! Let it happen! Who's the boss here? You or the feeling?"

And he writhed and screamed, even as he experienced an erection and a strong desire to discharge. He wiggled, contorted, whimpered, whined, and groaned for a solid two hours, sometimes looking and sounding like an adult, sometimes like a baby. He revisited this particular deep agony many times in the office, bit by bit allowing it to be there without running from it, letting the full impact of his own experience finally catch up with him.

At a group feedback session, he shared this insight: "This is what made me sexually addicted, I know it. I've hated this awful feeling inside me, of not being wanted, of needing so much touch and being rejected. It all came together (sic). I have been using sex to make me feel better, but I could never get enough. This awful feeling just came up again and again. I've never let it come close before. Now I know what's been driving my urges. I thought I was just a super-sex freak or something. But that's not it!"

My commitment as a therapist is to help unravel the threads that strangle the free-flow of natural health, and help reweave them into a reality that is liveable, workable, and in alignment with the true destiny of the client. Lust is a many-splendored thing. When it twists into inner and outer misuse and abuse, it cries out to be healed. Every therapist, then, is a sex therapist.

Archetypes: Hard-wired Circuits

An awareness of archetypes, the universal symbols uncovered in dreams and throughout world mythology, literature, and religions, is central to good therapy. Carl Jung coined the term archetype when he postulated that besides the individual unconscious mind of forgotten and repressed material, there also resides within us a universal or Collective Unconscious, a circuit board common to our structure as humans, that carries primeval predispositions to experience. Out of this global cauldron or repository of human possibility, we create symbols with which to translate our individual experiences into a mind-map of reality. Throughout history, in every culture (despite the differences in cosmology or theology), the images and descriptions used to create these maps are recognizable to all of us.

Archetypal images can enter an individual's psyche via imagination or dreams-- independent of worldly experience. The circuitry that enables this to happen is the same now as it was in humans aeons ago. For example, I, a twenty-first century American, can dream about a monster chasing me just as an eighteenth century European did, so regardless of time frame or culture, we share the same innate human capacity to use archetypal symbols to represent our experiences. My monster might look like the Terminator, and his like a dragon, but the terror involved in being chased by a brute of a creature remains the same. Archetypes strum a primitive and universal chord within us, awakening a deep sense of recognition and identification independent of culture or societal norms.

Darth Vader of Star Wars is the archetypal Dark Side, the fallen angel-like Lucifer who is to be mistrusted and feared. The Christ Child carries the archetypal sense of Original Purity, Grace and Innocence, worthy of adoration. Shakespeare's Jesters or Fools are the archetypal "Tricksters", who, according to Jung, bring about transformation. The Trickster stands outside conventional knowing or rules of behavior.

Archetypes refer both to entities, such as the Mother, the Hero, the Shadow, or the Cross, and/or to universal human situations, such as having parents, finding a mate, having children, or confronting death. Archetypes also manifest in symbols or characters that embody or personify common, universal personality characteristics (Evil, Good,

Strength, Cunning, the Free Spirit); human stations in life (the Renunciate, the Worldy Man, the Shaman); universal familial and relational ties (the Lover, the Mother, the Stepmother, the Father, the Sister, the Brother, the Friend, etc.); or universal forces (Death, Birth, Resurrection, Renewal, Transformation, Stagnation).

All the above mentioned are pre-wired blueprints for shared human experience, and those collective identities are as much a part of us as our own individual identities are. As an infant we experience The Mother in all her archetypal wonder, as a source of love, joy, pleasure, safety, comforting, and nourishment, without needing to know anything about that person. The archetypal Mother is ours, independent of our biological mother.

Our contact with other individuals is what triggers the archetypes within us. Archetypes, because of their transpersonal nature, are irresistible and compelling. When we fall in love as teens, we evoke archetypal energies of the Beloved, the Lover, or Eternal Friend, and gladly succumb to the persuasive aromas that waft over us, without needing to know anything about the particular individual. In this era, we tend to be drawn to movie stars and celebrities who represent strong archetypes. Their size on movie screens, combined with collective adulation, makes them indeed "larger than life."

"Mature" adults, too, fall under the spell of archetypes. "I have no idea how Charles and I got together. We've been married for twelve years and have never had anything in common. I think I just wanted to be in love so badly that I didn't notice the particulars all that much. I was also ready to have children." The archetypes of "being in love" and "bearing children" compelled her to action even in the face of strong arguments against her choice of mate. When archetypes meet reason or logic, archetypes win hands down.

We look for the Good King or Good Queen when we elect officials, honor sports heroes as our Warriors, and elevate someone like Walter Cronkite to Wise Man. We seek out and act out the inner world of archetypes in everything we do.

Culturally-influenced presentations of universal human characteristics and situations in movies, television, and literature can cause us to confuse archetypes with stereotypes, which dilute and often pollute their archetypal precursors. Archetypes embody the pure strain of universal themes and realities, whereas stereotypes manifest the un-healthy, limiting versions of loose generalities. Stereotypes are imbibed with the values of a culture and a time, thus presenting a false universal-ity that belittles the individual. Any generation that makes war uses stereotypes to dehumanize the enemy and to avoid self-responsibility. The Nazis stereotyped the Jews to the degree where ethnic cleansing made sense.

Whereas the archetypal Feminine, as another example, reaches goddess proportions in the heart qualities of wisdom, empathy, and compassion, the stereotypical Woman in our current American culture is depicted as overemotional and under-logical. While archetypes in-spire and unite us by their true universality, stereotypes make us lazy by inviting us to rest on generalities. Stereotypes keep us apart by falsely exaggerating differences into universal truisms. They sit at the core of racism, sexism, ageism, and other divisive concepts.

Archetypes remain forever rooted in the depth of the individual psyche, and therefore carry the potential to help the individual bear the fruits of fulfillment, whereas stereotypes grow in the mere shallow wa-ters of popular agreement, and ultimately leave the individual's spirit barren.

Archetypes and stereotypes are often improperly mingled and sometimes even directly mistaken for each other. Therapy that is effec-tive is designed to disentangle the two, because one nourishes and the other strangles the vine of life. As a therapist it behooves me to know the transpersonal level of my own being so I can address the archetypal level in my client to facilitate healing. In order to do that I need inti-mately to know "the story behind the story". When my client recounts her story I listen for the real impetus and drive behind the particulars of her behavior. I listen for her beliefs and assumptions about herself, and what it is to be a woman of her particular age in her particular situation. I listen in order to learn of the stereotypes that are blocking genuine empowerment and forward movement. I challenge those stereotypes with archetypal images drawn from my client's own creative imagina-tion so they can be defeated within her own psyche. Being reminded of archetypal reality is like waking up from a bad dream, and accepting the possibility of making a good dream come true.

Hearing the true "story behind the story" involves my listening to what my client really wants, and it is here where I rely on an archetype itself to guide me along as a therapist--the archetype of Enlightenment. I believe that deep down, people want to individuate, to feel, and to reunite with an inner simplicity and originality. People want to be liberated from any and all conditioning that keeps them bound, unnatural, and unreal--no matter what the seeming rewards of conformity or settling may be. They may have originally chosen a path of material comfort and safety at the expense of their ideals, dreams, and destiny, but they generally end up regretting it. My highly successful, baron-of-industry, 91-year-old client said it all when he said to me in a desperate voice, "I've done it all and had it all. I've owned mansions and yachts and hobnobbed with royalty, but I know along the way people don't like me and never have. I've alienated my own kids, and had a miserable marriage. I don't know how to love, and I want to learn. Is it too late for me?" Surely, in the archetypal garden of Transformation, the seed of change-of-heart just got watered. Throughout his time in therapy he went on to make great effort to reach out to his children and grandchildren in new and more honest ways. He went on to reach within to view his life from the vantage point of his own slumbering, awakening heart. He soul-searched and wrestled with demons--all for the sake of feeling. I saw him step by step let himself be reduced to a man with a new simple-hearted directness. He ventured to show his vulnerabilities and even speak his affections. His family and friends at first were mistrustful and cautious, but were soon melted by his sincerity.

For me to witness such a high level of inner work in an old man looking to salvage his life was like watching a real-life Christmas Carol. It confirmed that in the realm of what is truest and most worthy, the heart rules. It is the archetype I evoke and invoke in my therapy.

Archetypes and Personal Mythology: Mything You, Missing Me

We use each other to act out personal mythologies. Sarah has passionately pursued a quest to find the Good Father, something that never happened with her biological father. She may try a string of intimate relationships, setting herself up as dependent child, or she may get religion and strike up a relationship with God the Father, or she may do both. The archetypal Good Father myth unknowingly rules her life, and Sarah doesn't know that anything is amiss.

Although various archetypes crop up during our childhood, sometimes placing larger-than-life requirements on our parents, our personal unmet childhood needs fuel a mythological urgency later in life to find and merge with those archetypes again. Therapy, by the act of facilitating direct contact with unmet needs, and all the feelings and struggles they generated in our lives, takes the mythological element out of the picture. Paradoxically, the archetypes live on, more accessible than ever. After fully grieving the loss of the Good Father, and letting herself feel the reality of having grown up under a cruel biological father, Sarah found herself more able to receive "good fathering" in all its myriad forms, including wise counsel, kindly protectiveness, prodding encouragement. Before therapy, those were the very things that triggered her grief, which kept her from receiving the goods.

As children, we naturally mix archetypes and stereotypes with our experience of individuals, often losing touch with the individual altogether. In normal development we get weaned from the archetypal requirements placed on our parents, friends, and lovers to the point of accepting them all as flawed individuals. The same holds true for our self. Real self-love reflects an unconditional acceptance, independent of shoulds and image.

It is often the task of therapy to complete what "normal development" hasn't yet accomplished. With my client whose mother died when he was two years old, attachment to the archetypal Mother died hard. Out of a toddler's deep sense of need and loss, he continued to perceive and enroll women into that role, against vast amounts of "adult" evidence and better judgement to the contrary. Not having been naturally weaned by an unfolding history with the individual woman who was his mother, he had to learn to wean himself from a mother he never had. Not an easy task. True maturity means being able to find and appreciate, and even mourn, when necessary, the individual person independent of stereotype and archetype.

Separating archetype from stereotype, and archetypal myth from personal drama is like re-potting a plant that has outgrown its container. We belong rooted in archetypal reality as full adults, not wounded children.

The Question of Meditation

Does meditation usher in enlightenment, or is it yet another method used to repress pain? Dr. Herbert Benson documented in his book, <u>The Relaxation Response</u>, that taking quiet time to disengage the senses from external involvement, and using a simple word repetitively to get the mind focused, is beneficial. He maintained that the relaxation response of the body induced by meditation, regardless of spiritual content, offers extraordinary physical benefits, such as reduced blood pressure, heightened mental alertness, and increased vigor.

Arthur Janov, founder of Primal Therapy, suggests, on the other hand, that for someone who exists primarily in a state of repressed feelings, meditation is not only illusory but counterproductive to getting well, i.e., whatever falls short of dealing with the repressed feelings is a cop-out. Even some proponents of prayer regard meditation as merely "going blank." In Christian terminology, an <u>agnoia</u>, or a passive erasure of content, as opposed to the more proactive <u>metanoia</u>, or positive transformation, is a way of hiding from God, or even making room for demons. For Christians who believe this way, meditation is not only counterproductive, but downright dangerous.

How can you tell if meditation is right for you when you are undergoing inner work to release repressed feelings? Ideally, if you are not using meditation to escape from feeling, you can meditate as a means of disengaging from thought, thereby facilitating the natural centropic movement to the core feeling self. The time spent meditating can be a gateway to inner exploration, which can include healing past impressions and bodily imprints of pain.

If, however, you become more nervous or feel overwhelmed by your thoughts during the process, the odds are your body is responding to the quiet time with a desire to integrate a rising tension. If you find yourself "sleepitating" instead of meditating, it could be that escaping into the unconscious is the only way you know to prevent certain uncomfortable aspects of your experience from becoming conscious. Meditation in those cases does not serve any integrative function aside from sleep, which often serves as a buffer to pain. (Depressed people sleep a lot.) "Sleepitation" is not meditation, and the peace it brings falls far short of conscious inner peace.

When we are in a sleep state and dreaming, we experience images and stories and feelings. It is commonly believed that dream images and stories create the feelings in dreams, but I believe just the opposite: feelings generate the images and stories of the dream state. They generate the mind-stuff that comes up in meditation also.

Cognitive theories of psychology would have us believe that how we think determines how we feel, and although "frame of mind" influences feelings to a degree, both brain physiology and evolution show that the primacy belongs to the more primal and basic aspects first. Our primitive reptilian and mammalian brains dominate and dictate to the cerebral cortex, which processes that information in its own symbolic way.

The "thinking" brain follows the feeling and sensory brains, and acquires its raw material from them, out of which it forges story and meaning. In meditation, by practicing disengaging from the activity of the "higher" thinking brain, and staying attentive to the sensory, autonomic functions (breathing, heartbeat), we experience a grounding in our evolutionary and biological origins, and thus tap into universal renewal. Meditation that helps to link us to a sense of wonder, and connects us to a natural state of simplicity and feeling and automatically yields a transcendent, big-picture view of our immediate experience is true conscious meditation. We sleep to reorganize and regroup from the day's input. We meditate to reconnect with our Beginnings.

When mental activity is especially busy, and disengaging from it requires great effort, defenses against rising pain are inevitably at play. Whatever feelings or experiences that have been difficult or impossible to integrate (and so have been stored in the body or emotional memory bank) surface in quiet times. There is an unconscious impetus for integration pushing those feelings towards the cerebral cortex, or the thinking brain, for processing. The result in meditation is an overactive mind.

We can meditate as a way to gaze into the mirror of self, or use meditation as a means to shelter our gaze. Peace that arises out of honestly integrated suffering is long-lasting. Peace (or meditation) that comes at the expense of integration still wears the clothing of repression, and is not really peace.

"First try to discover your own childhood, then take the experience seriously. Listen to the patient and not to any theory; with your theory you are not free to listen. Forget it. Do not analyze the patient like an object. Try to feel, and help the patient to feel instead of talking to the patient about the feelings of others."
---Alice Miller

✳✳✳

"The main interest of my work is not concerned with the treatment of neuroses but with the approach to the numinous. But the fact is that the approach to the numinous is the real therapy and in as much as you attain to the numinous experiences, you are released from the curse of pathology."
---Carl Jung

✳✳✳

"The power to touch a heart--never underestimate that."
---Maharaji

Integration with Feeling: How Body-focused Psychotherapy Works

Why People Really Come for Therapy

There are different "levels" of therapy. Not everyone is ready to do deep work, or to make dramatic changes in their lives. Some people just want a little encouragement, or to be heard. They may simply want to feel cared for. Years ago when I worked solely as a massage therapist, I pre-screened my clients with an in-depth questionnaire to determine the best focus for each session. Once, in the middle of my specific queries as to aches and pains, my client stopped me short and said, "There is nothing wrong with me today. I just want to be touched." Good one. She cut through the sophisticated jargon and excuses.

Other people enter psychotherapy for the same reason--to be "touched" in a different way--by actually allowing me to enter into their inner lives more directly than they have let anyone else in. Those people don't necessarily come with a particular problem, but they are usually open, and that's fine.

Some people do bring specific problems, either those related to troublesome inward experiences such as anxiety, depression, low self-esteem, or creativity blocks, or to more outward experiences like relationship or work-related upsets. Learning new skills sometimes does the trick for these people, skills that include inner imagery, assertiveness techniques, or inner desensitization. For many, learning to see an old problem in a new light helps enormously. The therapeutic name for this is re-framing, and it remains a potent tool in the therapist's bag of tricks.

As a professional therapist, I have respect for most of the varied levels of therapy I have encountered. I marvel at how consistently people find their own solutions, often with minor intervention.

The Common Theme

Over many years of listening to an infinitude of problems in all types of people, I have come to realize that there is a common theme among people who come to therapy: they come to rediscover, reclaim, and reconnect with their hearts. I believe the whole range of "mental" problems, all psychological diagnoses, and most interpersonal conflicts, have to do with a disconnected heart. A disconnected heart inevitably involves repression that began in the formative years of life. Weeds on the surface have roots down below. Any therapy that does not take this into consideration is "mowing the lawn to get rid of weeds." The weeds have to be pulled up. "Uprooting" in therapy, as in garden work, is messy, and leaves holes. A master gardener makes certain new seeds are handy, as well as the mulch for cover, an adequate supply of water and sunshine, and whatever else is required to facilitate a healthy transition from the weeded turf to the newly seeded.

The process, though, includes dying. What this means is that in the uprooting of deep-seated unconscious imprints, it can feel as if part or all of the former mindset, i.e., sense-of-self, is dying. Because it is. When weeds are pulled up, the same sun that made them grow, now wilts, dries, and kills them. Consciousness is the cure.

When clients are ready for deep work, I purposely have them schedule appointments so that they have adequate integration time afterwards. (No business meetings or family reunions, please!) Deep inner work can be equated to surgery, where a certain amount of time is required for the incision to heal.

The Heart Has a Mind of Its Own

The heart has a mind of its own, and when we lose touch with it, we get confused, lose our way, and end up compensating for its loss with activities that don't satisfy us. Not only do we look outside ourselves for "things" or events to fill the gaps left by the heart's absence, but we also turn over the reins of our lives to the intellect. The intellect, or brain, simply cannot and should not do the job of the heart. Its binary computerlike ways render it incapable of adequately navigating the subtle waters of human interaction, relationship, and intimacy. The heart resides at the core of our personhood, and without connection to it, both inner and outer vultures recognize our debilitated state and move in.

Only recovery at the heart level is lastingly effective. More than "getting over an illness," recovery more often has to do with the rediscovery of something lost. Therapy means finding, touching, and finally giving the heart back its rightful position. If the core sensibilities I have been referring to as "heart" have been buried in the nether realms of the Unconscious, then therapy takes on the role of "salvage expedition." Finding and digging up the buried heart is not only at the core of our sacred journey as human beings, it alone is the real reason people come for therapy.

Off-balance, Right-on!

One time in the Intensive Care Unit I overheard a group of doctors huddling together about a critically ill patient that they were only able to stabilize with massive drug and life-support therapy, and who was nevertheless slowly slipping downhill. It made for one of the strangest medical conversations I've ever witnessed, and has become a hallmark of my Centropic Integration approach to therapy.

"We've got to do something radical at this point," said the nephrologist, "or else the kidney failure alone will do him in."

"I agree. He's not breathing on his own and the longer he's on the respirator the more he'll get hooked to it. Stabilizing him is just buying us a little time and he's going fast. If we don't come up with something , he'll be dead in a couple of hours--or even worse--on these machines for days."

" Yes, stability is not in his favor at this point, so let's just do something to knock him off balance, and then go from there."

"I like that. We'll destabilize him in the safest way we can, and hope he'll find some other resource."

So they did. With the suggestion of the infection control physician and the approval of the cardiologist, they put him on an alternating schedule of cooling him down and heating him up with a thermal blanket, adjusting medication and machine settings along with his own body's adaptive responses to the changes, weaning whenever possible. Like a fisherman alternately giving slack and pulling in tight, these doctors paced along with the patient's own primitive adapting mechanisms, jostling his primal homeostatic systems into gear, until, by some miracle, he pulled out of the downward spiral, stabilized on his own, and recuperated. They helped him access his own healing resources by first knocking him off balance from an artificial stability. What a metaphor for therapy!

The Boy At the Side of the Road: What Really Happens In Therapy

People ask me, "How can you listen to people's problems all day?" My standard reply is, "Seen a good movie lately?" Quality cinema captivates, entertains, and even uplifts. We weep for characters on the big screen, and laugh with them. They endear themselves to us through their humanity. But psychotherapy is even better, for participants embody the human drama in 3-D.

While people living a "normal" life hawk their wares out in the big world, I, as a therapist, trek into private mansions, tiptoe down dark staircases, discover doors locked up tight years ago, seek out hidden keys, fling open velvet curtains, and unearth treasures that have no price. In these interior basements, I find abandoned children, pale and light-starved. I get to witness the joy of the rescue and the relief of adult-child reunion. Interactive therapy lifts me into adventure, and reminds me that my heart lives to love and loves to live. In fact, I cherish the first moment when a client and I sit face to face in my little office. Our session begins modestly, like a first date.

"So what brings you here today?" or "What can I help you with?" I say. Inside, I am already wondering how this session will unfold. Will my client truly engage the angels and demons hovering around and within? How will she embrace them, or get them to embrace each other? How will she reveal her depth to me?

The hero's journey involves leaving the comfortable realms of the known, crossing over the frontiers of fear and aloneness, descending into the Valley of Death itself if necessary, and ultimately returning to the surface world renewed. The psychotherapy I practice happens under the banner of such transformation, and nothing less.

I believe everyone has the ability to navigate their inner journey successfully--no matter the level of psychological awareness, or education. I know when a client is sitting across from me that they have come here to find direction again. I feel honored that I have been invited to be on this little stretch of the way, for I am a fellow traveler who is being helped at the same time. When they blaze a trail for themselves, they are blazing one for me as well.

Were you to come to me for help, I would begin by observing you as you animate your stories with body movements, your tone of voice, the intensity of your gaze, your sighs. You would fill the moment with your essence, and with the secrets of your heart. I listen with more than my ears so that I can get a sense of who is really talking-- sometimes it's not who you think it is. Often, the voice echoes pain from long ago. One schizophrenic patient of mine, lost in the cryptic world of hallucinations, kept referring to "the boy at the side of the road." That "boy at the side of the road" frequently shows up in my office, appearing in different guises. The abandoned child remains hidden, but is not absent; he may lie dormant, but he is not dead. That's good news.

I see each client who enters my office as a hero in the making, about to brave at least a glimpse into the mirror of self-responsibility, inlaid into the mosaic of their relationships, and outlined by the frame of their family of origin. When the child gets lost, the mirror of the soul clouds over. The child's hiding place reflects the soul's secret shelter. How do we ever drift away from the child part of us? What primitive fears and hurts and survival urges compel us to cut off the very branch that connects us to the Tree of Life? Free the child, and you free the soul. Free the soul and healing will follow.

So here we are, in my office, and you are telling me your story. I should warn you that while you're speaking, I'm listening to the drums in the background, and if I can, I'll get you to hear them too. My tactic? To resonate with the mightiness of the song you are singing (no matter what your voice sounds like, what words you are using, whether you stay in one key, or whether you even know you are singing), and then chime in with sweet harmonies or discord or whatever it takes to make you hear your own melody. I'll even yell at you if I think it will help. Or I will sit with the grace and patience of a mountain, enjoying your song as it echoes through my valleys. I do this to enable you to hear for yourself.

As we maintain the therapeutic agreement between us, you will descend, and I will help you descend, into your private swirling pools-- the very waters Narcissus gazed into, but even deeper. Our initial plunge may stir up sand and cloud the waters, and you may doubt your progress.

"I'm more confused than ever," you might say.

"Hang in there. The dust will settle." And as it does, vistas teeming with life open before us. I will help you acclimate to your underwater world, and you will orient me. We will swim, and find everything you've ever thrown overboard in your life, even enter caves if we have to. Gliding through the subconscious with its dreamlike freedom from rationality and reason, we will locate old familiar scraps from your past, float them to the surface and forge them through our creativity into something new and livable. We will work hard, you and I, and experience exhilaration if we're lucky. Our work might be a salvage expedition, or a treasure hunt, or a swim with the innocent, playful ones---depending on where you lead us.

When we finish, again resting on the shore, then gradually shifting our focus to the simple reality of being together in my office, you and I might feel tired. A sense of peace pervades.

"Good job," I might say to you.

"Good job," you might say back to me.

After one such session that had been an especially fruitful and integrative experience, my 18-year-old male client opened his eyes to reemerge from a two-hour reverie. Searching for words to express warm feelings, he exclaimed, "Andy, this feels so right. I've been carrying this for years, and I finally get it." He paused, then said, "This work is so...human!".

"Thanks." Ah, he couldn't have picked a nicer adjective!

The Meta-Communications of Therapy

A therapist investigates his client's constructed world, and influences change. Unlike the dispassionate observer, which is the way scientists tend to see themselves, and which they believe is essential to their success, the therapist shows up fully present and involved. Maybe I as a therapist can learn to bracket my own opinions as I engage my client, but I still have my own constructed world-view, and can't help but perceive my client through it and incorporate her into it. I can't help it, nor should I. I enter the field as a human being, not in the guise of a tabla rasa that Freud suggested and recommended for therapists.

The aloof, blank scientific point of view is a myth. The new quantum physics shows us that the observer actually influences the behavior of sub-atomic particles--that they somehow respond to will. There is no such thing as a "neutral, impartial point of view." Out of a world of dreaming humans emerges our fundamental ability to influence each other into wakefulness (who really knows how this works?), so let's get on with it, and maybe even celebrate it. Screw the scientific point of view. Science attempts to sift everything through a sieve, to distance the observer from observed, when in fact, minimizing the "influence-factor" swims against the current of true life. Not only does the scientific reductionistic point of view put a strain on our attempts to process reality, but it artificially seeks to take us out of primary relationship with others. In therapy, this is counterproductive.

The therapist, as Observer and Influencer, exerts a therapeutic force before he ever utters a word. His beliefs about what is true and what is possible (in conjunction with those of the client) set the parameters for healing. A psychoanalyst who believes therapy takes years, and then has a client who is compliant with that belief, drags the whole thing out over a long period of time.

The unspoken assumptions in a system of human communication are more potent than the spoken directives or descriptions of "what-is," or what should be. They carry the meta-communication of the system, or the foundation of beliefs upon which the rest of the communication is built. When we read ancient literature or scientific studies, the meta-communications of that era are obvious to us, and often seem absurd. Navigational communication of long ago assumed a flat world, which seems downright silly to us now.

Metacommunications have a potency that can be harnessed in a positive way, and I try to accomplish that in my therapy. I base my work and interactions on a few fundamental assumptions, and I take a stand for them when interacting with my clients:

1. I know you know. Just as with Nature, where the shrub that carries the soothing antidote to the sharp thorns of the nettle plant grows nearby, the solution to problems are at hand. I assume my client has the resources within, and the capacity to find those resources that will significantly resolve his problems, integrate whatever it is that he has disconnected from, and eventually find peace. You could say I have faith in all of my clients.

2. I don't need to know. My theories about your inner world and the complexes that might reside there, or my mental illness classifications, are not what bring about life changes, and those factors do not have to predominate my experience of you in order for me to plan your care or treatment. I have faith in the process that exceeds my understanding of the particulars.

3. I know you are capable. I assume you can undo anything that has been done, and do for the first time that which you have left undone.

4. I know you are valuable. I acknowledge your intrinsic worth as a human being and as an individual. I honor your uniqueness and look deeply in order to discover the essence of you.

5. I know our being together in therapy will be helpful to you (and to me, too). I value the health-yielding effects of being present and honest, and believe our love will heal us both.

6. The truth shall set you free. I assume that truth and integrity are health-producing (even if they are not initially comfort-producing!)

7. There is nothing too large to overcome. The sub-assumption to this is: I know you are powerful. These two beliefs ride beside yet another

belief that brings true humility into the human condition and into therapy: there is nothing too small to trip over! (I've seen people have major issues over the smallest matters!)

Assumptions, as metacommunications, are the most powerful of beliefs, because even unspoken, they form the lattice for the vine of our consciousness to grow on. Our life-affirming assumptions yield fruit, whereas sometimes our conscious beliefs remain barren. A large part of the healing in our therapeutic encounter gets facilitated without words--even as we're talking. As a therapist I must be vigilant with my beliefs and ever-ready to challenge and correct my assumptions.

Carl Rogers, of client-centered therapy fame, proclaimed three fundamental therapeutic techniques that should reside at the heart of all healing: 1. unconditional positive regard---holding the client in a positive light, unconditionally; 2. the genuineness of the therapist, or congruence--by modeling an alignment of inner essence and outer appearance, the therapist engages and coaxes the real person out; and 3. accurate empathic relationship---in the process of accurately understanding the client's world, the therapist gives the gift of validation and strengthens a sense of authenticity.

I would add a fourth, and in my estimation, the most potent, unspoken tool for therapy: the focus on greatness. When someone sees you as unique, special, and even great, you can feel it. At first it might make you nervous. You might giggle without knowing why. Or squirm. But soon you will melt. A focus on greatness cuts through defenses like a hot knife through butter, and cuts the time needed for therapy significantly. The focus on greatness that the therapist offers his client is like the adoration many of us freely give to an infant. Who ever tires of staring at the beautiful eyes and face of a newborn, so perfectly made, and truly awe-inspiring the way it reflects a state of grace? It might seem outrageous to think we can focus like that on a grown-up client! Believe me when I say it is effective. Who would choose to resist that sort of loving regard? Few do. The real joy of this approach rests in its ability to melt seeming stones.

Therapy begins without words, and although words may make up the bulk of the conscious material, the healing takes place on a much deeper level. The exchange of therapist's and client's words, like the sculptor's hammer, chisel, and sandpaper, hew and probe the raw material until a shape begins to materialize. Through effort, a lasting smooth-ness results. What guides the hands of the therapist as sculptor are the spoken and unspoken cues of the client. Inconsistencies cry out to be confronted. Yearnings beg to be unleashed, and pain screams out to be released. When Michaelangelo was asked how he sculpted his David, he replied: "I cut away from the image in the stone everything that it wasn't, so it could simply be".

How Long Therapy?

How long does therapy take? Is it a long-term or short-term process? Some aspects of getting well require no time, and are much more a matter of timing than length of time. For a person with a long history of abusive relationships, for example, the unfamiliarity of a lov-ing, respectful relationship make it too strange to accept. But once the willingness to receive the good stuff and the responsibility for setting healthy boundaries are there, the shift can manifest in no time at all. Even after carrying a backpack full of stones for 24 hours, it only takes a few minutes to shrug it off. Healing sometimes occurs with little or no effort when one is ready, and wanting it to happen. Sometimes, no matter what the history, heaviness, or momentum of problems involved, it still only takes a subtle inner change to redirect the major path one is on. Just like a train hurtling down the track, which at a second's notice, by the flick of a switch, can change tracks without even losing velocity.

Deeper work takes more time and effort because of the defenses against pain that have kept the source of the person's problem imprinted within. This client must first of all enter the feeling level in order to achieve what I call "critical mass," a point when the forces of resistance are overcome. When critical mass is achieved, the person can feel again. With cooperation, strong desire, and concentrated effort, critical mass can be reached within weeks. Once on the feeling track, the process of therapy and inner healing proceeds organically according to the natural "unwinding" of the mind/body system. With deeply rooted trauma, it can be a matter of years. A general principle applies: the younger the trauma, the longer the therapy.

If one's goal is to function better in specific situations, then therapy as coaching might not take long at all. If, however, the goal focuses on integrating disconnected aspects of oneself, then reconnecting with feeling to enhance the quality of life, a little more time may be needed. Where else are you going?

Technique and Art in Therapy

Every therapist has a bag of tricks--techniques that signify his unique personal style and artistry. A host of practitioners over many years have contributed to the universal education pool, and their time-tested techniques are what counselors study when they enter the field of psychology. Sometimes someone comes along whose approach is so novel and effective that other therapists take notice.

Milton Erickson is one. Erickson, an M.D. with a Masters Degree in Psychology, was an eccentric genius and master facilitator who engaged his clients in very unconventional, effective, and sometimes amusing ways. The accounts of his sessions are hilarious. Once, a young woman came to him complaining that she was getting older and still hadn't found a mate. She went on to say that she was in fact afraid of men, and felt ugly, especially because of the gap between her two front teeth. She was depressed. Erickson brought up the subject of suicide, presenting it as the "escape clause," meaning that she could be consoled that if all else failed, suicide would always be there as an option. The notion of choice made her feel much better. Then Erickson came up with a brilliant idea, but wouldn't tell her until she promised to obey his every instruction without question. He had established such splendid rapport with her, and had piqued her curiosity to such a degree, that she agreed.

His instructions to her were to go home and practice spitting water out between her teeth until she had mastered the skill. She had to also promise not to commit suicide until she had succeeded. Even though she thought his suggestion a little crazy, she did it anyway. In a later session, Erickson got her to agree to a final fling: she was to go to a beauty parlor, buy and wear a gorgeous dress to work, and purposely seek out the man in her office who made her feel the most shy. Then she was to spit water through her front teeth on him when they met at the water cooler! The woman was appalled, but in the context of a last fling, she actually did it! The man, totally surprised, chased her down, and kissed her! The next day he ambushed her at the water cooler with a water pistol! They ended up going out, and eventually were married. Erikson loved being a director of human drama, and felt free to influence the players, the setting, the sequence of events--anything that appealed to his mischievous sensibilities. The man was a benevolent con-artist! My hero!

Communication specialists Richard Bandler and John Grinder, fascinated by the effectiveness of certain therapists of highly different approaches, (namely Milton Erickson, Fritz Perls, and Virginia Satir), conducted an intricate study of their therapy sessions to see if these masters had anything in common. They translated the results of their study into Neuro-linguistic Programming (NLP), a system that focuses on accessing the information processing style of the client as a way to facilitate rapid change. They noted that what earned Perls, Erickson, and Satir "genius" status was first and foremost how each of them uniquely and intuitively was able to "enter" the inner world of their clients. Their mastery wasn't attributed to a particular school of psychotherapy or philosophy, but rather to the practitioner's ability as a person to establish a loving and effective rapport with the client. Only on that basis did their craft turn into art.

Below is my list of common elements of outstanding therapists:

1. The willingness to go out on a limb and explore the more irrational (almost peripheral) elements of the client's presentation. The ability to pick up on the significance of body movements, changing inflections in the voice, or repeated themes, phrases, or icons that appear in dreams or in the varied stories the client tells, no matter how seemingly small or inconsequential. Genius therapists are highly and often mysteriously "on target", where others would miss or ignore the cues they follow.

2. The willingness to follow their intuition without knowing where it will lead—using a non-formulaic approach, independent of theories and/or diagnoses. This style directly involves trusting images and feelings that "pop in" in response to the client's verbal and nonverbal presentation.

3. A relentless focus on feelings, and the ability to suss out the emotional "charge" in a client, even when the client does not initially

recognize or fess up to that "charge."

4. The ability to "create space" for a struggling client to enter difficult interior places , by means of what I refer to as a "creative vacuum", where the therapist is simultaneously attentive, yet absolutely agenda-free and receptive.

5. The ability to uproot the "obvious" from the realms of the "assumed." Especially potent when what's "assumed" sits at the core of the problem and is dead wrong!

6. Using humor through irony, absurdity, and pathos as a way of getting to the core of the issue.

7. Engaging the "I-Thou" encounter with the client in order to give immediacy and potency to new information being uncovered, thus directly modeling and reinforcing the benefits of intimacy.

8. Benevolent trickery--this can mean the use of therapeutic double-bind strategies (like prescribing the symptoms the client is try-ing to overcome--"Let's see you bring on a panic attack right now"--thereby proving, either way that the client has some control), or any other strategies that emphasize the client's free choice.

9. The sense that nothing is taboo, that anything can be used for therapeutic movement and growth.

10. Story-telling--helping the client create a new life-affirming mythology to live by. Images and themes generated by the client carry the potency that needs to be woven into the fabric of these new tales.

11. A sense of transcendence—establishing the notion that "you are more than this." A good therapist conveys this both verbally and non-verbally.

True artistry in psychotherapy often calls on the Dark Side of the human psyche to be the wellspring for effective tools in overturning dysfunction. An effective therapist, like a competent surgeon, must be willing and able to dehumanize the client to the point of reducing him to the status of an "artist's medium." Furthermore, the therapist must be unwilling to let clients wallow in the comfort zone of intellectualism and story telling. Empathy and rapport-building, yes, but at times, no coddling, and no mercy. After all, weeding involves digging up the roots with a sharp lance. Surgery involves cutting with sharp scalpels and stitching with pinpoint needles. Deep-feeling therapy eschews collu-sion with suffering or ignorance, carries a ruthless disregard for excuses and reasons, and an uncompromising unwillingness to settle for less-than-wholeness. Therapeutic integrity dictates that nothing is too taboo or too sacred to confront, no bubble too holy to pop. A good therapist may be more on your side than you are, but unlike a parent who may rationalize his or her actions with: "I'm doing this for your own good," but actually is just passing on his or her own internalized repression, the code of the therapist flows forth from a foundation of humanism.

How to Recognize and Work With Feeling-fragments

Like an ancient alchemist assembling the five elements for transformation in the lab, the feeling-centered, body-focused therapist strives to bring feeling-fragments into consciousness, harvest the resulting emotional charge, and set the stage for integration. Feeling-fragments, components of repressed material, cycle and recycle throughout consciousness until they reunite into a whole once more, and then are finally relegated to the realm of neutral memory.

Feeling-fragments are buffered from consciousness by the body's defenses against pain. Pieces of an original painful feeling float around in the nervous system outside the conscious awareness in the form of anxiety, tension, driven thoughts and actions, phobias, and a myriad of other sensations and behaviors. The difference between consciously accessing memory (as in remembering what you had for breakfast yesterday), and being swept into the experience of the resurfacing of feeling fragments is not a subtle one. You can sense the "I" during conscious access, but not in the case of feeling fragments. Body responses, emotional tones, or meanings (what the person tells himself about an event or experience) can seem out of context, or even extreme, when feeling fragments are unleashed during a therapy session.

Initial listening techniques for the therapist require learning how to identify and distinguish feeling fragments from neutral memories. Other techniques revolve around learning to see the whole picture that is being presented, an exercise that is akin to assembling and aligning the pieces of a puzzle before finally connecting them. Finally, the therapist may need to come up with a highly-charged catalyst that can facilitate the merging of the separated aspects of a feeling into a completed gestalt, or point of wholeness. Attempting to link the pieces solely with "analysis" or "interpretation" tends to derail the integration process, rather than enhancing or quickening it.

A patient who repeatedly employs the same terminology, or even more directly, the same words or phrases to describe unrelated phenomena implies a meaning-fragment. My chiropractor client's wrist injury prevented him from practicing spinal adjustments, or in his terms, "doing what I hold most dear." When he described the collapse of a fruitless business venture, he claimed, "I lost that which was most dear to me." It turned out that this meaning of "losing that which is most dear to me" had resided in a core response when his beloved father died when he was five. Because he was not allowed to go to the funeral and face the finality of death, he had fragmented and spread out his grief that was later manifested in the theme of his current life: "losing what I hold most dear."

When a client repeats phrases, I then repeat those phrases back to him in the same context in order to help create a biological feedback loop into his or her consciousness. I keep the phrase active in the present while "gathering" other feeling fragments and bringing them into the current reality.

When a client repeatedly refers to certain parts of his body through talk or gesture, or indicates chronic physical problems, then I assume I am witnessing a body-response fragment. Sol, 53, with a recent diagnosis of prostate cancer, repeatedly spoke in a penis/sex-related language, calling men "pricks," "dick heads," "cocksuckers," and women were referred to as "ball crushers," and "cockteases." At one point Sol announced, "they'll take your dick if they can." This kind of talk made it obvious to me that we should investigate his teen years. In fact, Sol had had an affair with an aunt, over which he felt both proud and guilty. His father, it turned out, had also had an affair with the same woman, which made Sol feel hurt and angry. And deeply sorry for his mother. So much charge, and no way to process it as a kid!

When a single emotional tone pervades the various areas of a client's life, I think 'emotional fragment.' I believe depression is nothing more than fragmented, disconnected grief. Antidepressants combat the reemergence of these grief-fragments, thus running counter to the natural integrative processes. When strong emotional fragments of a feeling predominate the feeling-fragment scene, the therapist may decide to defer straight catharsis until other elements creep into consciousness. Many depressed people cry freely and even wallow in sorrow, so facilitating a tearful meltdown is not a cure for depression. Only when the weeping is connected to the true object of grief does the pool of pain actually drain out with some finality. Only when the link to the pain is broken does pain no longer make sense to the system. Paradoxically, this link can only break after first being connected consciously.

"Harvesting" for a missing feeling-fragment can actually be a fun exercise for the therapist, especially when the overall picture becomes clear enough that the fragment can be recognized lurking in the background before the client is even remotely aware that a psychic "soil-tilling" is underway. If the elements of meaning and emotion already reside in the conscious mind, then only body-response remains. A simple shift into body-awareness techniques coaxes the final fragment of consciousness to emerge. If a strong body-response (i.e., tingling in hands or feet, tightness in solar plexus, etc.) and a meaning (for example, "I cannot let myself feel," or "they hate me") coexist, then I make a move to elicit emotion. "What is the feeling there?" or, "What does that feel like?" If body-response (i.e., shaking, sweating) and emotion (fear) reside together in the consciousness, then I seek out the meaning that connects them (i.e., "What does this remind you of?" or, "When have you experienced this before?", or even more directly "What does this mean to you?")

It is important to note that these elements want to come together for the sake of biological integration and for gestalt resolution, so the therapist only has to bring them to light and let the natural centropic (or inward, integrative) forces ignite them into wholeness. The closer they come to each other, the more the charge of the moment intensifies, often reflecting an increasing level of resistance. The client will engage in all kinds of distraction gambits at this point, or, if feeling threatened by the imminent shift about to occur in his awareness of pain, he may segue into the more "dangerous" ploy of direct transference onto the therapist. As an East Indian female patient zeroed in on the chauvinistic, hurtful reality of her heretofore revered father, she turned on me with: "I hate you, Andy! How dare you bring this up, how dare you make me feel this way about my father!" That was immediately followed by: "I have never felt as much passion as I do right now. Do you ever engage in discreet liaisons with your clients?" She was serious! And had little recognition of the extreme nature of her love-hate projections!

Working with feeling fragments remains the main thrust of therapy because it parallels the body's own integrative processes, and takes into account the natural resistance to pain. If my explanation here sounds simple, then I'm glad. The reality is simple. The artistry of facilitation remains the great challenge because pain is real, and not just a "story." Therapy that deals only with the story and avoids, ignores, or denies the pain factor, does not get to the core.

When and How to Do Core Work

Core work involves repairing the foundation of the psyche. The glitches that mar the normal evolution of a sense of self in the formative years of infancy, toddlerhood, and childhood cry out to be healed. Ideally and archetypally, each person requires a loving, compassionate, comforting, wise mother and father for optimal mental health, regardless of whether that actually occurred historically. Obviously, it is not the job of the therapist to become a substitute for the Ideal Parents, nor do repeated "corrective emotional experiences" in group therapy make up for childhood loss, nor is it effective to simply imagine understanding and kind parents. The core work of shifting the child aspect of the psyche from the struggle mode to the at-ease mode, and shifting the reins of the psyche itself out of the hands of the wounded child, naturally takes place in the wake of feeling-fragment integration.

Too much filling in the blanks by the therapist, the method used in popular, generic Inner Child work, is like eating processed food: the more food is tampered with before it gets to you, the less benefit it provides. Core work requires the highest level of noninterference, and the most skillful artistry, yet it calls for much more than passivity on the part of the therapist. Just as grief-work is called work because it often must be facilitated and also involves challenging inner territory, so is core work "work."

With the child at the helm of the psyche, a myriad of struggle-strategies reign, and they simply don't relinquish hold easily. When all the formative years in the family have been a struggle, it seems like life itself IS a struggle, so with the end of struggle comes the end of life. Core work involves snuffing out the flame of unreal hope, and finally grieving real losses. Strangely, ending a life of struggle rings like a curse word in the ears of the baby who doesn't want to grow up, or the adult who doesn't relish self-reliance, yet at the same time, tugs on the heartstrings of the person who finally wants to get on with living and having fun. Core work inevitably stirs these primal conflicts.

Themes of core work often include what I call dethroning the parental figures, and letting them (or the imagined versions of them) carry their own karma or suffering. I continue to be amazed at how children take on the pain of their parents with the intention being not only to somehow shelter them, but also to magically keep them intact enough so hope for their love can abide.

Conflicting childhood feelings often become diluted, which later hinders proper integration and resolution. In core work, those feelings must be separated so that they can then fully emerge and become integrated at a child level. I am referring specifically to grief, hurt, anger, and compassion, emotions that often are felt simultaneously, then are intermingled, which brings on confusion, the end result being the feelings get stored away rather than resolved. An abused child can still love the perpetrator, even as he feels the hurt, the loss of a loving parent or guardian, and anger, all at the same time. The pleasurable sensations of sexual contact may confuse the issue even more.

The Core Technique

When the conflicted feelings of childhood unfold in a therapy setting (and not before), it is appropriate to help set the inner stage in order to facilitate the separation and clarification of those feeling elements. Below is an example of how I do that.

"Close your eyes. If you could travel back into time and find yourself as a child, how old would that child be?"

If the client picks the age of a traumatic scenario, then I encourage him to depict it as the memories come up with as much detail as possible, including sights, sounds, smells. This helps loosen state-dependent memories, which are the peripheral associations that the body uses as anchors for feeling charges, thus making the feelings more accessible. If the patient chooses an age well before a primal traumatic scene, then the focus shifts to a time before a splitting or repression of feeling, and indicates the need for safety before entering the "hot" zone. Eventually, I gently suggest that my patient "let the child get older now," and to ease him into the primal memories. If the client chooses a time and age after a primal scene, it generally introduces a more youthful or primitive mind frame already dealing with repressed pain. This too provides a doorway to the feeling realm.

"Three," my client might say.

"What do you see when you look at that three-year-old?"

"I see a three-year-old who is lost and sad."

(When a client says "sad," I note this as an emotional feeling fragment. If the client says something about the physical appearance of that child, for example, "I see neatly braided hair and chubby cheeks," I notate this as body-response feeling fragment. If the client focuses on a conclusion or belief state of the child, then I know this is a meaning feeling fragment. This notation system helps to round out the picture to include emotion, body-response, and meaning, so that the natural integrative forces can take over)

"What is she sad about?" I might ask, seeking the meaning element.

"She's all alone."

"And what is it about being alone that makes her feel sad?"

"Her Mother left her."

✳ "What is that little girl telling herself in that moment?" I prod.

"My Mommy doesn't care about me."

"Say that again."

"My Mommy doesn't care about me."

I continue, "What kind of a feeling do you have as an adult seeing a three-year-old feeling so lost and sad, and finally concluding, "my mommy doesn't care about me?"

"That makes me sad too."

"So just be sad." Then I say, "What is it like for the child to be with an adult who sees her sadness and weeps for her?" (Often more tears here.)

"The child feels good. Safe. Cared for."

✳ "If you could make some sort of body contact with the child, either to touch her hand, her shoulder, or to embrace her, what would you notice happening in the body of the child through your touch?" (This grounds the experience in bodily reality and keeps it from getting cerebral.)

"She's relaxing. Getting warm. She's hugging me back," the client states.

✳ "And in that micro-moment, what is that little girl telling herself?" I ask.

"Somebody cares about me. It's OK to feel sad." (At this point, the client has introduced the missing elements from her own childhood in an experiential rather than theoretical way.)

✳ "If this little girl really had someone like you with whom she could have had this experience that we are having now, what kind of woman would she then naturally grow up to become? Feel free to use your intuition."

She'd grow up to become a woman who feels OK about being alone, who feels good about herself, and who has healthy relationships," the client responded.

"As an adult, what does it feel like just to be in the presence of a woman like that?" (This shifting of perspectives between the child and adult aspects serves to "lubricate" the psyche that enters into a healthy fluid and flexible state.)

"It feels comforting. Safe. Inspiring."

✳ "And now let the image of that woman come into your body," I coach her. Take a nice deep breath and let yourself just try that on for size. You got derailed as a child and this is just you putting yourself back on track. How does it feel?"

"It feels great. I feel a lightness. I am smiling." (Note how so much of this remains at the body-sensation level. This is how the body gets "updated"--not by intellectual insight.)

"It is now time to let your mother see what you just did with this little girl. Let her see how with you the little girl feels safe, comforted, loved, and warm and relaxed in her body, from which she is able to conclude, "Somebody cares about me." Let her see how her little girl, under your care, naturally grows up to become a woman who feels good about herself, gets into decent relationships, and who is OK about being alone. Finally, allow your mother see what she did with that same little girl. Let her see how she planted the seeds of loneliness, abandonment, and of a desperation for relationship that yielded bad results. If she could see the mistakes she made, and the pain she caused, how would she feel?"

"She would feel so sorry, and so sad."

"Good! Let her feel so sorry and so sad," I said firmly. (Surprisingly, clients often cry for their parent at this point, showing an innate compassion even though that parent has hurt them).

"If this little girl had a choice of whether to come be with you, or stay with her mother, which would she choose?" (This introduces choice at a child level, something often not available in the child's youth. The child originally chose to stay with the mother and to leave herself.)

"She would come be with me."

"Now let your mother see that," I persist. "What would it be like for her to see her little girl choose to leave her?" (Often tears flow at this point--again showing deep levels of compassion)

"She'd feel lost and sad." (Amazing how often the client actually chooses the same words for the parent's feeling that she chose to describe those of the child a little earlier!)

"Let her feel lost and sad. You don't have to protect her from these feelings any more," I remind her. (How true that children protect their parents from their own pain by taking it on!)

"What is it like for the three-year-old to see her mother feeling so lost and sad?"

"Sad too."

"The little girl has a question for you, the adult, which is: "Is it me that is making my mother feel so lost and sad in her life? What is your answer to that?"

"No, it's not your fault."

"Say that again."

"No, it's not your fault," she repeats.

"And again."

(As obvious as all this is to adult sensibilities, this part of the work inevitably carries high levels of feeling, revealing that the child part of the psyche often carries the responsibility for parents' suffering, even though it's irrational. This technique yields much relief at a body level.)

I press on, " What is it like for a three-year-old to hear those 𝆑 words from you?"

"Really good! A great relief!"

"How are you aware of that right now?" (Again, this needs to be body centered.)

"I feel so light. My shoulder doesn't hurt anymore!"
O K. Let's review what we have done so far: by going back into time, the client provides the inroad to feelings, the clues as it were, then she brings the therapist into the central drama involved. The content varies, but the process of "harvesting" feeling fragments remains the same. It is important to maintain a natural fluidity between child and adult aspects, according to the state of the client. A forced focus on the child makes the experience rote or phony. Keeping it all adult denies the integrative process fullness, and keeps it intellectual and one-dimensional.

Pain stays repressed in its original form. Three-year-old pain hurts like a three-year-old hurts. No substitutes in this equation. By feeding back to the client her own perceptions of her child-self, and helping her focus on the missing elements of the emotion, meaning, or body-response (the holy trinity of my therapy), the stage is set for biology to take over and yield a full integration. This stage of the work helps identify the emotions of grief and hurt, and helps associate those emotions with the original body-sensations and existential conclusions ("Nobody cares about me."). The child (part of the psyche) is asked to choose adult or parent? ("If the child had a choice to be with you, the adult, or stay with its parent, what would it choose?"), and usually chooses the adult over the parent. The child is then relieved from responsibility for the parent's pain. All of these exercises require elaboration and reinforcement, but this is how the bare-bones of the core work technique works.)

The next phase of core work involves the same trinity of child, parent, and adult, but with a different twist. The goal is to introduce new healthy elements to the mindframe of the child. For example:

"If you could travel back in time and find that three-year-old and her mother, and find yourself witnessing the mother planting the

seeds of sadness and lost-ness in the child, how would you feel?
I would feel distressed."
If the client doesn't confess feeling some degree of anger, then I use a different strategy. I say, "If the scene I just described took place in a movie, and the camera was focused on the face of the child, in that moment, what are the expressions on the faces of the other people watching the movie with you?" A typical reply would be, "Outraged. Pissed." By once-removing the emotion around it, the anger can surface.

"Try these words to speak as an adult to your mother," I continue coaching, "How could you do that to that little girl?"

"How could you do that to that little girl?" the patient repeats.
"Again."

"How could you do that to that little girl?" the patient says.

"And now, as the little girl," I press ahead, "How could you do that to me?"

The patient asks the question, and tears spring to her eyes.
"That's it," I say, "Now hiding none of your tears this time, ask it again."

"How could you do that to me?" At this point, my client elaborates with her own dialogue. Great! Prompting is not usually required here, as the stage has been set."

"Now as an adult to your mother, "I hate what you did to that little girl!" The patient repeats it after me, and then I tell her to say it again.

Sometimes what starts as a gruff expression reverts to the hurt tone, and "how could you do this to me?" When that happens, it is showing how hurt and anger mingle and become diluted. If my client's tone sounds more like hurt than anger, I have her "downscale" by repeating, "how could you do that to me?", reverting back to the emotion of hurt.

"What is it like for the little girl to hear those words spoken to her mother?" I inquire.

"She is confused. She feels protective of her mother. Guilty." These are common responses to that question, which is OK, because now the client can clarify that these feelings have been mixed, therefore not integrated.

"Try these words as an adult: 'I hate you for what you did to that little girl.'"

The client repeats it, though it isn't unusual for a client to refuse to say those words. It feels too strong or severe.

"How does it feel to say those words to your mother?" I ask.

"Scary. True. Good. It feels right even though I feel bad saying it."

"What is the difference between those two phrases: "I hate what you did to that little girl" and "I hate you for what you did to that little girl?"

The client understands, "The former is about the person, and the latter statement about her actions."

"Now that you know it's about the actions, not the person, say this one again: "I hate what you did to that little girl.""

"I hate what you did to that little girl!" No hurt this time. It's more pure hate—separated from the hurt aspect.

Further dialogue makes it clear that focusing on the behavior of the person for the little girl, rather than the person who inflicted harm, "feels good, as though I have been right all along."

"And what kind of a person hates what that mother did to that girl, a good person or a bad person?" I persist. This addresses the child notion that hating one's mother is proof of badness, of unworthiness of love, of deserving punishment.

"A good person."

"Now go touch the little girl. Let her get the truth of what I am saying to her through your touch. 'Little girl, your hate is not proof that you are bad, that you don't deserve the love you want from your mother, or that you deserve to be punished. It is actually proof that you are good, because what you are really hating is bad behavior, and only a good person hates bad behavior." Tears usually come at this point.

"What does hearing that feel like to the child?"

"It feels like a great relief. It feels real good!"

"What are you aware of in your body right now?" I intend to anchor the new response into the bodily reality with these statements.

"I feel tingly in my hands."

"What is the feeling in your heart right now?"

"Very light."

"And what is your state of mind right now?"

"Clear."

"On a scale of 1-10, 10 being the most tingly, most lighthearted, and the most clear, where are you right now?"

"Seven."

"Excellent." Six or higher equals a promising response. Less than six indicates the need for more work.

"Take a nice deep breath, and let it go all the way up to an eight." I continue this, breath by breath, until she reaches a ten. This will anchor in the work we have done at a bodily level, creating a new response to the old material. From now on, touching on the subject of the mother will automatically trigger this new healthy response, thereby neutralizing the old one. Work like this is pivotal in turning around long-standing difficult patterns of feeling and behavior.

Finally, I say: "If you could now call in your mother to witness you at this level ten, what would it be like for her?"

"She would be happy for me." Or sometimes not. Responses vary here.

"What would you say to her from this Level Ten place?"
This is where the good-bye speeches come in, or the "I can't carry your pain for you any more," or "I'm sorry we couldn't get it together." (This is about separation.) "Level Ten" insures a high level of functioning. I then try call in others to the mind's eye of the patient who, people in her current life, whom it would be beneficial for her to dialogue with in this new stage of her development. Often the solutions to relationship problems become very obvious in this "rehearsal."

Note: The above describes the bare-bones stage and process of core work. In any given session of core work, I might spend much more time on a single aspect. Just like a dentist drills according to the extent of the tooth decay, different situations and people call for different levels and degrees of processing. Only when the feeling levels are fully explored and "excavated" from theory to gut reality do these techniques yield lasting change.

If the client remains attached to the image of the parent, and reluctant to have the child leave, or too empathetic to the parent's suffering, then I bring in other techniques.

Finding the Real Parent for the Child

If you can't bring Mohammed to the mountain, then bring the mountain to Mohammed. If the child aspect of the psyche seems unable to seek out its need-fulfillment by leaving the parent, then bring the real parent into the picture. Because the Unconscious doesn't know the difference between outer and inner reality (as evidenced by our body responses to images and feelings in dreams), I sometimes facilitate the proper separation of child from suffering parent by introducing the Whole or Real Parent to take the suffering one's place. Below are some guidelines:

"If you could travel back into time even farther, and find your mother as a girl. How old is she?" (How often the client will select the same age as they did for their own child-self!)

"I see her at three years old. She is with her father who is distant and aloof. Her mother has just died, and her father just can't handle the loss. He sends her to live with her Grandmother."

"What do you see when you look at that little girl?" I make note of which aspect my client tunes in to, and then introduce the other two, and I stay as body-and feeling-centered as possible.)

"She is so isolated. Separated from her brother. Forced to live with her Grandmother in the city after having lived so happily on the farm with her mother."

The technique proceeds as before. Have her show up as an adult who feels for the child. Let the parent-as-child receive the benefits of this new presence. Then proceed with:

"If your mother really had someone like you when she was three, and had a healthy upbringing, what kind of a woman would she then naturally have grown up to become?")

"She would grow up to become a feeling, caring woman."

"And what would it feel like to be the daughter of a woman like that?"

"It would be great!" I would focus in on the body response. Keep the process as interior as possible. Closed eyes help.

"This is your 'real mother,' the woman your mother was meant to be, and the one you intuitively struggled to bring out in her. Your intuition was probably right, but she never had anyone like you at that time in her life. Can you let the little girl part of you have her "real mother" anyway? It is what she wants, and something she will never get from the woman you have called mother.

Sometimes I emphasize this aspect: *"You will never have a mother who loves and cares for you in the way you have always wanted."* The patient needs to understand this in order to get on with appropriate grieving, and give up irrational hope. This occurring simultaneously with the introduction to her "real mother" creates a dual process: it empties the grief, and fills her up with simple relaxation and love. Clients seem to become weary from this exercise. I think it's the exhaustion of having struggled so hard for something not forthcoming . By splitting the parent into two distinct entities, the suffering human vs. the completed, "real parent," the client frees herself to feel both compassion for her wounded parent and fulfillment of her child aspect. These feelings no longer need be held in a mutually exclusive way.

The Child Must Die

If the child part of the psyche predominates, and that dominance has become a status quo that continues to prevent adult relationships in the present, something must be introduced into the system to alter the balance of power. The child will yield its place at the helm of the psyche only when her needs are met, or the possibility arises of having those needs met. We tend to manifest fierce loyalty to the needs of the child by letting that aspect of the psyche rule. It is difficult to relinquish this hierarchical model even though it renders adult living impossible. The flip-side also leaves the child in charge, because often the rapport between child and adult aspects has eroded to the point of being nonexistent or even hostile. Some adults hate their irrational, needy little selves and carry on interiorly just how they were treated as kids. Hostility towards this aspect of the psyche ironically also keeps the child aspect dominant. Ultimately, mental health calls for the adult and child parts of the psyche to meet in a mutually satisfying way, each complementing the other, but with the adult in charge.

Below is one method I use to shift this structure:

"If you could travel back in time and find yourself as a child, how old is that child?" I ask.

"Three."

"What do you see when you look at that child?"

"A miserable, unhappy kid. She feels unloved and lonely."

"Let that child now see you. Let her see how your problems in relationships result from her unresolved loneliness. How does she feel seeing that?"

"She feels awful. Her unhappiness has become mine. She feels really guilty about that."

"Maybe you have a system here where the two of you cannot be happy. Maybe she must die so you might live. Would she be willing to die for you to bring that about?"

This creates the bind: how can I just let the child die? Is this proper? Can I really live without the child part of myself? As therapist, I then justify this position with all sorts of psycho-babble, affirming my assessment that the inner dynamic of this person's psyche remains locked in an unworkable mode, and must change drastically if happiness is to find roots in her life at all . Whichever way the client chooses my "setup," it can serve as a fulcrum for change.

The possible responses: 1. "No, I cannot let my child die even if she is willing to die for me," which opens up the therapeutic doors of: "What is it like for a child to be with an adult unwilling to let it die?" and the positive infusion from that stand that follows. 2. "Yes, she is willing to die for me, OK, so be it" leads to the therapy of "How is it to have a child be so willing to die for the happiness of others?" which leads to other kinds of inner tenderness and self-appreciation.

I've even had one client actually go through with the death of the child, and it felt like the deepest, most restful sleep. The child aspect then woke up later! It just needed to be able to rest that deeply, in the repose of non-struggle. The death of struggle actually felt like the death of being to that client, because that is how deeply the experience of life as struggle had been ingrained. The Child Must Die technique carries extremes that challenge the rational approach, and certainly the prevalent feel-good "inner child" work of our times. This technique has to be used with great care.

Therapy as "Worm Stick"

Immediately after I graduated from New College in Sarasota, Florida, I moved to a rural community in south Georgia, where I had contracted to do a variety of jobs for two years. One of them was to work with the new day care center. Another was to work their worm farm. Now a worm farm is where Night Crawlers and Red Wigglers grow from little worm babies to full-blown fish bait in huge troughs of horse and cow manure, to be shipped out in peat-moss-lined Chinese take-out containers to the anglers and organic gardeners around the country. Not a pretty job.

Scooping the manure was OK with me because I could keep it at shovel distance. Putting the baby worms into the trenches was also fine, because slime levels stayed low. But what about harvest time? How in the world was I to extract the full-grown worms from their manure homes without getting crap all over me? Enter the worm stick.

Will, ancient Good-ole-Boy neighbor down the road, and worm farmer from the days of antiquity, saved me. "What you need, son, is a worm stick," he said.

"What's a worm stick?" I asked.

"Ah, a divine instrument! I invented it myself, and I have been manure-free ever since."

"Do you have one?" I asked, in my eagerness to be manure-free.

"No problem. Watch this!" And Master Will ambled over to some bushes near the worm barn, stripped off leaves from a likely twig, and cut it about two feet in length with his Bowie, then proceeded to whittle alternating ridges the entire length of the stick, and all around. The result? A denuded, ribbed masterpiece.

"This, young man, is a worm stick." Will squatted at the edge of the manure trough, and jabbed his worm stick about half way into the warm brown mass. He picked up another straight dead twig, and started rubbing it up and down along the ribs of its immersed partner. A little clunk clunk clunk noise ensued. He kept it up for about three minutes, and darned if I didn't see worms rising to the surface of the trough!

"No need to reach in and get all messed up," Will exclaimed, grinning proudly. "Not when you have a worm stick!"

"This is too cool!" I marveled at the growing number of writhing, wiggling little critters emerging to the surface. "How does it work?"

"Simple, really. I think the vibrations of rubbing the worm stick irritates them, forcing them up." The harvest proceeded virtually shit-free.

Deep feeling therapy is like a worm stick. (Oh oh, is this like Gump's "Life is like a box of chocolates"?) Deep feeling therapy helps bring reluctant repressed material to the surface. It carries with it a certain amount of irritation that prods at the unreal system to reveal its contents to the light of consciousness.

"Worm stick" techniques include: 1. loud music, 2. insults, 3. direct challenges, 4. put-downs, 5. negative implications, and, 6. introducing incongruency. Let me elaborate with a story:

Fred: Put Down, Get Down

Twenty-seven-year old Fred, looks like the Incredible Hulk-- massive chest and bulging arms. He has come to me for help about his self-image and bad living habits. In session four, he is still ranting about his weight. "I'm too fat! Look at me! I need to lose thirty pounds, easy. It's my lifestyle, I know. I party with my friends, drink too much, and wham: I'm huge! I get so caught up in having a good time, I forget what is good for me. If I don't exercise in the gym every day for a few hours I'm a goner!"

"Fred," I asked, "Have you ever heard of 'anorexia?'"

"Yeah, what does that have to do with anything?"

"You remind me of an anorexic thirteen-year-old girl."

"What's that supposed to mean?" he smirks.

"Don't you get it? The same obsessive thinking about being fat, hooked on exercise in a compulsive way..."

"OK, OK, I get the picture....."

"Wait, I'm not done. Anorexic girls often get so absorbed in their self-image and weight loss because it is seemingly the only area of their lives they can control. It's like a symptom of feeling out of control. Some of them actually feel guilty about taking up space. Or they feel unworthy of nourishment. Or they are mysteriously acting out revenge against a controlling parent."

"Can we change the subject?"

"Sure. But tell me again about how disciplined you are at work, and how clean you keep your home environment..."

+++++++++

(Comments: Fred went on to explore the difference between how he feels inside and the macho image he projects. Always much bigger than his peers growing up, he established an identity as a "large" person, and dissociated himself from feeling small. He did eventually touch into a core sense of tenderness and vulnerability. He later confided in me that the image I presented of him as an anorexic thirteen-year-old girl really bugged him, because as incongruous at it seemed externally, it hit home inside. Also, I got away with my "snide" attitude only on the crest of an excellent rapport with Fred.)

++++++++++

About loud music: sometimes, as a way to access more right brain aspects of my client's inner world, I will have him or her recline with eyes closed in the office Lazy-Boy, and then play loud music for about twenty minutes. I'll say: "Let the feel of the music take you where you may not want to go but may need to go. If you don't like the music, just let it blend in as background music during your process of getting in touch within." Tribal drums, Gabrielle Roth's Bones, Tangerine Dream, Peter Gabriel's The Last Temptation of Christ, the soundtracks to Last of the Mohicans and Emerald Forest--these evocative sounds serve as "worm stick" irritants to help bypass intellectualism and other avoidance strategies. Evocative music touches us like nothing else, and stirs the heart strings into action. I generally use the discordant, high energy, more abrasive music first, then taper into heart-space instrumentals such as soulful piano or plaintive violin, and finish with soaring celestials.

Thank you, Will, for the Worm Stick!

The Question of Touch in Therapy

Touch is our mother tongue, linked at the mammalian level to "switching on" and normalizing all bodily functions at birth. Newborn kittens not licked or handled, die. Human babies inadequately touched regularly fail to thrive. Increasing tactile stimulation with a woolen under-blanket alone stimulates infant weight gain, decreases fussiness, and improves immune function. Tiffany Field, Ph.D., of the Touch Research Institute of Miami, Florida, has verified via scientific studies what common lore tells us: touch is vital, necessary, and therapeutic. Over fifty hospitals in the United States fund and maintain massage programs, recognizing that such a high-touch approach to patient care yields shorter hospital stays, quicker healing times, overall improved customer satisfaction, and fewer lawsuits (which makes treatment-related touch cost-effective all around).

In mainstream psychology, touch between therapist and client is taboo. Fear says touch will lead either to improper sexual conduct or to a lawsuit, or both. Popular books, movies, and television shows (The Prince of Tides, Primal Fear, Melrose Place, etc.) often depict therapists having sex with their clients, with dramatic and dire results. So the message is: avoid touch altogether. Besides, by showing up as the warm, touchy-feelie therapist, you might interfere with, or gloss over, the more difficult aspects of therapy, thereby confusing the transference process. Remaining untouchable insures clean projections. Touch messes that up and confuses boundaries. Touch may also serve to increase or distort the power differential in the already unequal relationship between therapist and client, and influence self-esteem in a destructive way. Touch may therefore be an abuse of power on the therapist's part. Those are the cons.

The pros go like this:
1. Touch increases and quickens the process of transference, and doesn't automatically confuse it. (Transference is already a form of confusion!)

2. Touch provides emotionally-corrective experiences (especially for treating someone who's been physically abused), and reintroduces the idea and reality that touch can be good and part of a healthy relationship.

3. Touch, as a highly charged, non-neutral event, "pushes buttons", bypasses defenses and quickens bodily awareness and feeling-access.

4. More significantly, touch helps mobilize inner resources for healing by stimulating release of thymopoeitan, a hormone which oversees the maturation of T-cells.

5. Touch reinforces boundaries (that's how kids learn them), and does not confuse them.

6. Touch humanizes the difficult process of therapy and adds the necessary element of safety and caring.

The potential to abuse touch in therapy remains, as does the potential to abuse antibiotics during medical treatment, but that doesn't mean they shouldn't be administered wisely and prudently.

What sort of a message does the avoidance of touch really give to a client anyway? That touching is unnatural? And not part of healing? Wrong! Caring, conscious touching injects a powerhouse of life-affirming meanings directly into the bodily neuropeptide network, and greatly facilitates overall healing. Touching is good therapy, and good therapy is touching.

Centropic Integration:
Inner Access and Transformation

The Beginnings

Centropic Integration (CI) is a body-oriented psychotherapy modality that my friend and colleague, Dr. Camden Clay of Atlanta, Georgia, and I developed in the 1980's out of our own personal growth work, based on our desire to create and be a part of a therapeutic community. We synthesized elements of John Ray's Body Electronics™, Stanislav Grof's Holotropic Breathwork™, and added our unique form of core-feeling counseling. The essential tools of CI are sustained acupressure point holding, evocative music, and emotional facilitation. We first applied it in a group workshop setting (which evolved out of years of "healing parties" that we hosted) and soon modified it to work in the one-on-one setting.

The Definition

Centropic (in physics, a "movement towards the center") refers to the natural tendency of humans to return to unfinished core experiences or issues for the sake of completing them, and integration refers to the reuniting of disconnected parts. Centropic Integration has as its theoretical foundation the science of psychoneuroimmunology (PNI), which focuses on the biology of memory storage via the neuropeptide system. The goals are to apply those physiological principles to the realm of personal experience, and to use the influence of a group of loving supporters and/or the therapist to bring about desired change in a rapid way. We set out to demonstrate that inner healing does not have to take a long time.

Theoretical Foundations

There is something about humans that is absolutely impressionable. We come into the world with our nervous system wide open, and whatever we encounter, we bring inside and make it a part of ourselves. We naturally absorb the language, cultural norms, customs, and rules of our environment. There is the well-known story of a family that was vacationing in the wilds when their vehicle turned over, and everyone but the infant girl was killed. A pack of wolves found the infant, and a lactating she-wolf adopted the human baby and raised her as her own. (Yes, this sounds like The Jungle Book, but it's a true story!) The little girl grew up with the wolves, scampered around on all fours, ate raw meat, and howled at the moon. As far as she was concerned she was a wolf. Some people discovered her eleven years later, took her back to civilization, and made every effort to remind her of her true nature. The question: was she or was she not a wolf? She was certainly wolflike in her behavior--a true testament to the extreme impressionability of the human creature--yet in genetics and form, never actually a wolf. (It is interesting to note that the little girl died at the age of 13, the natural life span of a wolf in captivity!)

Essence vs. Programming

That story illustrates the difference between, and the potential for, misalignment between essence and programming, which to some degree holds true for each of us. As we grow up encountering and collecting life experiences, we adopt beliefs, cultivate likes and dislikes, and develop a sophisticated self-image and world-view along the way. Unfortunately, during this process, too often our underlying nature of pure, unburdened enthusiasm and happiness is forgotten and covered up. The notion of "learning" becomes the permanent filter through which life is experienced. Eventually, we "mature" to the point where all new input is routed through established memory circuitry, and the past ends up encroaching upon each present experience, by superimposing on it old meanings, associative emotions, and conditioned gut-level body responses. For example: a physically abused child placed in a foster home shirks away from the new genuinely loving touch of her adoptive family, and remains locked into abusive memory pathways. Her former negative conclusions, along with her knee-jerk self-protective body-responses, reinforce a reality long gone.

The past becomes our present. Nonintegrated traumatic events or unmet needs tend to be continuously recreated and repeated with new players. It is as if the body gets stuck. I believe a person's current health problems may be a direct outcropping of unfinished emotional and interpersonal business, or in other words, the body's pantomimed response to internalized past programming. What started out as external stressors have been absorbed, becoming internalized stressors, flooding the system with damaging reactions long after the traumatic circumstances have changed.

The seemingly random process I am describing wrecks internal havoc, sometimes via blatantly traumatic events, and sometimes more subtly and incrementally. A sociological study, recording what the average three-year-old in the United States hears from significant adults in a day's time, showed most of the messages to be negative, limiting, and inhibitive. Just as the little wolf-girl grew up with wrong impressions that molded her sense of herself, we, too, absorb a myriad of negative and limiting impressions that occupy our nervous system (in the form of beliefs and mind-maps of reality) and make them the core of our self.

It's In the Body

The science of psychoneuroimmunology states that these negative programs take root in the physical body. In order to make it through overwhelming or painful situations (this can include physical, emotional, or mental pain), people tend to fragment their experience and "hide away" the pieces in the recesses of susceptible tissue and organs, where they are biochemically encoded in their entirety onto neuropeptide molecules. The network of neuropeptides and receptor sites located throughout the soft tissue of the body is what we refer to as "body memory," occurring at both conscious and unconscious levels of awareness. Arthur Janov, author of The Primal Scream, claimed that neurosis, or the splitting up of the whole-brain responses to painful experiences into fragments in order not to feel is one of our unique human survival adaptation methods. Once this splitting (which is basically a numbing of feeling) has occurred, a natural longing for wholeness remains, and it is this longing that mirrors the biologically driven centropic impulse to reintegrate what has been cut off.

After years of witnessing hundreds of clients undergoing natural integrations in the emotionally unfettered environment of our workshops and Centropic Integration sessions, empirical investigation demonstrated to Dr. Clay and me that not only do the memories tagged with a higher emotional charge have a stronger impact on the psyche and the body, but that all experiences stored in memory can be retrieved. Cam's and my belief is simple: consciousness is the cure. Bring these hidden elements of the psyche, especially the heavily emotionally-laden ones, into awareness in the context of a loving, permissive, and embracing setting, and healing results.

The Approach

Centropic Integration as a therapy modality has a threefold approach. First, a whole-brain, highly-charged desired outcome is instilled into the system, and then the process of accessing and releasing all earlier life-negating programming by encouraging the client to feel repressed pain is inaugurated. The third branch of this method is what we have come to call positive peer pressure, the life-affirming influence of a healing circle, or in the one-on-one setting, the therapist. Personal and individual deep feeling--comprised of meaning, emotion, and body response (reflecting the triune nature of the brain)-- is the key to Centropic Integration and the life-impacting changes it facilitates, and that which separates it from other emotional release-oriented therapies.

Setting the Banks of the River

Before the reservoir of suppressed or unconscious feeling is tapped directly, it is important to set the parameters within which the release is to occur, ensuring that not only will blocked energy be freed, but that the client will be propelled in an empowering direction, shifting from current reality (point A) to where he or she wants to be (point B). A release that occurs without presetting the banks of the river too easily ends in a nonproductive breakdown, which is unnecessary.

Focus on Feelings

A typical session begins with a face-to-face encounter, with the therapist asking open-ended questions relevant to the client's medical and personal history, and then shifts to focus on emotionally charged material as it arises.

Common questions are: "What are you aware of right now in your body as you tell me about your brother?" or "What is the feeling being expressed in your voice as you mention the hospital?" or "If your heart had a voice right now, what would it say?" The client's disclosures about the unfulfilled or disappointing aspects of her current reality inevitably reveal underlying existential themes or messages linked to simple core feelings such as grief or loss of innocence. Simple questioning then easily reveals childhood conclusions linked to those feelings which over the years have diminished healthy self-esteem, trust, boundary-setting, and relationships in the adult context, and which of course are no longer relevant. Pain that has been unmasked exposes Point A in all its limitations, and makes letting go easier.

An Aligned Statement of Desired Outcome

The CI facilitator then helps the client to focus on and arrive at an aligned statement of desired and meaningful outcome. For example, "If you could have your life unfold in whatever way you desired, what would it be like?" Some examples of answers are: "I choose to be able to touch others with love without taking on their pain", or, "I choose to know and feel my own heart even if it means feeling pain and disappointment", or, "I choose to consistently stand up for myself even in the face of others' anger and disapproval." Point B choices bring about a sense of possibility of balance and integrity in particularly problematic areas of life.

With both Points A and Point B fully aligned with a meaning, emotion, and body response, the parameters for change (the "banks of the river") are set. Any additional emotional release in the next hands-on phase of the session automatically serves to move the person further along the path to his or her outcome.

Accessing the Memory

Centropic Integration uses sustained hands-on point-holding along acupressure meridian lines to access the body-component of stored fragmented memories. The acupuncture lines of the endocrine system hook directly into the circuitry of the limbic "loop" in the brain where emotional memory is processed. The client lies in a supine position, while appropriate points are determined through a simple system that corresponds to the endocrine glands and various emotional states; we also can assess the client's body response with our hands, seeking points of trigger reaction, or tenderness to touch. Points can be held by one or more participants, with one person taking on the role of facilitator. (Notice how I didn't say "therapist" this time. Cam and I have always felt that this work belongs to the people. A person can be an effective, sensitive facilitator of inner healing without necessarily being a psychotherapist by trade. What they do need is personal experience and some practical training.)

Breathwork and Altered States

The first 60-90 minutes of point-holding are devoted to deep synchronous breathing by client, facilitator, and other participants, accompanied by evocative and emotional music designed to activate and release the abreaction process. Tapping into the long tradition of various cultures that use music to evoke trance states or deep feelings, ranging from tribal drums to a huge pipe organ in a cathedral, this phase of CI elicits both emotion and right-brain, imagery-infused thinking.

Heat, Resistance, and the Body Electric

Just as the electrons in an electric heater generate more heat when we turn the resistor up, acupressure contact points reflect the client's resistance to change: as heat--physical heat! The points get hot to the touch. Resistance, a term often used in psychotherapy to mean the cumulative effect of inner defenses against feeling pain, manifests as a physical phenomenon. All the energy that has been devoted to repression of feeling, when forced to a head, burns. At this time the client may be experiencing images and/or body sensations that either symbolically or directly indicate the spontaneous reemergence of stored unconscious information that may have to do with nonintegrated memories.

The centropic impulse for resolution, coupled with the client's desire for a new outcome, brings the electrical potential at the resistance points up the scale enough to match and finally surpass the resistance. The blocked portions of experience flood forth in emotional catharsis and/or realization, while at the same time biologically integrating the meaning, emotion, and body-response aspects of repressed pain. Point-holding and evocative music thus help "flush out" hidden, peripheral features of experience, making the integrative results of CI dramatic compared to conventional "talk therapies". With conscious catharsis, the Gestalt achieves wholeness once more. (I imagine that if we could monitor the process microscopically we would see the fragmented pieces of the neuropeptides melting together and naturally flowing towards and settling into their proper receptor sites.) The electrical flow of corrected nerve conduction overcomes internalized blocks and surges into any body part where dysfunction had previously resided, often initiating a period of intense burning sensations (the kundalini of Eastern philosophy?), while at the same time the "mind" is flooded with insight about the original issue involved in the trauma or injury, and also about related patterns of behavior. The knowing and understanding of self from this experience is not interpretive, but direct.

The In-filling

The final phase of the session, the "in-filling", which reaches beyond the abundance of insight and the burning inner fire, takes on a spiritual quality hallmarked by serenity and deep body relaxation. Clients report this as a time of integration, a sense of personal victory, and healing, full of recognition and connectedness. The amount of time that has elapsed is about two hours. The session ends with the cooling, pulsing, and releasing of the points, followed by a sense of "afterglow," which can last for hours and sometimes days.

Final Notes

The healing that occurs through Centropic Integration begins with a direct bodily encounter with one's own locked-up pain and resistance to feeling, and ends in renewing daily life with empowering choices and revitalized hope. Unlike the cognitive therapies that effect experience by consciously altering the thinking process, with Centropic Integration cognitive insight happens spontaneously, as a natural outcropping of deeply processed feelings. Follow-up sharing, especially in the intimate group setting of a Centropic Integration workshop, enhances cognitive anchoring. Changes and insights facilitated by a natural integration at the body level endure over time.

Power Tools for Inner Work

In addition to the techniques of core work, the general principles of watching for and gathering feeling fragments, and holding to the unspoken life-affirming metacommunications I've outlined already, there are other hints I want to offer that will help facilitate inner access during the therapy process. The techniques fall into the categories of rapport-building, confusion-generating, or integration. They are tools for the therapist that will interrupt or derail dysfunctional patterns of thinking or processing, and encourage access to feelings:

1. Attend to "what-is," not what "should-be." This can be a challenge, especially if what is happening seems to fit into a past pattern, concept, or experience. Be vigilant about this.

2. Breathe. Be aware of your breathing in order to stay centered and to reign in any interference with what-is. When in doubt, breathe. Disengage from the "story" aspect of presentation as often as necessary. Be attentive to your client's breathing pattern, especially when it becomes shallow, or rapid.

3. When the story starts becoming too intellectual, shift focus.

4. Be honest. Honesty does not imply cruelty. "I am having trouble taking you seriously" may be far more effective than saying, "That's bullshit."

5. Take risks. "That's bullshit" may provide the perfect jolt.

6. Use pivotal questions such as, "What is the feeling?" or "What is your body response to that?" in order to help stay on track. Be relentless with these questions, because they address the two more "primitive" aspects of feeling fragmentation.

7. Feel first, understand later. Beware of the impulse to interpret or explain.

8. Use the "native" words and phrases the client uses. If the client says "Mom," you repeat Mom, not Mother.

9. Go for specifics. About everything. "What hurts? How are you aware of that hurt right now?" Specifics lead to feeling fragments.

10. Confusion is OK. Let it go long enough to stimulate sufficient frustration or dissatisfaction, often necessary for forward movement. No need to push clarity prematurely, or at all, because a client will often reach for intellectual clarity in order to hide feelings.

11. Use shock to interrupt patterns. Frame the topic at hand in an opposite manner. "I'm glad you are resisting this because it seems like we're progressing too fast." That statement is both confusing, and therapeutically double-binding.

12. Go for the emotional charge, overt or covert, in the spoken or the unspoken, or where action and feeling are aligned or misaligned. Pay attention to the quiver in the voice, the smile that comes after expressed discomfort, the provocative clothes.

13. No taboos! Who says you can't talk about mutilation, masturbation, or murder? Whatever your client is hiding is more likely to be something at the fringes of her sense of "OK-ness" , and so, speaking about taboos in any arena automatically invites her particular withhold to surface.

14. Respect the humanity of the person, and nothing more--not their "holiness," their wealth, social status, fame, achievements, or self-image. A healthy disrespect of whatever a client has been hiding behind helps to move them into the real. Even if they have been hiding behind a disability or a painful childhood! Hiding is hiding! This takes some guts. I've had "famous" clients with whom I initially felt intimidated. Nevertheless, everything but their humanity is fair game!

15. Be creative. Notice what pops into your own consciousness at every phase of your client's presentation. These images and/or feelings pro-

vide the best analogies, metaphors, or real human feedback.

16. Ask your client to exaggerate and intensify. Have them use movement, sound, facial expressions. What starts as a whisper often ends in a scream. Exaggeration escalates to the real.

17. Have your client repeat key phrases or gestures. Tell them: "Say that again" or "Repeat that motion with your hands". Often the emotional wave that accompanies the statement or gesture made by the client releases only after the second or third repetition. They simply didn't hear themselves the first time. This repetition also makes the client more sensitive to the impact of their self-expression.

18. Ask permission before touching, either before the session, immediately before contact, or both times. Physical contact should not come as a surprise. Respect of boundaries is paramount.

19. The Distillery Technique
        "Imagine a special machine that is able to distill out of whatever you put into it all the life-affirming aspects of that substance. Now imagine your (Mother, Father, etc.) as energy. Whatever image appears. Have that energy turn liquid. Notice the color and consistency of that liquid. Put a bit on your tongue to get a taste of it. Put it into the collection chamber of the still, and turn on the flame. Notice the color of the vapors that rise from the boiling liquid. Then let the vapors recondense into the collection vial as the liquid which contains only the life-affirming aspects of your (parent, spouse, etc.). Notice the color and texture of this new substance. Now drink it and pay attention to your body-response as it circulates through you."
Generally, the initial substance will contain noxious qualities, and the final product healing ones. This exercise punctuates and reinforces the knowledge that as an adult your client has the ability to distill out from parental/family influence the good stuff, and discard the bad. Children, on the other hand, tend to "swallow whole" or introject the parent, and don't distill or separate out what's not good for them.

20. When your client enters a self-negating space, have him list his faults, and as you write them down say "good one" or "great!" This

takes the sting out of what is generally a "feel-bad" experience and puts it into a constructive framework. Praising "the bad" or the weaknesses confuses the judgemental system.

21. Trust yourself more than any technique. Make it up as you go.

22. Shift to body focus as a way to bring awareness in. Intellectually, or even emotionally, it may be easier to keep the problem "out there." Then return to feelings or meanings, and you will notice that the client is closer-in with them. Go back and forth between a focus on the body, on feelings, and on meanings.

23. View your client as your teacher who is about to reveal something that you have been pondering for years. Ask the questions you really want the answers to.

24. At first, agree with whatever your client tells you, no matter how self-serving or delusional it may seem to you. Agreement draws the client out, and helps with rapport-building. Agreeing with defenses, excuses, or rationalizations sometimes makes the client rally for her real self. Think about fishing: sometimes you let the line stay loose, give a lot of slack, and only reel in at the proper vulnerable moment.

25. Disagree with whatever your client claims to believe in and argue about it relentlessly, especially if she is trying to convince you that she's right. Work the argument around to your client's core belief about her life or herself. Be sure that your arguments still exemplify your advocacy for your client's well-being, even though you're being "disagreeable". Then abruptly shift to the feeling level, dropping all argumentativeness. This can dramatically make evident the difference between struggle and non-struggle, and can help rattle her whole argumentative approach. When it comes to feelings, there's simply no argument. Hopefully this "mini-drama" sets the stage for reevaluation and re-framing.

26. <u>Deathbed dreams technique:</u>
  "Imagine yourself on your deathbed. You have only a few moments

left to live. What is your experience when you look back over your life?" This conjures up regrets and remorse like nothing else.

27. Be absurd. In statements you make about the client and in your reasoning about those statements. Set up a "collapse of reality" moment when you let all that you have been saying fall apart, as you either confess to the absurdity of it or contradict yourself. This generally loosens the hold the intellect has on the client, and delivers the unspoken message about the unreliability of the intellect as a navigator of irrational waters. Do this technique if your client is too "reasonable".

28. <u>Spit in Their Soup Technique:</u>
    The idea of this originated with Alfred Adler. No one would keep eating soup you have spit in, he said. Make some unpalatable association with something the client has used to avoid feeling. For example: "You have turned to food as your comforter, but food has not been the friend you think it has. Food has been your seducer and deceiver." Or another: "I believe your son is really trying to get close to you. What you have called 'discipline' has just been a way to keep him away,' and, a final example: "You think what you have had with your father is 'closeness,' but to some it would be called 'emotional incest.' If the client accepts even a hint of your negative association, her behavior will change.

29. Tell little stories that make a point, using metaphors. They can come from your own life experience. This helps to shift into right brain functioning which is more conducive to feeling.

30. When dealing with phobias or dreams, go for the feeling behind them. Phobias are old feelings that latch onto an item or situation. Dream images, too, are generated out of nonintegrated feelings.

31. Listen for themes. Distill out the "generic" version of any conclusion statements your client makes, and feed it back to her. See how she resonates with the generalized "I-statement." She might say: "The judicial system in this country makes you spend money even when you haven't done anything wrong," or "Men don't really like a woman who

is both smart and pretty." Suggest she say: "I get punished just for being who I am."

32. Look for blind spots—what is obvious that the client doesn't see. Coax her into seeing it. You can even say, "What aren't you seeing here?" as a lead-in.

33. Generally speaking, don't work harder than your client.

34. Make process-comments in addition to content-comments. Feed back the unspoken aspects of what the client is sharing. For example: "Your eyes are getting moist as you say that about your brother," or Just as you started talking about your feelings you jumped into something else altogether. What was that about?"

35. It's OK to cry in front of your client, or to be real in any other way. But remember, as far as therapy goes, it's the client's turn.

36. <u>Be the thing technique:</u>
        My client suffered severe environmental sensitivities, and had no defense against common "germs" (her word), so I told her, "Be a germ. Speak to me as if you were a germ." She said: "I make whoever comes in contact with me miserable." Then she started crying, because that was how she felt as a child in her family. It's a powerful technique.

37. Silence. Better to err in the direction of saying too little than saying too much. Use silence to punctuate especially poignant statements. Periods of silence convey zero external pressure and may serve as the most potent of tools to draw out repressed material.

38. Escalate the zero pressure of silence to become a negative pressure of what I call the "fertile vacuum" technique. A vacuum commands drawing power (as in "vacuum cleaner"). The difference between silence and the Fertile Vacuum Technique is degree of intent. You, as therapist, have a feel for what is about to surface in your client, and within your own heart and mind, create space for it to emerge. This is akin to a prayerful attitude on your part.

39. Dismantling a skewed polar reconciliation system. Two signposts of a skewed polar reconciliation system are: an incessant unhealthy struggle with parts of oneself, and/or a marked lack of empathy for others. If your client presents herself as a Pulverizer, a Minimizer, or a Maximizer, the therapeutic approach remains the same: let the opposites emerge. When a client claims, "Part of me wants to run and part of me wants to fight," do whatever it takes to have both parties show up at the same time. Shift the focus to the body. "Where exactly do you feel that in your body right now?" Or perhaps say, "If you had to locate that in your body, where exactly are those parts in contact? (If they're not in contact, direct your client to have them meet.) It is in this direct contact of opposites that a transformative alchemy can happen. The mysterious "Third Element," the heretofore unknown new resource, is forged out of the encounter of opposites. Get these "enemies" in the same ring, and let them duke it out. Keep your client focused, albeit uncomfortable, until the moment naturally unfolds into something new.

Final comment

Even when these techniques don't work as directly as desired, with strong intent behind them, they still serve to wear down the unreal system of the client and make room for feeling fragments to emerge and reunite. I believe this is what the mind/body system "wants" to do naturally anyway. So, chip away, therapists! Don't even let "failure" get in the way. There is no failure when it comes to deep feeling therapy techniques because feelings unfold as the client would have them unfold anyway. At the risk of being seen as too lighthearted in my approach, I say: in therapy, be real, be sensitive, be creative, go for it, and have fun.

The Course of Therapy:
What Recovery Looks Like

The questions are bound to arise: what does recovery feel like? Does emotional pain simply end one day, to be replaced by something else the next? How does the journey unfold?

Rivers rarely follow straight lines; rather they meander along slopes and gradients on their way to the sea. Deep feeling therapy also follows nonlinear pathways, as therapist and patient meander through the interior landscape of memories, feelings, defenses, and pain, and the outer one of current relationships and life situations. Just as repression finds its way into the system gradually, starting when we are children, the therapy that attempts to release it also happens bit by bit. Each person is unique, of course, but some generalizations can be made around the healing that takes place after deep-feeling therapy.

I have divided the general progression of the therapy experience into seven distinct phases:
1. Presentation of Problem
2. Discovery
3. Touch-in
4. Feeling
5. Grieving
6. Emptiness
7. Reinvestment

The Presentation of Problem phase is when the client's complaints tend to be situational, occurring in the present, and generally external-oriented. For example: "I am having trouble in my marriage," or "I'm having panic attacks." She might be hating her job, or obsessing over something or someone. This could be referred to as the story phase, superficial phase, or symptom phase. In the previously-used garden analogy, it's the time when weeds are first seen in the garden, or first recognized as unacceptable, or the harvest isn't what was anticipated. With a problem-solving, cognitive approach, therapy often begins and ends in this phase of engagement. The therapist will help the client identify and strategize her way through the maze of presenting obstacles, framing the client's objectives in terms of behavior. These therapists offer goal setting, homework assignments, journaling, deadlines, and follow-up evaluations. Sometimes this degree of intervention works, significantly improves the quality of life, and the client leaves satisfied.

But for others, therapy needs to go beyond problem solving. They have come to realize that their troubles are not due to lack of management skills, and they may even recognize some patterns in their difficulties. The client's inquiries probe deeper: they might want to know why they feel perpetually incompetent at work when they are as well-trained and experienced as anyone else, or why they feel so shy around the opposite sex. And they might express how disturbed they feel because they hurt so much. A client like this then enters the Discovery phase, where elements of the story are examined, probed into, confronted, and challenged. This could also be called the confusion phase, or the resistance phase, because not only are there no easy or quick answers, but there is a reluctance to face or feel the perplexity and clutter around the issues that have come up. Defenses serve to buffer the person from discomfort or pain, so it is in this phase that the therapist begins to introduce the option of doing something other than defending against discomfort: simply experiencing it. "OK, you're uncomfortable, so what?", becomes my prevailing attitude. "Be with it, keep going." In this step, the client is learning to move beyond the cloud of discomfort by no longer resisting it, but rather by exploring it. To pierce this "cloud of unknowing," in order to know the real truth of her situation, the client must fight, overcome, or bypass her own defenses against feeling.

What happens next is what I refer to as the Touching-In phase. While talking about her situation, the client inevitably stumbles into feeling, and is often surprised or embarrassed over sudden tears that flow when she is flooded with memories. A deeper layer of response to what she assumed to have been limited to external problems emerges. More diverse elements from her history are now becoming a part of the bigger picture. She might say, "That's how it was with my brother and me," or "I used to hate sitting still in school." I call these elements feeling fragments. They are hints that inevitably lead us to the deeper significance of the surface events. The touching-in phase is hallmarked by the collection of these fragments into the central arena of consciousness. It is as though the actors who have been waiting in the wings come onto center stage one by one, meet, and interact with each other. Seemingly innocuous recollections and associations spontaneously create a platform upon which the underlying feeling can present itself. Their relevance to either the current situation or to an inner integration is not always apparent, so the probing penetrates deeper. Using the psychoneuroimmunology model, this phase marks the early emergence of neuropeptide chips that contain the emotional and body response, as well as meaning-fragments from past dissociated painful events. Just as the images in a dream help us to understand the feelings behind them, these fragments herald the return of repressed pain. The focus of therapy at this phase is still primarily on the problem-at-hand, on what was originally presented, and so the feeling fragments mostly go unnoticed as such. My belief is that the external precipitating event, or the presenting problem, has little to do with the true mind/body integration at hand. I believe the integrative impulses of the body dominate, compelling us unconsciously to extract from our current external situation those elements that resemble closely the original imprinting of pain. We then use those present-day elements to rekindle the necessary fire of an emotional charge that is needed to weld our disjointed past experiences together again. Whenever this occurs, the unfinished past rules the present. We unconsciously repeat the past to heal it, but of course, as long as we remain unconscious to it, simply repeating it isn't the answer.

In this phase of therapy we are just beginning to make these past elements conscious. Let me remind you that these memories come up naturally and spontaneously, requiring no external prompting from the therapist. It is these memories that comprise the core moment from which a lifelong associative string of impressions has lead the client to experience the present problem in the unique way she does. The defenses that were originally set up to block the pain around those past experiences also block natural creativity, and the ability to see in a novel fashion. Defenses thus keep us stuck and limited.

As the process of gathering feeling fragments picks up momentum, the client will find herself crossing over into the Feeling Phase of therapy. Feeling is the whole-brain, whole-neuropeptide, simultaneous in-touchness with the sensory, emotional, and meaning components of an experience. It is a qualitatively different experience from the fragmented phase, in which confusion reigns. In a connected feeling state, the client's experience begins to make sense--naturally and without effort. True insight comes from seeing from the inside, and that happens through feeling. Feeling unites the past with the present, and liberates it for the future. As the client progresses through this phase, she learns her own unique style of recognizing feeling fragments and connecting them into feelings. Janov refers to this as "sinking into feelings." She will find herself spending more and more therapy time in the "feeling zone." Memory fragments emerge then integrate into whole feelings more rapidly and naturally, with less resistance. At some point in the work, where the defense mechanisms crumble altogether, or at least significantly subside, the client achieves "critical mass" in the integrative process, where the cumulative forces of expression and feeling have matched, overcome, and dominated over the forces of repression. Then and only then is the client predominantly a real, or feeling person once again.

Conventional logic claims that the past stands as the backdrop to the present. In this phase of therapy, however, the client relegates the present to stand as a backdrop for the past. Events in the present, even seemingly inconsequential ones--TV commercials, movies, a love song on the radio, parents interacting with their children in the mall, the aroma of baking cookies--suddenly trigger all kinds of emotionally charged responses, and take on a heightened, associative, reminiscent quality directly relevant to the emerging flood of feeling fragments. Clients often find themselves withdrawing from day-to-day involvement in order to stay in touch with the outpouring of impressions. "I was drunk with feeling," they'll say, "I didn't care whether I was laughing or crying. It felt so good to feel and keep feeling!"

Sometimes clients at this point will display addictive behavior with their feelings by entering what I call a "feeling-junkie" phase, which poses the danger of skewing the life experience by hiding out in the past as a way to avoid the present. A feeling-junkie attempts to keep the present in the background long after its natural recession for the sake of integration has passed. At the other end of the spectrum, behavioral therapy discourages any focus on the past, and channels all psychic energy into measurable, present-day "corrective" tasks--a fine strategy for undoing unhealthy wallowing, but otherwise in direct opposition to how early childhood impressions actually get imprinted and uprooted.

On the tail end of this return to the past comes the Grieving phase of processing. With a reconnection with feelings, the client eventually reaches a point of sensing the unfulfilled needs, mostly intact within her in their original pristine form, from her childhood. I'm referring to the need to be touched and held, respected, appreciated, valued, adored, guided--basically the need to be parented.

Needs make up the deepest layer of feelings, and not having them fulfilled, hurts. In this phase of therapy, remembering the hurt, perhaps feeling it for the first time, triggers grief. Grief is the body's natural response to loss. The client often grieves what she never got, focusing on those ages and stages of development where she disconnected herself from feeling her needs. Because needs also drive behavior, in this phase of therapy, insights about the client's true motivations throughout her history come to light. This is also the phase where the false hopes of childhood come to an end--the motor that drove our madness gets turned off.

And this leads to the next phase of Emptiness. Unreality grinds to a halt. Nothing to strive or struggle for. It's a quiet phase, with not much to talk about. Clients often continue their withdrawal from social contacts beyond their immediate family. They frequently quit stressful jobs, which their newly sensitized systems can no longer tolerate. They may experience a heightened sense of neutrality, or indifference or detachment, which takes some getting used to. Their feedback might be: "For a while I was scared that I just didn't care anymore, but I soon realized I was normal, that I wasn't as overinvolved as I had been in the past."

The final phase of the therapy experience is what I have labeled the Reinvestment phase, where natural interest, caring, and the desire for involvement all reemerge. The charge carried inside by repressed feelings no longer pushes the body to discharge, and therefore most driven behavior ceases. Memories and past events resonate more neutrally. The world itself shows up as what it is, and no more. Nothing symbolizes anything. Sex is just sex, not conquest or peace or worthiness. The boss is just the boss, not Mean Daddy, or the enemy, or the Punisher. Not as many villains or saviors walk the planet. Just people. Nothing presents as catastrophic or urgent as it once did. Setbacks and failures, although experienced as upsets, no longer carry the tidal-wave magnitude of devastation as before. Rejection hurts, but doesn't kill.

The importance of kindness becomes self-evident, and kindness becomes easier. Life is simple and normal--no more, no less.

Short Notes on Family and Couples Therapy

Another Gorilla Story

I knew a gorilla in Atlanta named Willie B., who was raised in solitude in the zoo from his earliest days. I remember the blank look on his face as I stood by his indoor glass-enclosed cage. After years of limited zoo life, he too stopped swinging in his tire swing or climbing in his barren jungle gym "tree", and just sat staring out into nothing. Even the zoo people worried about him, and after much brainstorming they arrived at a wonderful (sic) human solution to Willie B's blahs: they bought him a television! He became, at 350 pounds, the ultimate couch potato, but now instead of staring out at nothing, he stared out at nothing on television. And so he went along, month after month, until one day something wonderful happened: someone stole his TV! Forcing the zoo people to come up with something else, and thank goodness, they thought of bringing in some other gorillas. Just as our mall gorilla earlier in this book, Willie B. had a rough time of it initially. He just didn't seem to know what to do---even with a very willing female his own age! Another bad case of contact deprivation.

Just like gorillas, we just don't do well in isolation, and in fact , even pairing off into two's is not enough. We too need our extended tribal family. We humans only really thrive in a community setting. Community carries within it the same root as communion, or communication, and therein lies our connectedness as a species, and our well-being as individuals.

The classic study of the women with breast cancer who participated in a support group as compared to the control group of women with similar diagnoses, who did not , clearly emphasizes the efficacy of group support in lengthening survival times, quicker healing times, and higher incidence of spontaneous remissions. We need tribe for our health.

Some social psychologists emphasize the "systems" approach to mental health, which focuses on the entire family unit as the patient, and recognizes the individual's symptoms as inseparable from those of the family.

Families: Bond or Bind?

Families are a hoot to work with. Like segments of a stained glass window that together make up a single living tableau of the psyche, families magnify all the ingredients that go into both the glory and the dysfunction of each individual member. If we were to take a magnifying glass to the psyche of any one person, we would see his or her family of origin etched into the synapses.

The individual's patterns of thought and information processing are often reflected in the family's patterns of interaction. When I was a kid, my favorite comic books were of the "Origin Story" type, like how Superman created his Fortress of Solitude, or how Zorro got his mask, or how Bruce Wayne first got the idea of being Batman. Bringing in the family after working with an individual client for a while is like that sort of comic book---and the story makes so much more sense.

Family dynamics manifest along three basic vectors of relationship: generational, gender, or parent-child. A healthy family draws clear generational lines. The parents' relationship as an entity needs to maintain clear boundaries around it, without involving the children. In unhealthy systems this generational boundary breaks down. Children become the pawns in the battle of the spouses, or parents take sides in sibling rivalries. Sometimes parents compete for the love of the children, as a form of one-upmanship.

Sometimes gender plays into the picture, with different treatment or attitudes towards each sex. Expectations for boys and girls vary, sometimes creating friction or a sense of unfairness.

A family manifests an extended entity, greater than the sum of its members, and yet intimately reflecting the psyche of its players. Some people are better at three-legged racing than others, meaning that connectedness to the family can either enhance or hinder the forward movement of the individuals in it. Some cultures clearly favor the family entity over the individual, and others favor the individual.

But every family relies on spoken or unspoken rules of cohesiveness, and employs things like loyalty, guilt, tradition, or love to enforce or encourage them. Sometimes the responsibility for the family cohesiveness is meeted out in a skewed manner, with one member carrying too much. Enter the Peacekeeper or the Enabler.

Even inorganic systems need a safety valve, or something to handle waste material. An internal combustion engine has the manifold which channels waste products to the air. A steam engine has an escape valve to release extra energy. The plumbing of a house needs a sewer or septic tank. A family system will often appoint one member to play such a role. One of the Star Trek: the Next Generation™ plots involved the discovery of a tar-like entity who had been created out of his civilization's bad characteristics. He served as the collective garbage dump, and was abandoned to live out a solitary existence so that the others from his world might thrive, free of their own negativity. (Thank you, Gene Roddenberry.) Enter the Scapegoat.

The therapist's job is to ascertain what's healthy about the particular family system and what's not. The measuring rod often comes down to "is this life-affirming or not?" Appearances can be deceiving. Sometimes what looks like closeness, caring, intimacy, or something else seemingly beneficial or positive, just turns out to serve as a hindrance to personal integrity. An individual may be so caught up in unhealthy family roles for the sake of the stability of the family entity that she may be committing what Sidney Jourard called "altruistic suicide". Although the family seems committed to the wellness of the designated patient, the unspoken commitment remains in favor of the status quo which requires the individual's self-sacrifice. Only when the family can learn to accomplish the same level of intactness in a way that no longer requires the death of one of its members will that individual get well. To treat the individual without addressing the entire family structure misses the real illness.

Because of the collective nature of the unconscious material, family systems may present seemingly unravelable complexities and insurmountable obstacles. It's hard enough to work with individual unconsciousness! Yet because each family member carries his or her own impetus towards autonomy and health, the system thereby contains a synergistic drive towards "the truth". Even a single candle in a large dark warehouse illuminates a vast area. One real feeling melts mountains of resistance. The odds favor consciousness. Darkness is, after all, only the absence of light. Dysfunctional family systems that refuse to change in light of a member's pain, and would seek to continue invalidating that person's experience, must crumble. The truth shall make you free, but not necessarily comfortable

.

Couples

When two people enter into a relationship, two worlds and six brains meet and inevitably collide. Navigating the waters of relationship in a way that yields growth and healing must take pain, defenses to pain, and each person's personal history into account. Remember: nothing is too small to trip over! Anything can trigger the past and old hurts. Often women in relationships are deemed "irrational" and men "unfeeling", but the truth remains we are all double-agents, each with our irrational and/or unfeeling times.

Rest assured that you are inflicting any unconscious pains you endured in childhood on those you love. Relationships are the quickest route I've experienced for uprooting and bringing to light any blind spots within the psyche. That's why a primary relationship is so great to be in, and can feel so bad sometimes. It comes with the territory. If you're an unfinished product, that is. And if you're not, please call me, so I can tell you you are.

The journey of inner integration, the central topic of this book, eventually comes down to self-responsibility. Nothing closes the gestalt on past hurts and needs un-met than to see how much of that I'm currently inflicting on those I love, or how much I've passed on. Relationship work may initially actually be embarrassing, and should continually be humbling. It remains the true proving ground for inner development.

A committed relationship is like a pressure cooker: its hermetic seal increases the effects of pressure and heat in transforming the raw to the cooked, from the undeveloped to the mature. A relationship is also like a gem tumbler, which works OK with a single stone, but quickens the finishing process with two stones. When rough edges of each stone collide, they both polish faster and more evenly. OK, so these metaphors include heat, pressure, and colliding--experiences that don't sound pleasant.

Therefore, any guideline to healthy relationships must proclaim: SAFETY FIRST. A person must feel safe to be fully true to his or her experience before real intimacy can show up. Hidden aspects of experience often carry an unspoken resentment to the partner for making them unacceptable and having to go underground. Nobody likes to hide, yet we will if we feel unsafe to be who we really are. Safety is a perception of the primitive Reptilian brain within us, and when we feel threatened, defenses engage no matter what we believe or tell ourselves with our conscious mind. Both my wife and I are therapists, but when we're fighting we get just as defensive as anyone else. We've had to come up with strategies in the face of our angers and hurts that foster a strong focus on safety first, so that time processing these things is kept to a minimum, and becomes an enhancer of our intimacy rather than a block to it.

The reptilian brain harbors the famous "fight-or-flight" response hard-wired into our nervous system, and inherited from our prehistoric ancestors. When we feel threatened, our primitive tendency is to run or fight. "Oh, yeah, what about what you did to me? You never listen, etc.". Beyond fighting or fleeing, our primitive defenses also include other animal responses to danger (again, thanks to the Imago™ model): 1. fight, 2. flight, 3. freezing, 4. hiding, and 5. submitting.

Fight is lashing back. Match fire with fire. Keep the other away. Claw to claw.

Flight is running, fleeing, avoiding contact. "You'll never get me".

Freezing. Like a deer facing headlights. Like a bird, although being pursued by a fox, holding perfectly still. A make-believe cloak of invisibility. "If I don't rock the boat, this conflict will just pass".

Hiding is actively going out of sight. Not just madly running like the flight response, but actively finding something to hide behind. We hide our hurts behind anger. We hide our feelings in attitudes.

Submitting is what wolves do in facing the Alpha male or female as a way to stay included in the pack. Submitting is a false-vulnerability defense we use to stay in a hostile system. We agree, and let the other's style dominate. Unlike healthy surrender, submitting breeds resentment because it affirms an inequality that hurts the self.

Step one in working with a relationship is to recognize the different primitive defenses at play. Some persons or couples focus in on a few, some cover the entire range. When we engage defenses, we impair progress towards intimacy. Thank God we embody more than our Reptilian brains!

The next guiding principle in sorting out the clashing worlds and feelings in a relationship is: TAKE TURNS. Instead of the natural tendency to barrage back and forth with hot lightning bolts and comebacks, take turns venting, and make an agreement to do so. Next, let the "receiving" partner ACTIVELY REFLECT back the words, feelings, and OK-ness of the venter's expression.

"I hate the way you disregard my feelings! Damn you for acting so superior! When you denied what you'd said, I felt like clobbering you. I still feel like clobbering you!"

"You hate the way I disregard your feelings. You damn me for acting so superior. When I denied what I'd said you felt like clobbering me. You still feel like clobbering me. You seem like you feel angry and hurt by me. That makes sense to feel like that when disregarded and in the face of superiority".

The very act of mirroring the venter's words and feelings, with an added OK provides the single most vital ingredient to getting along in the rough spots: feeling heard. When I feel like you've really heard me and have even a spot of empathy for me, I won't linger on things. I'll just make my requests for next time, and move on.

MAKING REQUESTS FOR NEXT TIME, and HAVING THE VENTEE MAKE SOME SORT OF COMMITMENT STATEMENT TO HONOR THAT REQUEST make up the final stages of the process.

Again:

1. Take turns

2. Reflect back the words, feelings, and OK-ness of what your partner says until he or she feels heard

3. Make behaviorally-framed requests for next time

4. Make a commitment statement to honor those requests next time.

OK. This system sounds good. With practice, a couple can

realistically come to "take turns" in ventilating. It's all very adult. What about those times when hurt feelings keep both parties from full-fledged adulthood? Children (rightfully) want the adult to do the work in resolving, guiding, helping, comforting, understanding, approving, giving permission, etc., so when two people come to each other with that child mind-set, the blame-game ensues. "Well, you're not being very loving here..." "Yeah, what about you?" Endlessly, back and forth, with neither taking any transcendent step towards resolution.

Empathy skills come in as paramount here because they work at an adult level and appeal to the heart of the child. Here's some lifelines to keep in mind for those times of hurt feelings. Don't wait for your partner to deliver them. Do your best to muster up enough empathy to say them, and the odds are you will successfully switch from the anger/attack tracks to something more reconciliatory.

"What do you need from me right now?" or "What do you need to hear from me right now?" or "What do you need to happen here to make things all right?"

Another Word About Anger

Because anger carries and conveys innately destructive energy, and we humans instinctively slip into defense-mode in the face of annihilation or even danger of harm, it seems that anger could only be destructive to a relationship. It can escalate to violence and result in wounds. Why do anything but avoid it?

A couple that successfully weathers anger without capsizing the relationship is off to a good start. A couple that successfully integrates a healthy style of expressing anger and using that expression to propel the relationship into new areas of intimacy is well on the path of wholeness and growth. Anger can and should be rocket fuel. Although it contains primitive self-preservation undertones, its expression carries a great deal of self-abandon, and the kind of risk-it-all attitude necessary to help a relationship shift into a new mode of honesty and empathy. Anger sits on top of other more tender, vulnerable feelings, specifically to protect them. To keep a lid on anger or to channel it into "reasonable" case-building against your partner and to promote your point of view, directly interferes with the flow of deeper feelings and inhibits intimacy. Ironically, then, inhibiting anger exerts a destructive influence on the relationship---more so than its free expression.

When a bomb squad is called in to handle a potentially danger-ous explosive devise, it first establishes containment. Make it safe so when (or if) it goes off, nobody gets hurt. In relationship terms con-tainment comes in the form of agreement. "OK, we're going to take the time to hear each other out, even if it gets vigorous, loud, or irrational." The bomb squad then takes one of two primary approaches: detonate or diffuse.

Diffusing anger at the onset by going directly to any underly-ing hurts or vulnerabilities, works mainly for more experienced inti-mate communicators. Most of us still need to explode first with loud self-righteous attacks and defenses before we even begin approaching the underlying tender parts. So I say, without waiting for sainthood, take the detonation path with a will. Let her rip. Give free vent to re-sentments. Make it personal. Make it specific. Dr. Brad Blanton recom-mends the phrase "I resent you for......." over all other forms of anger expression, because of its direct, face-to-face, feeling qualities that actu-ally speak of intimacy and self-responsibility. Anything less yields less gain. I've done this, and I tell you, it feels good, and gets good results. Without having to be rational, in control, good, mature, adult, a full venting of resentments empties the heart and mind of their poison, and opens the psychic space between partners for deeper realities to flood in. Forgiveness naturally flows in the wake of full expression of anger. Stifling anger for the sake of reaching forgiveness inevitably aborts the real process of reaching it. That supposed "shortcut" ends up making the whole damn mess take longer.

Emotional Aikido

Years ago I witnessed George Leonard, author of The Ultimate Athlete and a black belt in aikido, in his late sixties at the time, fight fifteen young men in a demonstration of his martial art. He looked like he was doing T'ai Chi at the beach, swirling around with outstretched limbs as he grasped his opponents' wrists and arms, gently ushering them to the floor one by one. Afterwards, when I asked him how he did it, he answered in a Zen-like fashion: "I let them do it". Unlike other martial arts like karate where the response to being attacked is to step back to block, kick, or punch, aikido involves stepping closer in and letting the attacker's aggressive energy become its own undoing.

The couples' communication strategy I call emotional aikido follows the same principle, and can have the same disarming results. Instead of avoiding the uncomfortableness of confrontations, I recommend stepping in closer, and digging deeper into the feeling level. The idea is based on the belief that anger and aggressiveness both sit on top of underlying hurt or tenderness. To shorten the time spent in angry exchanges, get to the hurt as quickly as possible.

Emotional aikido involves stepping in closer to the feeling reality of the other by being more honest and vulnerable about your own.

For example: Ashley complained about her older brother's incessant aggressiveness and disapproval. Recently, when she was on the phone with him, describing her plans to take a natural nonmedical approach to treat her cancer, he voiced outrage and anger.

"What do you mean, you're going to eat raw vegetables? That's crap. You'll starve to death before the cancer gets you!" Based on a long history of intimidation with her brother, Ashley normally would have just frozen up, kowtowed, mumbled some apologetic words, and hung up. Instead, after some coaching in the ways of emotional aikido she responded with: "Are you saying that because you care about me?" Note the brilliant aikido move in that! He either had to admit he cared, which is more vulnerable, or say outloud that he didn't in which case his true stance would be revealed and somehow be more workable. When he replied in an angry tone, "Damn right that's why I'm saying this," Ashley said the following: "Well, I appreciate that you care about me. It's just your tone that I can't stand. I wish you could speak to me in a more caring tone." Her brother paused in silence for a long time, totally disarmed and at a loss for words. Ashley felt empowered.

The practioner of emotional aikido seeks out and imputes positive motives in his opponent, so that there's nothing to resist or fight against. Ashley attributed "caring", and it worked.

When Ernesto attended a family business meeting he was met with an onslaught of reproaches from his father and brother for an impending decison to leave the company and set out on his own. Instead of his regular aggressive and hostile defensive response, his new emotional aikido approach went like this: "I don't blame you for being upset. I'd be upset too, if either of you announced to me that you planned to leave. I love the idea of a family business. It's been a great way to keep this family together, and I honor you for it. And now the family can help me stay connected in a business of my own." Even as he made moves to separate, he aknowledged and appealed to their sense of unity, and disarmed them. "Their icebergs of doubt and upset, just melted on the spot," he reported, "And before I knew it we all became sentimental about our years together in business, and we were thanking each other."

Corrolaries to the aikido principle include:

1. In a fight or disagreement with your partner, own your shit as rapidly as you can. The longer the gap between a disagreeable event and your taking responsibility for your part in it, the longer the delay of intimacy.

2. Focus on the good, and on bringing out the best in your partner rather than on pointing out the bad. This doesn't mean be pollyanna and ignore bad or hurtful behavior. What it does mean is that it works better to reinforce the behavior you do want than it does to condemn what you don't want.

3. Cultivate faith that things will work out, and focus on that experience of faith, even when things look bleak. Faith reaches out beyond the current understanding of the mind. An old girlfriend told me once, in the middle of a fight, "Trust the love", and it disarmed me.

4. Keep respect a practical matter, and not just a theoretical one. That means actually allowing your partner to be, think, and feel differently from you. Respect first, react second. Without having to get morallistic about this approach, suffice it to say that it works as a strategy. People don't resist much in the face of respect. In fact when they feel heard and accepted, they will be much less likely to disagree.

5. Find and fight for common ground. This is similar to saying fight for the relationship rather than fight your partner about any particular issue. Focusing on what you both want actually sets the stage for getting what you individually want, faster. Again, no moralism necessary. It's simply a strategy that works better.

Respecting History

Feelings ride central to relationship work and healing. Inevitably, not only do the current worlds of two seperate people collide, so do their pasts. Whatever is repressed in one gets pushed on by the other by the nature of the impulse to integrate---in both. What my partner represses in herself inevitably interferes with my natural flow. That's why being together can be so helpful: help is built-in at home. And it's harder to hide it.

Before the adult level of working things out fully takes place in the form of requests and committed statements, the irrational, feeling level of integration can be facilitated by helping the venter get into full feeling. With practice, a style of inter-personal integration comes about where the question, "What does that remind you of?" naturally arises, and a sensitivity to personal history can soften the blow in the present. "I did the 'superior' thing because my father always called me 'stupid' when I argued with or disagreed with him in fights." "I over-reacted to being criticized because, it still carries a feeling of rejection for me". "Your comment made me feel disregarded like I did so much of the time growing up". Who can't soften to the pains of a child? People who know their own pain tend to be easy to live with, because in owning their own pain they don't have to inflict it outwards to keep it at bay. Feeling people have no need for enemies, and therefore deal with conflict reasonably when it comes up, and don't seek it out. Feeling remains the key to personal healing, and for healing between people too.

The Three-legged Stool Model of Relationship

A relationship is like a three-legged stool. It's a picture I use and offer to couples to assess and measure their relationships. The stool's legs must be of equal length to maintain balance. A stool with tall legs is elevating, and a stool with short legs, less exciting. Obviously all three legs must be present or the stool cannot stand. If at least one or two legs are significantly shorter or unequal in length, the chair cannot stand without a constant hand on it to keep it from wobbling or toppling.

First leg: compatibility. Nothing mystical about this. It means similarities, and includes values, likes and dislikes, religion, intelligence, interests, etc. The main areas where compatibility rules are: God, sex, money, children/parenting. A rule of thumb dictates that a relationship boast at least a 70% compatibility level to "make it". Exceptions can work when the ratings of the other two legs are high.

Second leg: commitment. This refers to how committed each person is to the entity of being together, in both communication and riding out both the good and bad times. Commitment can be measured in the compatibility leg as well, but the relationship itself needs a separate score on its commitment level, which is a synergistic summation of the commitment of each person (yet not just the simple sum). This means that the commitment level of a relationship can be strong even when the individual commitment levels vary from each other. Commitment makes up the glue that holds growing, developing individuals in relationship.

The final stool leg is magic, sometimes known as chemistry: the ineffable quality that makes being together better than not being together, the combined subjective "feeling" of the rightness of the relationship's being. Magic includes but is not limited to sexual excitement or romance. Magic includes a sense of destiny, and keeps flowers growing in the field of routine and familiarity.

Often when I ask a couple to rate their relationship, each in private, the similarity or disparity of their ratings also indicates the health and unity of their togetherness. If one person is living in a "level 10" on a scale of 1-10 in all areas, and the other rates the relationship at a "5" or "6" at most, the stool becomes a wobbly one even if each person's rating alone looks stable.

As far as the length of the stool legs: high is exciting and more risky, has a higher center of gravity, and is thus more vulnerable to the "shearing" forces of interactions with the world outside the relationship. Short legs make for more stability but less excitement.

Of course a three-legged stool with no legs at all epitomizes rock-solid equilibrium and zero excitement. Neither compatibility, commitment, or magic figure into the fabric of this sort of a relationship, and by the standards of this model, it is no relationship at all. Such people co-mingle without really relating.

Some people hold their relationships together despite a great variance in compatibility, low commitment, and minimal magic. These are the relationships that require a constant hand to hold the stool upright, and whose work is justified under the banner of "potential". This model does not measure by potential, but only by actual. The relationship that requires the constant hand to even keep it upright has been called "codependent".

How's your stool?

Mango Smoothie

"Aren't relationships all about compromise? You can't have everything. I don't like some things but I just accept the bad with the good. It's better than nothing." Sounds reasonable, no? Yet, I hear words like this all the time from clients to justify bad relationship choices. I tell a person who rationalizes like this, the following story to help clarify how good and bad elements often can't be weighed in a linear fashion to decide ultimately what to take in or be part of.

If I make you a fruit smoothie, and add to it the most luscious of tropical fruits, like mangoes, pineapples, bananas, kiwis---all your favorites----and then right before your very eyes, and just before I hand it to you, I take an eyedropper full of liquid cow manure and squeeze it into your drink, and swill it around, will you drink it? It's not enough manure for you to either smell it or taste, but you know it's there. Can you drink it? Should you drink it?

I've gotten a wide variety of answers to this dilemma. One woman told me: "It has good elements in it, and if I can't taste or smell the manure, what's the difference?"

Another: "No way I'd drink that! Just knowing about the manure makes me want to throw up!"

Or how about: "Well, it depends on the circumstances. If I'm starving and that's all I have, then OK, but otherwise I'll say 'no , thank you'".

Some will question with all sorts of potential qualifiers: "Is there any way I can accept the smoothie now, keep it until I learn how to distill out the manure, and drink it later?" Or "Was it a healthy cow?" Or "Doesn't pineapple juice neutralize the nitrogen of manure?"

How do you answer?

Money and Relationships

Money is funny. Despite it's make-believe, unnatural origins, it has wormed its way into the human psyche, and the deepest workings of relationships. How a couple deals with money often reveals the true dynamics of their relationship. I'm sure this could make for a book on its own. So here's just one quick take on the subject, illustrating the feeling-principle in action even when it comes to money:

Tony and Melissa: What's Mine is Mine

"But it's my money. I had it before we got married. You had nothing, and now you have a lot. Why do you complain all the time?"

"You're cheap! I'm married to a millionaire, so why can't I live like the wife of one?"

"You don't know the value of money!"

"So that's why you spend five thousand on clothes for yourself, and then give me one thousand for my wardrobe?"

"You have so much more than you ever had before. How can you bitch like that?"

The banter continues till a heated deadlock. They look at me for help.

"Let's shift the focus a little here," I say. "Tony what's it like to give so much to Melissa and have her respond with 'you're cheap'?"

"It pisses me off! I feel unappreciated. My generosity's going unacknowledged. I feel taken for granted, and used. That hurts." His voice softens.

"Oh, Tony. I don't mean to hurt you. You are generous! I'm so grateful for your taking me and the kids into your home and heart. I know you want us as your family, and I appreciate that so much."

"So, Melissa, what's it feel like to have Tony spend more on his clothes than he gives you for clothes? And when you have to ask him for spending money?"

"I feel belittled. I feel treated like a child, and not an equal in my own marriage. I feel put-down. It pisses me off! I was the baby in my family, and now I'm treated the same way as an adult. I hate it! I feel like property, like you love your money more than you do me! That hurts." Her voice softens, and eyes mist.

"Melissa, you and the kids are the best thing that's happened to me. I love our family. I don't want you to feel like my property, or like a second-class citizen in your own marriage. I've just been trying to teach you to be careful with our money. To respect the money is to respect me."

"Tony, that's the first time I've ever heard you say 'our' money. That's the first time you ever said anything about money along with caring for me and the kids. That makes me feel like there's hope. I know you care. It's the stupid money that's stood between us. As long as I know you care, I'm content. When you complain about my spending, I've felt like the money was more important to you than me." They're both soft now.

This sort of shift from "you-statements" to feelings, eventually helped bring about a shift of the money structure. Tony started sharing his financial dealings with Melissa to keep her informed, and they both made up a budget together. Melissa made a point to show her thriftiness to Tony as a form of her respect. Once the feeling level opened up, both Tony and Melissa could more directly deal with each others concerns. Interestingly, when Melissa totally upheld Tony's prenuptial money as sperate and untouchable, Tony softened and made more of it available to Melissa directly without her having to ask for allowance. It's not that each of them suddenly dropped his or her position, but rather that each of them softened the edges around it. Contact at the feeling level made things liveable. Paradoxically, with that contact the money didn't matter so much.

The Power of Positive Choices

Shelley woke up feeling nauseous and she had a stiff neck. She didn't really want to get out of bed or go to work, but her strong work ethic and Affirmation Training class dictated that she assert her way out of her condition. A haggard face was reflected back at her in the mirror, to which she spoke: "I feel great. I am ready to go to work. I have never felt better in my life." Shelley gritted her teeth, dressed, and went to work. What's wrong with this picture? Affirmations that declare something is true in blatant denial of current reality may end up serving the forces of repression by teaching the subconscious mind that you are a liar. Healthy or desirable outcomes will not be the result.

On the other hand, affirmations spoken in the form of powerful and meaningful choices mobilize the heart and will to yield a sense of purposefulness and direction. They can creatively stretch your world according to your heartfelt desires. Framing desires as choices rather than false or even hopeful statements takes the unnecessary, punitive "shoulds" out of the picture.

I help my clients reframe their self-realization and deep wishes into powerful affirmations in order to engage the internal neuropeptide feedback loop of information with the conscious mind's intent for good, conscious, and real outcomes. What follows is a composite list of empowering statements I've collected over the past decade. Notice your own body-response as you read over them. Feel free to incorporate the ones that resonate for you on your list:

I choose:

* to be true to myself and let the chips fall where they may.

* to challenge: "I am not getting what I need, therefore I don't deserve it."

* to allow myself to feel good.

* to recognize and reclaim my sense of innate lovableness.

* to affirm how right it is to be in tune with the needs of a child and for adults to appropriately defer their own needs.

* to affirm my love and appreciation of family.

* to recognize that there is such a thing as healthy disengaging which is different from unhealthy isolation.

* to be truthful first, optimistic second.

* to no longer internalized my anger, but learn to externalize it safely.

* to let myself be irresponsible sometimes.

* to no longer associate saying "no" to others with a heartless detachment, but rather, associate it with a healthy self-caring attitude.

* to beware of any tendency to want to do the "easy" thing, as opposed to doing the "right" thing.

* to affirm my right to expect things for myself.

* to be pain-free, even though pain has given me purpose and meaning in my life.

* to grant myself a pain-free existence even though nobody granted me a pain-free existence when I was a child.

* to feel the pain from my past until it is just a memory, rather than using the pain to connect with others out of context.

* to affirm that I can choose positive direction even if I don't know positive destination.

* to affirm myself as a champion of innocence in this world.

* to recognize that although my family's style was to avoid feelings by

focusing on science and intellect, my style includes a strong interest in the feelings and suffering of others.

* to recognize that love, besides being a warm feeling, involves a real sensitivity to the reality and needs of another.

* to do my inner work of connecting with my hurts, so that I don't have to "use" other people to help me connect with them.

* to recognize that taking responsibility for my own well-being includes seeking out meaningful support for myself.

* to take a stand for myself, even going so far as to say, "Your way is not my way."

* to recognize that the "mean" side of myself has had the job of protecting me, and to see that I can now be directly assertive

* to recognize that in the present, I can ask specifically for what I want when I feel unloved, even though in the past, as a child, I felt I couldn't.

* to recognize that I can walk away from what I don't want.

* to be vigilant with my own mind, without being hyper-vigilant or uptight about it.

* to feel my aliveness, even if pain is part of being "alive."

* to connect with the vital, feeling part of me.

* to affirm that I have become the kind of attentive giver I always wanted my family to be for me.

* to affirm my desire to be in love with life again.

* to recognize regrets from the past as primarily a factor in my present, and deal with them as such

* to recognize that I can be connected to my heart in ways other than through the hope of a child for perfect love.

* to challenge the conclusions of a child when he says, "I'm not being loved because I am not lovable"

* to recognize how hope has prevented me from fully integrating my pain.

* to affirm that my heart no longer runs on hope, but rather on passion.

* to let myself feel the painful feelings from the past, so that resistance to feeling can no longer rob me of the intimacy I want in the present.

* to recognize that anything less than consensual, pleasant sex is not acceptable.

* to recognize that my needs are more than just complaints; that in truth my complaints were the result of my needs being unmet and/or violated.

* to recognize that it's not good to obey bad or harmful instructions.

* to recognize that I am not responsible for the happiness of others.

* to feel and deal with my lonely, sad feelings rather than punish myself for having them.

* to affirm my growth in taking care of myself and in no longer assuming that I am the cause of whatever is "wrong" in my relationship.

* to fully know and affirm that there is nothing wrong with me for wanting what I want, or not wanting what I don't want

* to accept responsibility for what I want and don't want by clearly expressing that to others.

* to recognize I can be as direct as I want to be

* to realize that "protecting" someone from the truth is actually preventing them from moving beyond the lie.

* to know that I can say "no" to certain behavior without saying "no" to the whole person or to the special-ness I want with them.

* to no longer have to earn the right to feel good.

* to affirm that I deserve to receive, independently of what I put out.

* to recognize that to be quiet out of fear of speaking is not a positive quiet.

* to distinguish between the "good" pain of pushing myself beyond my current limits, and the "bad" pain that comes from denial of my real needs or feelings.

* to admit how exhausting it is to be strong on the outside when I am really in pain on the inside.

* to recognize that my being out of the moment and out of touch with my feelings has robbed me of right relationship.

* to commit to taking care of myself.

* to acknowledge that I want adventure and stability in my life

* to confess my transgressions and express my remorse to those I have hurt.

* to be aware of how I leave the moment, and focus on what I am avoiding by doing that.

* to affirm that I am not stupid for not knowing what I never learned, and that I can now learn it

* to affirm that numbing out my pain for all those years, although it took its toll on my health, worked as a survival choice.

* to move beyond my suffering, even though it has become the most familiar way to be in the world

* to recognize that suffering is optional

* to learn how to appropriately put my needs first.

* to let myself receive without having to be ill to do so.

* to fully equate the self with other, and no longer replace the self with other.

* to acknowledge that uncertainty can be OK when it is not tainted by anxiety or confusion, and that it is not the same as anxiety or confusion at all.

* to recognize that my "fulfillment thermostat" was set at a very low level as a child, and that I no longer settle for that.

* to recognize that the true bond of love is based on "two separate people," even though that seems paradoxical.

* to know the void and emptiness that appear when I stop struggling for love as "neutral," and be comfortable with that.

* to realize that the love in my heart is not put there by the people I love, and that it belongs to me and fills me, whether they receive it or not.

* to challenge the notion that because my parents suffered, they were somehow noble and excused from being there for me as a child

* to recognize my depression as a survival technique, and affirm that I no longer need to depress my pain to survive.

* to challenge the catastrophic thinking that "if people knew me as I am, they would have nothing to do with me," and "I have to be perfect in order to have other people have anything to do with me."

* to affirm that I don't have to be perfect to be OK

* to affirm: "It's OK to reject that which isn't good for me at all levels in my life"

* to be present as I am, beyond appearances

* to declare a healthy end to my suffering, recognizing that years of carrying it has served to make me humble.

* to recognize that I have only known myself as a sufferer, and to now challenge that notion, and get to know myself as a happy person.

* to let other people feel their own pain.

* to be able to give my love without taking on the pain of others

* to reveal myself more authentically to those I love, and that includes not only my strength and independence, but also my needs and vulnerabilities.

* to recognize that a truly caring person gives from her own full cup, and that means filling it first.

* to be honest with myself and others, to continue to reveal myself, to lead with my heart, to be a real person.

* to beware of entering a relationship due to the fear of being alone.

* to acknowledge myself for taking heartfelt risks to move forward

* to recognize that I can manifest strongly even when things are falling apart.

* to affirm that whatever in me is dissatisfied with less than my heart's desire is a good impulse.

* to affirm that I can be hurt and angry without becoming vengeful.

* to affirm that the life force within me is stronger than the death force.

* to challenge the notion that because "suffering brings about change," if I want to change, therefore I must suffer

* to be patient with myself as I grow and develop, the way I would with a child.

* to recognize that sometimes the most healing thing to do in a relationship is to honor the separateness.

* to take a stand for my true vision, my true standards, and my true values in life, even when I feel fear

* to recognize that I value and am deeply touched by kindness, and feel good about what that says about me

* to affirm and recognize that my future belongs to me, no matter what has happened in the past.

* to grieve the fact that I wasted many years "loving what doesn't love me back"

* to recognize that I cannot force another to have real contact with me, that I can only reach out to make real contact myself.

* to trust that feeling my true pain without resistance to it is the fastest way through it.

* to know that the child without the adult is lost in the moment, and the adult without the child is lost without the moment!

* to recognize that abdicating my right to make waves is to disempower myself.

* to learn the positive aspect of making waves.

* to make the fundamental choice to be true to my heart, and let all secondary choices flow from that.

* to reaffirm my heart's ability to know who is good for me and who is not.

* to affirm that I want to be with someone who wants to be with me.

* to no longer tolerate abuse in any form.

* to challenge the belief that "bad things happen to me because I deserve them"

* to recognize that people reach for higher standards for themselves when they feel good about themselves, and struggle to live up to others' standards for them when they feel bad about themselves.

* to fuel my greatness with inspiration rather than "the need to be good"

* to let in and enjoy the sense of absurdity and humor in my life, and use those as stepping stones to positive change.

* to take a firm stand on being true to myself, especially in my own home--no matter what!

* to let myself feel what it's like to be the object of protective anger, and learn to incorporate that into an ongoing healthy, inner fierceness of integrity.

* to affirm my anger as part of my caring, unlike anger that comes from not-caring.

* to know the healthy aspect of surrender, independent of the notion of "caving in"

* to be able to live by the credo : Meditate and fight!

* to recognize that it is honest self-revelation that keeps perception of self and reality-of-self in alignment.

* to validate my own experience without having to get lost in another's

* to navigate the waters of my aloneness without becoming isolated.

* to now be the driver, and no longer the driven.

* to recognize that I have confused love with taking on others' burdens, and now separate the two.

* to reject over-responsibility for others, even if they love me for it.

* to learn how to feel great without having to do "great" things for others.

* to recognize that sometimes doing for others breeds dependence and resentment.

* to acknowledge that doing well in a medium that is not really mine is not enough for me.

* to recognize that my moment is this moment.

* to affirm my values of the artistic moment over the finished product.

* to forgive myself for having been fooled into living as if I am less than I really am.

* to recognize the truth of "no one believes in me the way I do" as reflecting a level of self-love, not an absence

* to create clear communication even when I am uncomfortable

* to no longer be "nice" at the expense of my own needs.

* to recognize the massive confusion I have been subjected to in my family system, and acknowledge my strong constitution for having survived it.

* to recognize my depression as a form of fierce loyalty to my own inner child (my heart) and its unfinished grieving process.

* to affirm my desire to live and have fun.

* to reject as much of my childhood conditioning as is necessary to be free, even if I have nothing left but myself.

* to recognize that the best way I can help my friends be happy is by enjoying my own happiness in their presence.

* to affirm that the risk of opening up when I talk, is better than talking without opening up.

* to affirm that I am not the same person I was before, and therefore I am free from the past.

* to let my grieving of wasted time serve as a reminder that I have no time to waste.

* to recognize that "I can do no right" is just as blind as "I can do no wrong".

* to affirm that I don't have to be "on" all the time I'm with others.

* to challenge the idea that "I need to be connected with everyone I'm with" and replace it with "I need to be connected with myself no matter who I'm with".

* to acknowledge that I'm moving from defining myself by the responses of others, to defining myself in my responses to others.

* to challenge the idea that "to be true to myself, I lose relationship" and replace that with "to be true to myself yields relationship".

* to recognize that the adult realization of "it's all inside me" is different from the child's conclusion that "it's all my fault".

* to recognize my healing process to include both taking bold adult steps, and letting myself sink into and feel all the kid feelings that come up in face of those steps.

* to recognize two main ingredients of maturity: the ability to see the other's point of view, and the ability to accept loss.

"We are psychological beings and not logical beings."
----Dr. Brad Blanton

✳✳✳

"Yesterday's truth is today's bullshit."
---Dr. Brad Blanton

✳✳✳

"Why am I so introspective? I had no place else to go."
----patient

6

Case Studies & Stories: Therapy in Action

Jerry: It All Hurts

Jerry had had a history of migraine headaches since age eleven, for which he had taken medication numerous times. He had noticed that during times of stress the episodes were particularly intense. I was working with him in a group setting where he recounted a life of frustration and lack of fulfillment. He told the group of relationships he had been in and then stated, "Every time I get into a relationship, I get hurt."

"Close your eyes and say that again," I suggested. He did, deliberately and softly.

"I'm getting a headache," he announced, a slight wince on his face.

"Say it again and let the headache happen," I advised him.

"Every time I get into a relationship, I get hurt."

"Again!"

"Every time I get into a relationship, I get hurt." This time he paused, then biting his lower lip with his upper teeth, and holding his breath, a single tear oozed from his right eye. "To love hurts," he whispered. The tears welled, his energy was wavering, but he was still in control.

"Say that again. That's it right there!"

"To love hurts." This time, the emotions swelled, the control walls started to bend, and more tears funneled down Jerry's cheek.

"Say it again!"

"To love hurts!" he began sobbing. The dam had finally burst, and Jerry's face and body quivered with the letting go.

"Feel that pain, Jerry. Just feel it with no resistance this time, without doing anything about it." The feeling was over the wall, freely flowing now--the body releasing what had been held for a long, long time.

"So what did you choose to do when you realized that 'to love hurts', Jerry?" I demanded.

There was a pause, a slight reflection, and the answer spilled out: "To not love."

"Feel it, Jerry. How does it feel 'to not love'?"

Another full pause and a reply, as if his life were being summed up in two words, "It hurts."

"Feel it, Jerry. That's the existential corner you've painted your-self into. Just feel it and be with it."

In a flash, a life-strategy based on avoiding pain had been re-vealed. The core belief stood exposed: to love hurts; to not love hurts. Opposing forces held within the body, leaving Jerry in the middle zone of neither loving nor not-loving. No feeling. Jerry, working as an ac-countant, had "lived in his head" for years. Carrying this unresolved dilemma had created the prodigious amount of pressure inside his head.

"So, Jerry, what's your new choice here? Understand--there's pain at either end, and let's face it, avoiding the pain didn't work." The room was thick with a delicious silence as the whole group sat poised for his answer...

"I choose to love," Jerry whispered, with a peace and resolve that shone on his wet cheeks, "even if there is pain." He sighed. Every-one else in the room sighed. It was sweet and true. Jerry had made a good life-affirming choice for himself, and we could see that it was...well, livable.

Jerry now sat charged with the same emotional energy that had fed the fruitless strategy of avoiding pain. Once the body response had lined up with the new choice, it became part of the domain of the subconscious. No litany of affirmations would be necessary to maintain the vitality around that choice. A new path of least resistance had been born within his being.

"How's your headache?" I asked.

"What headache?"

Phase two of Jerry's session involved some gentle acupressure point-holding, along with mellow music, to help him rest in the new-found peace of a life-strategy that suited him. In follow-up appointments, Jerry reported a marked decrease in the migraines, both in intensity and frequency. Migraine headaches were now experienced more as red flag indicators around his issue of choosing to love vs. choosing to not feel pain, and when he felt one was imminent, he knew how to ward it off.

Ruth: Haunted By My Past

Ruth was in her 30's and physically fit. Her complaint was her relationship history.

"I just broke up with a man, and I'm upset because I might not be able to maintain a long-term relationship," she cried, concerned over the prospect of being alone, without the intimacy she wanted.

"I've been in therapy for years, but my relationship pattern has not changed. I'm with a man for about a year, and at a certain point in our relationship, when we should be getting closer and moving towards commitment, I get a panicky feeling. I start thinking that he is trying to invade my space, and then I do something to push him away and it's over. I know it's me, and I can't help it." She wept as she spoke.

During the first part of the session we talked about some of the particulars around her relationships with men (including her father and brothers), and I also asked questions about her medical history and some of the details of her childhood. (I noted that Ruth was a breech birth which means she emerged from her mother feet first.) I listened for signs of the "three brains" as Ruth spoke. The emotions expressed were sadness and yearning for intimacy, and the emotions verbalized were panic and loneliness. The noteworthy meanings or themes that Ruth wove into her story included "invading my space," "I'm stuck", and "there is nothing I can do".

When I asked Ruth to try on for size what it would feel like to go beyond that stuck point in a relationship with a man, she didn't get far. Tears continued to flow. I figured that whatever was preventing her from getting past that spot in order to reach an outcome was locked in more at the physical level than the emotional or mental. We continued on to the sustained acupressure point-holding part of the session. Ruth lay on the couch in a supine position while I placed my fingertips on two endocrine-related acupressure points on her torso (Remember: the endocrine system is hooked into the same part of the brain that processes our emotions. Pressing endocrine points therefore accesses the same circuitry, which can help the "hidden" neuropeptide chip to surface.)

As I held Ruth, she began breathing a bit deeper and more rapidly than usual, which I had requested, and then I played a recording of evocative music to stimulate feeling. (Music, because of its direct emotional appeal, has been used for centuries to arouse or calm.)

After a few minutes, Ruth informed me that her upper outer thighs were cramping, and said that it felt a little strange to her. I was aware from her history that this symptom wasn't related to any medical problems. Another few moments passed, and Ruth suddenly opened her eyes, looked into mine, and asked, "Andy, has anyone come into the room?"

I looked around over my shoulder, then back to her and replied, "No, why?"

"I had the distinct feeling that someone came in." She continued breathing, noticing an increase in the leg cramping and a growing sense of "nervousness".

"Are you sure no one entered?" she asked with a pleading tone in her voice.

"Yes, I'm sure. Who does it feel like it is?"

"I sense a masculine presence," she whispered, her arms shaking slightly. "I'm scared and I don't know what I'm scared of!" Ruth started to sweat, very lightly at first, then profusely. Soon she was shaking, sweating, and her legs were cramping.

"Andy, I feel really panicky right now and I don't know what it's about, and this has been interesting, but I've got to get out of here. I don't believe in ghosts, but I have the distinct feeling that there is a man in this room trying to get inside my body." (Aha! Here are the two elements I had noticed before: panic and "invading-my-space!")

"Stay with it, Ruth! You're getting to it! Let it happen! Let the man come to you and reach you this time. No resistance this time!"

Ruth took the inner leap. She inhaled deeply, as if to brace herself and let it happen. Suddenly, her body relaxed, a broad smile appeared on her face, and she crossed her arms in front of her.

"I know who it is now," she said, almost whispering, "I know who it is." Her body was relaxed, the shaking and sweating had subsided.

I inched a little closer, still holding her points, and whispered back, "Who is it?"

"It's the doctor," she said matter-of-factly, and yet clearly realizing it for the first time herself. "I see it all now—the leg cramps, the man invading my space, the fear--I finally get it!" The enlightened glee was evident on her face. The acupressure points were burning to the touch, hot from the body's resistance to the integration, but this time the resistance didn't win.

(Ruth was reliving her unique birth experience with the imprint it had left on her nervous system. Before her birth, Ruth's mother and the doctor had known she was in a breech position. The doctor--a man--did in fact reach inside the mother three times in attempts to turn the baby around before delivery. It was the mother who experienced a man "invading her space"--because he was! A physically painful event charged heavily with emotion and meaning was imprinted into the body of baby Ruth, an experience of such intensity that her newborn nervous system simply could not handle it! Her body/mind system, however, retained the memory of it and acted out the "desire" (actually, the centropic impulse) to integrate it by repeatedly bringing the fragmented pieces forth into situations in Ruth's adult life that resembled the intensity of emotion, meaning, and body response of the original moment. This was the ghost of a feeling she'd been carrying within her all these years that emerged through projection onto the men she was in relationship with. It accounted for the "ghost" in the room the day I worked with her. Now the complete and original scene had surfaced into consciousness, and now all three of the neuropeptide chips were united.

What Ruth had carried for thirty-plus years, and talked about in therapy for ten, was simply reintegrated and released in two hours! The good news is: it's not a matter of time, but one of timing. Now Ruth could be in the man-woman arena with a healthy level of commitment and intensity, and without the ghost of her past haunting her.)

Jill: Back at You

"There is this voice inside me that is always judging me," the woman across from me complained. "It never lets up! Always telling me what I'm doing wrong, and how stupid I am. I feel terrible most of the time, and I don't even want to go out. I'm so depressed."

Thirty-eight-year-old Jill had been clinically depressed for six years, and before that was never really happy. She sat slumped forward in her chair, shoulders rounded and heavy.

"Do you hear that voice now?" I asked.
"Not really."

"Well, close your eyes. Call it forth. Evoke it. Let it be here to judge you. I want to hear it."

Jill sat quietly, conjuring up that judgmental part of herself.

"I can't seem to find it. It's not judging me right this second."

"So this is the so-called judgmental part of you that has made you miserable for years? And it can't seem to find anything to criticize you for right now?!!" I demanded.

"No," she replied sheepishly.

"Then I say it's incompetent! How can you give any power or authority to a part of you that is so totally incompetent??!?"

Jill laughed heartily. "You're right! It IS incompetent! And I can judge it as much as it can judge me!" She laughed through the remainder of the two-hour session.

(This technique worked because it was funny. Notice how I took on the role of the critic by focusing in on the word "incompetent." I used a critical context in order to dismantle the Critic. I called its bluff, and publicly humiliated it. By the way, even if Jill had actually found the critical voice in that moment I told her to, she would have proved to herself that this critical self is under her control.)

Jona: Hope Does a Body Good

Jona had been struggling with myeloma for ten months, and during his illness, he had been through many ups and downs. One day he and I discussed hope.

"I'm afraid to feel hope and then have what I'm doing not work, because I'm setting myself up for disappointment. If I don't hope so much, I won't feel as hurt if it doesn't work out."

"You mean, the higher you fly, the harder you can crash?" I asked.

"Right."

"What does hope feel like?"

"Like making a plan and being able to carry it out."

"That's not a feeling, Jona. That's a definition based on the future. And if you define hope that way, nothing will change. What does hope feel like?"

"Like the good feeling I get when I've made a plan and carried it out."

"That's a feeling based on the past---having carried something out. Close your eyes, Jona. What specifically does hope feel like?"

"A lightness in my chest, and an open feeling in my head."

"Now feel it and recognize it. This is hope in the present---independent of the future and the past. This is yours now. There is no such thing as 'false hope,' because hope exists in the present."

"Mmmmm. Thanks, I accept that!"

Enrico: Heavy Heart, Heavy Blood

"I cheated on my wife for an entire year, and she never knew. I kept the secret for the next fourteen years, and then she died of cancer. I never told her, and I never received her forgiveness. This has weighed on me all these years, and I still feel so guilty!"

Forty-three-year-old Enrico, a slender Colombian man with graying temples, looked imploringly at me. "Wouldn't I just have hurt her by telling her? I knew the affair was over, so why inflict more pain?" He vacillated back and forth between his guilt and his rationalizations, never fully embracing either.

"Have you ever wondered if your secret affair played into your wife's illness?" I inquired, going for a nerve.

"Oh, please don't say that! I feel so guilty! I know I did wrong, but telling her would have hurt her more. There was no need---I loved her!" He fidgeted in his chair as his anxiety escalated.

"I think you've been fighting your guilt for fourteen years, and it's time to stop fighting---because you are guilty! Face it, Enrico, what you did was hurtful to your wife and to your marriage! Maybe more than you know!" I was merciless, acting on the hunch that Enrico needed some sort of a push to get him off the fence he had been straddling all those years.

Enrico, head in hand, cried in anguish, no longer fighting his guilt, but rather, letting it wash over him in waves of sobbing. Finally, through his quiet whimpering, he whispered, "But she loved me...."

I softened my tone, because I could tell Enrico had broken through the cycle of wrestling with his guilt. "Enrico, I ask you--now, in death, after all these years--is your wife more concerned with all your years of suffering over this, or with the suffering you caused her?" Hesitating slightly, Enrico replied, "She is concerned about my suffering."

"So, Enrico, let that in—that is forgiveness. You have done the time for your crime."

Enrico broke down again. Aware that he was a religious man, I pushed a little more: "What is it like for God to see you accepting this forgiveness after confessing your guilt?"

He lit up. "It is a state of Grace. I feel a lightness in my blood!"

(Interesting last comment! Enrico had been diagnosed with leukemia two years after his wife's death.

I marvel at how I got away with being such a bad-ass with Enrico, but obviously I so accurately entered his framework of thinking that he accepted my rough manner and took it to heart in a way that unloosed him from the back-and-forth state he was in)

.

Rachel: A Good Beginning

Background and history:

Rachel, 51, had had a long history of both food and environmental sensitivities as well as chronic infections, candida albicans, and other medical problems. In immunological terms, her system was manifesting both overactive and underactive responses simultaneously, demonstrating a core biological confusion about what is good and what is bad for the system.

Rachel's relationship record involved one "loser" after another, yet the memories of various partners that she recalled were ambivalent. "Monty cheated on me regularly, but I miss the stability of being with him." (stability?!)

"Now Richard, he conned me out of money, and even directly insulted me before he left, but you know, within the bad he was very brilliant and a hard worker." (...within the bad? Strange choice of words, no?)

At age 15, Rachel's parents divorced. As early as age seven, Rachel had sided with her mother, a beautiful, superficial socialite. Rachel hated her father, a dullard of a businessman who liked his orderly routine life, went to bed early, and only tolerated the social scene his wife dragged him into. He made Rachel work for her allowance, and stressed values of a deeper nature. He was strict and no fun.

After the divorce, teenage Rachel pushed her mother to marry the richest man in their home country of Belgium, but that relationship also collapsed three years later, and her mother ended up penniless. Rachel's father found himself isolated and lonely as he aged.

Instead of the healthy maturation process of distilling from each parent the "good" and discarding the "bad," (which is how we synthesize from the raw material of our parents' character a new and relevant sense of self) Rachel had chosen (swallowed/introjected) one and rejected the other. Ironically, she had taken in primarily bad influences and cast out the good--a dominant theme throughout her life, from relationships to her body's immune responses!

Would cognitive awareness of all this influence change? Hardly. The therapeutic task involves reaching the body/mind system with information it can respond to with a high feeling valence factor, thereby tapping into the mind/body electricity responsible for bringing about transformation. That level of charge often reveals itself spontaneously when repressed material surfaces..

Treatment plan: to "harvest" relevant emotional charges from two distinct areas:

1. the arena of Rachel's 30-year old son Adam, who had a long history of feeling rejected and unwanted, a history that included boarding schools, numerous psychotic episodes, and general unhappiness. He was now once again in Rachel's care. She genuinely felt bad about him and her past treatment of him.

2. the seven-year-old aspect of Rachel's psyche—the Rachel who made the original choice of Mother over Father. We needed to explore her confusion as a child in the midst of a loveless, highly polarized marriage relationship, and what led her to make the choice she did.

The Work:

Rachel began Session Seven in a chatty manner, telling me about her relationship history with men. About fifteen minutes into it, she suddenly turned silent, and stared off into space.

"You're so quiet," I offered.

"I'm just tired," she said.

"Close your eyes for a moment, and just let yourself be tired."

"OK," she sighed.

"You sighed."

"I've lived such a party life, and I'm tired of it," she explained in a monotone voice.

"Where do you notice that tiredness in your body the most right now?" I asked.

"Right here," and she gestured to the center of her chest with her hand.

"Rachel, keep your hand there. If that part of your body had a voice of its own, what would it say? Right now, first words...."

"I'm so tired."

"Say it again."

"I'm so tired," she repeated, and a tear rolled gently down her cheek.

"Rachel, I'm going to move in and put my hands on you now. Is that OK with you?"

"Uh huh,' she said lightly. I repositioned the recliner chair she was sitting in, and placed my right hand at the center of her solar plexus as I reached behind her and placed my left hand on her lower back. I could feel a release beginning to happen. Rachel's journey of inner exploration shifted into higher gear with this contact at both the physical and feeling levels. With her eyes still closed, Rachel engaged a deep feeling inner reverie.

"I've lived like a party-girl the way my mother has, but I've ended up with nobody, alone like my father. My poor father," she said wistfully. "I miss him. He really was sweet. I think I may have done him wrong by siding with my mother all those years. I may be more like him than I believed. Gads. I've followed my mother's path with my father's nature--no wonder I'm so sick!"

"And no wonder your son is so sad," I added.

"Oh, God, it's true. I passed all that onto him! I've been so confused. Oh, my poor boy!" And she began to weep. And weep. "Why did I choose my mother?" she blurted angrily through her tears.

"What's the answer to that?" I reflected the question back to her.

"I was seven! My mother was so pretty, and so much fun! I loved dressing up with her. My father is so boring." (She slipped into first person, present tense, the sign of true regression....)

"That's it, Rachel, keep your eyes closed. Be there. Talk to him."

She complied readily. I withdrew my hands, and backed away.

"Daddy, why can't you play with me? You're always so serious. You just make mother's life so boring. Let's have fun! I hate you, I really do!" she said, weeping, then continued her monologue. "No, I don't...I just can't love both of you. I don't know how to love both of you!" Rachel wailed those words. Don't know how to love both of you. I do love you, too, Daddy. I'm so sorry." She was sobbing. "I'm so sorry. I'm so sorry. I didn't love you. I'm so sorry. I'm so sorry, Adam. I didn't love you either, and now you're so sad and sick. I'm so sorry." Her head was in her hands as she sobbed violently. "I'm just seven. I don't know how to love both of you! Help me! Please love Daddy, Mother! Please love Daddy. Let me love Daddy! Mother, let me love Daddy! He's my Daddy. Let me love him!" These were the pleas of a seven-year-old. "I hate you, Mother. You make Daddy feel so bad! You make me make Daddy feel so bad. I hate you! You're so mean! I hate your fun! I hate you! You hurt Daddy."

The phrases carrying the highest emotional charge were repeated, as if to let the feelings they described fully wash over Rachel. The confusion of a seven-year-old had emerged from its locked-up state, intact and in its original form. Love and hate for both parents. Through grief and remorse, Rachel emerged calm and clear. Suddenly her history made sense to her. A good beginning.

(My comments:

The immune system has the multiple tasks of recognizing that which is good and that which isn't, then it must "kill" the bad, making the fundamental distinction between self and other, and to keep 'otherness" away. As a child Rachel confused her deepest bodily responses by introjecting her mother's style, and rejecting her father's, despite some deep leanings towards valuing him. Because of the principle: The body follows what is in the heart and mind., this personal extremism and confusion translated into an equally deep confusion at the neuropeptide messenger molecule level manifesting the imbalanced excessive immune responses.

Even Rachel's language and mind-set reflected her core confusion of good and bad, highlighting how highly charged material thoroughly infuses the system. Because the neuropeptide communication network that unites nervous, endocrine, and immune systems goes both ways between what we have called "mind" and "body," we can anticipate that Rachel's cathartic, integrative feeling work will normalize the "inner flow" along the network, and thereby help set the stage for physical healing. Because the neuropeptide system pervades the body with emotional charge and information, integrating and feeling feelings are central to the process of making someone whole. To feel is to heal--not because of a particular school of psychotherapeutic thought says so, but because biology dictates that it is so.)

Esther: Good Analogy

"I'm really doing fine in my life. It's my daughter I'm worried about," announced my new client, Esther, to me as she settled in her chair. Esther explained, "She's 25, newly married and out of the house, but she still calls me every day, with one crisis after another. I feel for her, so I help her out, but I'm not getting to take care of myself much."

"So you're doing fine on your own, though, right?" I asked casually.

"Oh yes, I'm fine, it's my daughter who is the mess."

"What would she do without you?"

"She'd totally fall apart."

"And then what?"

"I don't know. I've never let it get to that point."

"So you're going along, doing fine, and then your daughter comes in with a crisis, and what happens to you?"

"I get all nervous and anxious and involved, and I end up feeling terrible."

"How long does it take for you to go from feeling good to feeling bad?"

"Not long at all. Minutes."

"You have a serious plumbing problem."

"Excuse me?" Esther said, a perplexed look on her face.

"I said you have a serious plumbing problem."

"What on earth could you mean by that?"

"Whenever your daughter pulls the plug in her bathtub, your tub drains out!"

Esther sat quietly, taking in the analogy. "You're right," she said. "That's a serious plumbing problem. How did our plumbing systems get connected like that anyway? I never get to finish my bath this way. Thank you. It's silly, but it's true. Her plumbing belongs in her house, and not in mine."

(Commentary: Sometimes a single analogy hits the spot the way it did for Esther. She went on to implement new boundaries and strategies with her daughter, but all based on the fundamental impact of the initial "plumbing" exchange. Perhaps it's the right-brain nature of analogies and metaphors that makes them so potent.)

Lydia: I'm Not Supposed to Be Here

'I'm not supposed to be here. This is where people die. I can't die here. I need treatment--the strongest chemo and radiation possible.

I want to live. I have to see my grandchildren grow up!" Lydia lay in her bed at hospice, emaciated except for swollen legs and abdomen. Her breathing labored, she poured out her concerns to me.

"Look what I've done to myself! I've smoked for over forty years and have destroyed this beautiful temple God has given me, and now I've got to fight!"

"Isn't it too late?" I asked.

"No, I can't believe that! How can I be at peace knowing what I've done? I must fight so I'll know that I did all I could to save my body. Then I can be at peace."

"Do you think you could ever forgive yourself?" I questioned.

"Maybe, if I fight with all I've got, and get the strongest treatment there is..."

"What about forgiving yourself first?"

"No, that's not possible. If I did that, I'd lose my motivation. I'd just give up."

A long pause followed and we sat in silence together, Lydia's inner turmoil still apparent in her wrinkled brow and restlessness.

"Are you hurting?" I asked.

"Badly. I can't stand it, but I need to fight this thing."

"Lydia, have you ever done something that inadvertently hurt someone else?"

"Yes, why?"

"Who did you hurt?"

"My son."

"How did that feel to you?"

"Oh, horrible, when I realized what I had done. I felt terrible about it."

"Then what happened?"

"He was mad at first, and then he forgave me when he saw how sorry I was." Her eyes moistened with the memory.

"And how did that moment feel to you?"

"Just wonderful. Actually, bittersweet. Even though I hurt him, and that was for real, he still loved me."

"What did that feel like in your body in that moment?"

"It was warm, and I relaxed a lot. We cried together and hugged. It was very warm." A tear leaked out and down Lydia's cheek.

"Lydia, that's the feeling forgiveness creates. It is a good and a powerful healing thing to do for yourself. Couldn't you find it in your heart to forgive yourself now? You certainly are sorry for what you've done, right?"

"Oh, yes."

"And you want to do what is best for your body now, right?"

"Right. But what about the will to fight?" she demanded, already relaxing her shoulders and slowing her breath.

"What about: 'forgive first, then fight like hell?' You've already done so many bad things for your body, isn't it time to do something good for it now?"

"Yes, you have a point. 'Forgive now, and fight like hell too.' Yes, that feels very good." She lay back, mulling over a new approach.

"And think about it, Lydia, if you do such strong chemo and radiation, you might not even be up to forgiving yourself after."

"True. I can't put that off. I am sorry for what I've done." She glanced up, fixed her concentrated gaze on mine, and the tension melted from her face. "Thank you," she whispered.

Jason: From Pornography To Perfection

"I'm into pornography," Jason confessed. "Actually, not the hard stuff. I'm hung up on big tits. I can't get enough of them. I've been collecting pictures for years, and spend hours on the internet. I'm in awe. I swear it's an addiction. I just can't look enough or get enough." So went Jason's opening to session number six, as his hands fidgeted along the edge of his seat. He looked both agitated and excited.

"Close your eyes and say that again," I suggested.

"I just can't look hard enough or get enough," he repeated.

"Stick with the 'I can't get enough,'" I said.

"I just can't get enough. I just can't get enough."

"Get down on the carpet and say that again."

He stretches out in a supine position on the floor, and repeats, "I just can't get enough, I just can't get enough--hey, I'm getting turned on!"

"Now say it without words," I urged him.

He opened and shut his mouth, almost gingerly, like a fish. He gasped and began writing around.

"I want to live. I want to live. Let me live! I want you to live. I can't live with you. Mommy, let me live! It's a strong feeling. I don't understand what I am about to say, but now suddenly I'm thinking of myself in high school and this girl, Fran, whom I had a crush on."

"Talk to her."

"Fran, I have feelings about you I've never had before. I don't know how to be with you. I....I....adore you! I just adore you. You're so melancholy and so pretty. I feel so moved by you. You're so....soulful. I adore you. Thank you for letting me kiss you. I have such deep feelings for you. I want you. God, do I want you! Like nothing ever before. Fran, I worship you!"

"Now go back to Mommy."

"Mommy, I can't be with you. I want to adore you, but I don't. I think you're a woman of heart too, but you just don't live like one." He began to sob. "Let me live, I want to live. Let me live, Mommy. I want to live. I can't live with you." More tears.

Jason started talking about an old memory. "I'm in the car now, going to nursery school with my older brother. I've saw him enter kindergarten so I wanted to go, too. My Mom made special arrangements to let me go with him today. I'm around three or four. My brother is in the front seat with the driver, and I'm in the back seat with a neighbor girl. It's around Christmas time, I guess. We get to school and there are lots of kids. I'm scared. My brother goes away to his class, and I'm left in the large group of kids. I don't know anyone. I'm afraid, but I want to live." He wept as he told the story.

"What happened next?"

"A lady helped me sit at a table and gave me a sprinkle-covered cookie and some milk. She was very nice. I'm scared, but I want to live! I like this. I like all these people. I like the world. Mommy. Let me live! The world is a good place!" Jason began to scream the words, tears pouring out of his eyes.

"I like this, Mommy. Let me live! I want this! I'm scared, but I want this! I can do this!" A small pause. "I'm back with Fran."

"Talk to her again."

"Fran, I adore you. I love adoring you! You are so beautiful, and so gentle. I just adore you! God, what a feeling in my heart right now!

I'm gushing! It's so strong! I've been so scared of the world, of my feelings, but I want to live now! I want to live. Mommy, let me live! I have to live! "More tears and pleading. Jason sobbed quietly for ten minutes, then opened his eyes and looked into mine.

"How're you doing, Jason?"

"Fine, really. Very fine." He rolled into a sitting position. "Wow, how did all that happen? Don't answer. I know. Darn it if it doesn't make sense to me. I feel the connection between my awe and fascination of breasts and the yearning of my heart to be in awe and fascination with my mother or with a woman. I can see now how those memories fit into my obsession. And you know those memories weren't like photographs, either! I was there! I felt the feelings. It's as if this were the origin of something I've been carrying around with me. My mother always played it safe, and did everything in her power to keep my brothers and me from doing anything dangerous. Or anything else for that matter. I begged her to let me go to nursery school. I had to beg her to let me have a bicycle. She was always so afraid to let me go, to let me live. And I was afraid too, and her fear didn't help me. I haven't thought about Fran in a long time. God, I loved her. I felt so overwhelmed by my feelings for her. I never said those things I said today to her. I listened to my fear instead, and that same fear has kept my heart from adoring anybody or anything. I've prevented myself from getting too excited or too involved. And that's not good enough for me anymore. Great, I'm 34—I feel like I've wasted a lot of time living halfheartedly! But I don't care, I'm here now, and I get it. I can't blame my mother for anything anymore."

I listened to Jason's flood of insight. "What about the big breasts?" I asked.

"Big breasts have been my vicarious link to my lust, my passion, my awe. In a weird way big tits have been the measure of my aliveness. I don't feel bad about it at all. I love womens' bodies. The whole Feminine thing. I've been fascinated by breasts ever since I saw a deck of playing cards that had pinups on them, and then later I kept copies of Playboy hidden in my room. Breasts have been the taboo, the danger! What I really want. What I'm really interested in. What I really feel turned on by. The secret mystery that remains covered up! I put all my excitement about living into that. I feel that today I reclaimed that energy for my heart. And that feels right. You know what else? I feel like my eyes are somehow physically more open than before." He glanced around to test the scope of his visual field. "Yep, I see more! This is totally cool!"

Congratulations, Jason.

****

(Comment: Jason tapped into the deductive, associative string of consciousness that contained a "theme" in the form of repeatedly repressed feelings of excitement. Because repression basically doesn't work, his excitement tied into his fascination with pictures of nude women. Yes, it was addictive, in that he couldn't seem to control himself. He felt driven. Once he let himself touch into and follow the vein of feeling fragments, he went all the way back to the "Mother Lode": feelings and fear-based ways of dealing with the world as influenced by his overprotective mother. Not that I had to say any of this psychobabble to him at all. He got it by feeling the child-level of experience within. He naturally shifted between his toddler, teen, and adult frameworks to create what I consider a work of art. I especially like how he physically noticed his eyes more open at the end of the session. What a great metaphor!)

Jake: I am Worthy of Feeling Lousy

"I just feel so nervous, like I've got to keep moving or something bad will happen," Jake proclaimed while sitting in my office.

"Then what happens?" I inquired.

"I end up eating when I'm not hungry, going to movies I don't want to see, drinking alcohol, or arguing with my wife. I end up angry at myself. Then I think after all that I deserve to feel bad."

"What if you didn't do any of those things?"

"I think I'd feel lousy."

"Don't you end up feeling bad anyway?" He thought about it, and didn't reply. "What if you just let yourself feel lousy to begin with?"

"I'd feel bad a lot of the time."

"How do you know that? I'd like to suggest that you try something different! Let yourself feel lousy! See what it's all about!"

"It wouldn't be easy," he declared.

"To feel lousy?"

"To let myself feel lousy."

"Well, are you worth the effort?"

"I think so."

"Letting yourself feel what you really feel is an act of self-love and self-affirmation."

(Ironically, trying to feel good and avoid feeling bad by self-stimulation, distraction, eating, etc. turns out to be exactly what prolong suffering. Also, did you notice how I put feeling lousy in the categories of "effort" and "being worth it?" And he bought the re-frame well, so now instead of "deserving" to feel bad, he's "worthy" of feeling his feelings.)

Tracey: Lazy Be, Worker Bee

"I can't help it, I'm lazy and not motivated. I start things and can't finish them. I have great ideas, I just don't like following through. It isn't easy being in college like this," Tracey, a bright freshman at Smith College, declared. "And my folks are giving me a hard time for goofing off. I got straight A's in high school, you know."

"So what else are you doing in college?" I asked.

"I'm in the Poetry Society, and I hang with my friends a lot."

"So when you're 'lazy,' what's going on inside you?"

"I know I should be doing something, like studying or researching a report, but then I am all the more determined to hang out"

"How do you know you should be doing something besides hanging out?" I asked.

"What do you mean 'how'?"

"What reminds you?"

"I can hear a voice tell me."

"And then the urge to hang out is stronger."

"I know it's laziness, but I can't help it," Tracy acknowledges.

"Well, I think it's a good quality, that you can repeatedly in the face of schedules and deadlines choose the immediacy of a stress-free enjoyment—that's true poetry!" Tracy looked surprised. "I wouldn't be so quick to let go of that quality either," I continued. "To be able to make an island of peace in the midst of busywork is a great gift. Look at your parents. What happened to their poetry? Aren't they hard workers?

When have they ever enjoyed themselves as much as you're enjoying yourself now in college?"

"I'm not there to enjoy myself."

"Says who? Have you ever heard your parents reminisce? You think they look back fondly at all the hard work they've accomplished in their youth? I doubt it! They remember their fun times, and you're just better at it than they ever were!"

"That's absurd. I like to produce and do a good job with my school work. I am a good student, you know."

"Look, you started off by telling me that you like to hang out, so I know you're primarily a poet, and now you're telling me you're a worker too. That's fine, as long as you don't let the work thing get out of hand."

"I won't. But your speech about the virtues of laziness is nuts."

"Sorry, I gave it my best shot."

(Commentary: Tracy's "laziness" was a response to her parents' voice in her mind. She was rebelling against them and their approach. So I just replaced the Parental Admonisher with an adult voice that praised laziness, and she rebelled against that, while at the same time taking in adult support for her poetic nature. That which was originally framed as a failure in her mind [succumbing to laziness] was now replaced with a free choice to "not let work get out of hand." Both her poetic nature and her working nature were affirmed, and I think she felt good about the whole thing. I think she also liked outsmarting her adult therapist.)

Julie: Confuse and Conquer:
Overdrive Pacing to the Rescue

Julie's mother was dying in her Florida retirement town, and Julie blamed herself. "It was my decision to sell the house where Mom and Dad were living, and get them down here to retire." Her voice was dripping with self-recrimination. "If only I hadn't pushed the Florida thing, and all of us moving here!"

The nurturing hospital staff and chaplains each took a turn at cheering her up, using consoling tones and very rational explanations aimed at vindicating Julie. "It wasn't your fault, dear," they'd say. Julie matched each of their incoming soft strokes with verbal self flagellation, growing harsher with each utterance. "It was me! I wanted us to be in 'stress-free' Florida. I took my mother from her New York friends. I pushed it!" Her tone of self-blame didn't waver, except once when she included her husband in her guilt trip. I jumped in.

"What do you mean, my husband and I? Now you're including him and blaming him, too? Aren't you being a little easy on yourself?"

Then she broke! This is what she had wanted to hear! Finally someone outside herself had now spoken in the one voice she could hear. Sobbing, she wailed—"I'm so ugly!," as though she were confessing her true crime. "Look at me!" She pulled out a driver's license and thrust the photo under my nose, as the final documented proof that she was indeed ugly. "Look at me. I used to be so good and so pretty as a little girl. And look at what I've done to my poor mother!"

She couldn't stop weeping. So I escalated my punitive verbal attack. I knew she was a New Yorker, so I slipped into a mild street talk: "Just listen to one more thing here, honey, and tell me honestly--because you've obviously fucked up enough already…" She hung her head in anticipatory shame. (At last, she was thinking, someone who really knows how to punish me!) My voice was pitched, ready to deliver the final blow" "Did you or did you not do what you did for the unity of the family?"

Julie very sheepishly whispered, expecting the final merciful execution, "Yes."

"OK, then," I continued in my prosecutorial tone, "That's beautiful, not ugly! Come on, Julie, you did it for them as much as for yourself. You know they couldn't handle the cold winters up there anymore, and the dirty streets, and the traffic. You wanted them to have what you have down here. You wanted to be near your mother and give her a good thing. That is beautiful, Julie. You're beautiful for doing that for your mother."

We sat silently after that. I imagined smoke spiraling out of Julie's ears as her mental processor ground to a halt. The voice of The Punisher (even louder than her own!) has told her she is beautiful. And it rang true. Suddenly Julie looked up, dazed and wet-cheeked. She looked like she had just snapped out of a bad dream. She quietly thanked me. A calmness had set in, and even as she stood up and wiped her face, she radiated gracefulness and self-acceptance. "Thank you," she whispered again as she walked by me to return to her mother's bedside.

(Commentary: What I did with Julie I call overdrive pacing. It's something I modeled after the overdrive pacing they sometimes do with "run-away hearts" in an Intensive Care Unit. When hearts burst into a rapid, uncontrolled gallop that drugs can't halt, the doctor will sometimes hook up an external pacemaker, and turn it up as fast as necessary to "capture" the natural electrical firing mechanism of the heart, and then gradually slow it down.

Only by capturing and over-driving her own punitive style and tone could an intervention effectively calm Julie down. Any third party listening in would have easily heard the absurdity of my mismatched tone and content. But Julie didn't notice it until it was "too late," and her heart had already slowed down and normalized. Was she confused by what had happened? Yes! Because the shift took place by entering her framework of thinking, and by dismantling it from the inside.

Overdrive pacing works so well with depression! I never cheer-up a depressed person!)

Joseph: Planting a Good Seed

Joseph bemoaned his horrible childhood and the years of abuse he had suffered. His body was riddled with all sorts of physical ailments, including a rare form of lupus, and carried a variety of "emotional problems," which he could name. He believed himself weak and frail by nature.

After listening a while, I burst out with, "God, Joseph, you're a mess!" He was taken aback by my candor, especially the way I used a phrase he might himself use to describe his condition. "Anyone with your history who didn't have a strong constitution would be dead by now!" I went on and on, appealing to Joseph's sense of having been traumatized, and his own logic about it, to reinforce the idea of "strong constitution." I listened attentively, intermittently shaking my head from side to side in a gesture of utter incredulity. "You must have an amazingly strong constitution to have survived all that!"

Soon, even Joseph, whose talk and outlook are overloaded with suffering , doom and gloom, and self-depreciation, made a reference to his strong constitution, and I knew a good seed has been planted.

Robert: Save Me, Save Me Not

"I'm not going to answer your question about whether I'm sui-cidal or not, because I know you have the duty to turn me in if you think I'm going to hurt myself," 23-year-old Robert stated in an agi-tated voice, his sharp sad eyes piercing into mine.

"Well, I won't lie to you. You're right about that. But I still need to know how you really are doing. Robert, it's important. You must tell someone the truth. Let it be me. Let it be now."

"OK, if you're being honest with me, and you want me to be honest with you, then I have one request," he said.

"What?" I asked.

"Do you promise to be honest with me? No professional bullshit?"

"OK, I spare you nothing," I agreed.

"You have been working with me for almost a year now, and you see I haven't really gotten anywhere. I still go into deep depressions, and I hate my life. I can't seem to change."

"What do you want to know from me?" I asked.

"Can I really get better?" he stammered, his look crazed and lost, like a child looking down at a wound that he can't believe is really bleeding.

I thought hard and fast of all the hopeful things I could say, of all the diagnosis-related jargon I could whip out, of the wonders of chemical therapy. It all seemed like one big platitude. Instead I said, "Robert, look at me, because I mean this. I promise you, if I ever come to the conclusion that you're not saveable, I will personally help you find the pills to kill yourself with!"

Robert evidently allowed something in, for he gradually relaxed.

(Commentary: Robert pulled out of his downward spiral, and has since leveled out and progressed in therapy. I have reflected on this interac-tion many times, and remain amazed at how important it was to honestly affirm Robert's right to die in the face of unrelenting misery. I think that helped him as much as my "positive" assessment of him did.)

Jessica: Slight Error

Twenty-seven year old Jessica had always been uncomfortable being a woman, and came to therapy to resolve the matter. She was seeking peace and insight. She had done a lot of work around gender issues in past years of intensive therapy and workshops, long before she came to see me.

"There is one scene from my past which I keep revisiting in therapy, that seems to hold the key," she suggested.

"Oh, what scene is that?" I asked.

She closed her eyes and went inside herself. "I'm not two-years-old. I'm standing at the entrance to our living room. I'm crying. My diaper is hanging at my ankles. My mother sees me naked and says "nasty," an awful expression on her face. I feel so ashamed of my naked-ness and my genitals. This is where I got the idea that it's nasty to be a girl."

"You have gone over this scene in therapy before, right?"

"Yes, many times."

"So you don't mind if we do something a little different here today, do you?" She didn't object. "OK. This time, I'd like you to be your mother, just before little Jessica enters at the doorway. What are you doing?"

"I'm sitting in the living room, reading the paper, no, a maga-zine. I'm taking a little break before my husband comes home from work. Dinner is cooking in the kitchen."

"What's for dinner?" I asked.

"Turkey!"

"Wow, you actually remember that?"

"Yes, I have a great memory."

"OK, now slow the memory down. And apply your memory skills."

"I'm still my mother, right?" she asked, and I nodded.

"OK, I hear a sniffling noise coming from the kitchen, and I look up from my magazine to see little Jessica crying."

"That's it. Slow it down even more. Be very specific in what you see."

"OK, I see tears on Jessica's face. I see her sad little mouth. I look down and see her dirty diaper at her ankles. It's poopy and smelly....."

Suddenly Jessica started laughing hysterically. She jumped up in her chair and fell back into it laughing. Interestingly, her eyes were still closed.

"What's so funny?" I asked, smiling at her infectious outburst.

Jessica opened her eyes and replied, "My mother said 'nasty' about my diaper, not my genitals! My diaper was nasty! And this is the 'pivotal scene' in my life, the one I've based my being so out of sorts as a girl on? This is too absurd!"

(Commentary: Sometimes our memory of an event distorts the event, even though the feelings are valid. If Jessica really had been carrying this scene as "the pivotal scene," this update of her memory made a big difference. I did what I did on a loose hunch.)

The Power of Positive Loving (and Beware of Positive Thinking)

People have the uncanny ability to torture themselves with just about anything--even with something that seems absolutely healthy and good. One young married couple I worked with at the Institute demonstrated this very dramatically.

Susan and Ron were in their mid-twenties, were from the mid-West, and had been married since high school. They stood out as an "adorable" couple. She, frail and thin from advanced liver cancer, modeled a gentle spirit of softness. Ron doted on her lovingly. Having heard about how positive thinking and attitude in general effects health, Ron took it upon himself to keep his wife "up" and motivated. Because he wanted Susan to live, he made sure she would never have a down moment. He kept her busy and motivationally "pumped" from early morning until bed time. But Susan still seemed to be "slipping away." Ron approached me in desperation.

"You have to help Susan!" he pleaded. She's losing it. I'm so afraid she'll just give up on me. You must tell her how important her will to live is, and how she has to fight!" His voice betrayed his own sense of loss of control and panic. Ron was losing it, too. So he wheeled Susan over to my office, and departed with, "You can do it, honey," then he planted a tender kiss on her cheek.

The moment the door closed behind him, Susan burst into tears.

"I cant help it! I feel so overwhelmed! I don't know if I can do this. I don't want to disappoint Ron!" And she sobbed and sobbed, trying to compose herself and apologetically wiping away tears. "I'm trying so hard, but I'm so tired."

I said, "Susan, for just a few moments, let yourself give-up. That's it, just close your eyes and lean back, and give up. See what that feels like."

Susan sighed, reclined on the office sofa, and let go. More tears came, followed by a steady stream of her fears, regrets, yearnings--all pouring out in little stories and memories. She described the kind of funeral she wanted, even down to the type of flowers and music. Of course this sort of talk had been completely taboo with Ron, who wouldn't hear it. The stories gushed at first, then slowed, and finally Susan just rested. Her shoulders had worked their way down from her earlobes, her breathing had evened and deepened.

"I feel really calm right now," she said with mild amazement. "And actually I feel relieved! The pressure in my abdomen is way less, and I can breathe!" Even Susan's facial muscles relaxed into a gentle serenity. "Ron is trying so hard to help me. He's terrified of losing me. I love him so much, but I just can't do it his way any more. I need space to be myself." She settled into a glow of quiet empowerment. Rather than her "negativity" draining her, as Ron had feared, making room for the "down" feelings to surface and be expressed drained them out of her system, creating an inner space for something else--peace. Susan left my office pushing her empty wheelchair back to the main building where Ron anxiously awaited her.

Later he came up to me, jubilant and curious. "What did you do to Susan? She has renewed energy for the first time in weeks! How did you snap her out of her funk?"

"Actually, Ron, I didn't. I let her get into it." And I proceeded to gently confront Ron with the reality of the unhealthy pressure he was unintentionally inflicting on his wife.

"But what about 'positive thinking' and that book, <u>You Don't Have the Luxury of a Negative Thought</u>?" he asked.

"Ron, the power of positive loving is stronger than the power of positive thinking, and loving means embracing Susan even during the down times." He got it, and lightened up. Positive thinking can be a powerful tool. Be careful to use it in a way that goes along with your biology, and not in a way that hinders it.

Cindy: Which Came First?

Cindy had a long history of "environmental hypersensitivity." She became ill from the chemicals in new carpeting, mold in the air, sulfites in foods, hair spray and cologne, and fluorescent lighting. She had come to me because of depression.

"What are you depressed about?" I asked innocently.

"What do you mean, what are you depressed about? I'm depressed about my hypersensitivity!" she declared, in a huff over my naive question.

"I think it's different from what you think. I have been working with a mind/body approach to healing for many years, and this is what I have found to be true, and what I believe is true in your case. Depression is a way to depress, or numb feeling. It's a very viable way for your body to handle hypersensitivity by making it less sensitive. I bet you couldn't handle your condition without being depressed as a biological way to be 'insensitive.'"

"That's ridiculous," she replied. "I can have this hypersensitivity without being depressed!" I raised my eyebrows in a gesture to concede that what she said was a possibility. I think this was the fastest turnaround I ever facilitated.

Charlene: Who's a Dreamer?

Charlene was 46, had bushy red hair and thick glasses. Her husband committed her to a mental hospital when she turned manic and started talking "nonsense." After a stay of three weeks, she "snapped out of it," and has been fine since. We were in session #4, and Charlene brought up that episode, becoming more and more agitated as she spoke.

"I knew I had to act so normal then. I hadn't expected to be taken to the hospital. I don't want that to happen again. So I know I can be normal. But that day, things became very clear. I got a sense of my

Mission. I realized I was the Messenger. All day I could see it more and more clearly. The signs were all there, and no one else could see them. I knew the Dreamers needed me to get them the message. Without it the children were in danger. Their future was at risk. Like science fiction. A woman came out of the drug store and she didn't even know the Dreamers recognized her!"

I interjected, "I get a sense of urgency from what you're saying."

"Of course! Without the Message the children were in danger! But I had to be so normal, when it was screaming at me in everything!"

"A message that was loud and clear to you, no one else noticed?" I demanded.

"Then I saw the frisbee in the store window, and it had a dove on it! I needed that dove to complete the message, so I went in and bought the frisbee. Of course I told the clerk some made-up story about a family picnic, because I couldn't make the real Message digestible. I wanted to though."

"So it was an important message that you had to keep secret?" I asked.

"Because I had to be so normal...."

I broke in again, "All I know, Charlene, is that somewhere in all this there is a good intent for children. How did that good intention get so buried in this complicated story?"

"Yes, I had to get it done so the Dreamers would receive the Message in time to save future children."

"When I think of dreamers, I think of people who are asleep, who are unaware of immediate surroundings. Who would that be in your life?"

"My parents," Charlene replied with on hesitation.

"You saw and knew things they didn't see?" I persevered. Her speech was slowing down, and suddenly her shoulders slumped and her head hung down slightly.

"No one wants to know what my heart sees and knows," she cried. And then she began to sob. Her tears and posture regressed to those of a child. Finally, the feeling that generated all the mania and strange imagery had emerged in its original form.
****

(Comment: Charlene probably did see and know something as a child that

her parents didn't see or know--the love that was missing in the family. Her cryptic tale of needing to get some information to the Dreamers mirrored her sense of urgency to somehow enlighten her parents--something that never happened, thus the anxiety and pain never left her. The childhood feelings mismatched her adult self-image so they came out in a "crazy" form. Reconnecting at the feeling level returned a natural parasympathetic normalizing to her system, even though the mood was melancholy. Better sad and real than manic and unreal, no? Was Charlene's experience a "schizophrenic episode with psychotic features?" Probably, but who cares?)

Ronald: How Did This Happen?

Skinny and frail-looking, 35-year-old Ronald, in overdramatic tones, recounted his long history of physical ailments, and isolationism. He'd never dated, and still lived at home with his widowed mother with whom he had a "close relationship".

"I don't know what I'd do without her," he mused.

"Isn't she getting old? I nudge. "I suppose she can't do without you."

"If I left, she'd face a great void."

"What about when she dies?" I nudge again.

"I would cry. I'd face a great void too. I might be suicidal."

"You know," I mused back at him, "the death of a man's mother makes for a rite of passage that strengthen's the entire system as a separate entity in the world. Maybe you need to go through that passage to get well. Although I warn you: your mother might get ill and even die if you step into it too quickly. She's grown so dependent on you. I'd go so far as to say her life is in your hands." I shrug my shoulders with a resigned sigh, and raise my eyebrows. Ronald looks confused. I go on: "It's up to you, if you get well here, but there is this risk...."

Ronald stammered and raised his open palms to shoulder height.

"How did this happen? How did her life come into my hands? Did God do this? No, that can't be. Did I? No, I don't think so." His brow is crunched with the heaviness of these thoughts. "She did this! What right does she have to put her life in my hands?!" Ronald was outraged. The weaning had begun.

****

(My comment: OK, I tricked him with some slight-of-hand talking. But I still believe what I said: that his wellness somehow hinged on separating psychically from his mother. I just nudged him in an inevitable direction. Why get suicidal later, when he'd given up most of his life already?)

Shelly: Too Shy

"I'm very shy and withdrawn most of the time," complained 23-year-old Cindy quietly.

"How withdrawn are you?"

"When I talk, I freeze up and get self-conscious".

"You're aware of getting self-conscious when you do it?"

"Well, yes."

"So that's 'self-aware' in addition to "self-conscious'".

"I guess".

"Are you feeling self-conscious right now?"

"No, not really."

"So you're aware that you're not self-conscious right now?"

"Right".

"Well, what you have here is a wonderful, wonderful gift".

"How can you say it's a gift? I'm miserable with it!"

"Which part? The self-awareness or the self-consciousness?"

"The self-consciousness! I stumble and freeze and don't know what to say.....It's awful!"

"What a wonderful gift!"

"What are you talking about?"

"Just why aren't you self-conscious right here and right now?"

"I don't know. I guess I came here to talk about myself and that's what I'm doing."

"So you're doing what you came to do and the topic is you. That's what yields self-awareness. In other frameworks, you get self-conscious. It's like an alarm system telling you when you're not doing what you came to do, or when you're not including yourself in the topic enough. What a gift! Where did you get your training?"

"Just natural," she mumbled shyly.

"Now you just need some answers to basic questions and you'll be fine. Like: 'What am I doing here?' and 'How can I include myself in this?' So if you don't know what you're doing someplace, find out! And if you don't know how to include yourself more, find out! And let your self-consciousness make you uncomfortable enough to do that."

****

(My comments: Notice we didn't do any inner child or past-oriented stuff. Totally focused on how to get a grip as an adult, by reframing the 'problem' into workable bits, and actually assigning self-consciousness a new job. In subsequent sessions, Cindy practiced and rehearsed all sorts of new tactics to reinforce this new frame. We eventually did dip into her past to uncover how her shyness served a definite function in her family. Tears over time and childhood lost solidified Cindy's forward movement.)

Client Stories

Life With Feeling Makes Sense

Once deep feelings surface in therapy, and the integrative forces of the body/mind system successfully yield closure to painful imprints, life begins to make sense. Patterns of unconscious behavior, both large and small, suddenly stand out clearly, and you might think: "How could I have been so blind?"

The following are patients' commentaries on their therapy in light of their deep inner work. Notice the sense of being extricated from tightly woven dramas---a liberation that comes not just from knowing about the family or personal history involved, but from knowing the history as it flows forth from feeling. Notice also how repressing feeling at different developmental levels of childhood results in different degrees of suffering. The rule of thumb in this regard: "the earlier the repression, the more widespread the damage to the psyche".

The adage: "change your mind and change your life" contains great wisdom. When your worldview is altered, so is your world. A person riddled with repression inevitably carries a world riddled with struggle. True organismic change comes about by reaching and emptying the recesses of repressed feeling at levels below the conscious mind which then undoes warped higher levels of thought and belief that came about to mask pain. Feeling feelings clears the mind, and unclutters the world.

Jacob: Enough Already

My mother lost her family in WWII, and wanted to have a large family of her own to make up for it. When I was born as the third son, my mother doted on me. She tied my shoes till I was six, anticipated my needs and centered on me with all her might. She often looked at me and thought of my namesake, her dead brother, and heightened her attentiveness to me to avoid her emerging grief. Her care of me was designed to support her repression of her feelings. My job was to make up for her lost family and her feelings of loss. Even her touch of me was primarily to console herself and keep her grief at bay. If I ever got angry at her or grouchy over her smothering ways, she would look so sad, that I'd get a horrible guilty feeling, like my anger, my insistence on having my own needs, was making her sad. So I accepted her doting, at my own expense, and came to just whine whenever she didn't anticipate my needs well enough. I never owned my own needs, or got to responsibly ask for what I wanted. Her need to be needed overrode my need to be myself and grow.

The more I grew, the less I needed her, and the closer she got to her own painful feelings, and the more guilty I felt. "Mommy, let me grow up! I'm sorry about your dead brother, but I can't make up for that! Feel your grief and leave me out of it! Feel your grief and let me in on it! But don't use me to make up for it!" If she had felt her grief one way or the other, we could have been close. There might have been an intimate, yet sad, moment together. "I'm sorry your brother is dead". I could have cried with you.

I always felt I wasn't enough in my relationships with women. The paradox is that when it comes to making up for my mother's lost family I AM NOT ENOUGH, nor am I supposed to be! I can't be enough for you in your life to make your pain go away. It doesn't work that way. I didn't know that till it all came up in therapy. Now I know. I am enough.

Raymond: I Ain't Stupid

I've had this thing my whole life about being stupid and incompetent. Being the youngest of my family, I was always treated as both. "What do you know? You're the baby." "Let your big sister do that". My mother dressed me till I was seven years old, salted my food till my teens. When we shopped for clothes, she'd ask me what I wanted and then proceed to override my choices with her own, reinforcing the fact that I was too stupid to even know what I wanted. (Actually, now I know what she did as stupid parenting! If you give a kid choices, honor them!)

In school I made it my mission to be the smart one. I needed the teachers and my grades to assure me I was smart, because I felt stupid inside. Whenever I didn't know the answer to a teacher's questions, I experienced anxiety attacks. I was afraid the truth of my stupidity would be uncovered. I even cheated on tests to keep up the appearance of being smart.

Many years later, in Med school and then working in the hospital, with its overwhelming amount of technical and medical information, and high level of responsibility, my fear of being discovered as stupid and incompetent haunted me. Long after that period, I continued having nightmares about feeling totally inept with my patients, and getting caught by my supervisor!

In therapy, I've uncovered a major primal scene behind this lifetime of insecurity about my intelligence, a single incident which by itself didn't make for the pattern, but fully exemplified the essence of it. At an emotional level, I'd never progressed beyond that stage.

When I was about two years old my mother gave my older sister an empty perfume bottle. I wanted it, and cried and whined to have it. My sister rightfully refused to turn it over to me. Unfortunately, my mother intervened and made her do so. When she did, she called me "stupid". Before she handed it to me, she secretly filled it with clear water and left off the top, so when I tucked the treasure into my pants pocket, I got myself all wet. I cried again, and when my mother came to change my shorts, she laughed at me. My sister laughed at me too, having successfully wrought her revenge. I felt stupid, bad, isolated, ridiculed, shamed, and of course, furious. Like Scarlet O'Hara, in the movie, Gone With the Wind, vowed never to be hungry again, I resolved, "I'll never be stupid again!"

I misunderstood that at a heart level I wanted to have the special feeling with my mother that her gift of the little bottle to my sister represented. I misunderstood that it's not stupid to not know what you don't know---that I simply didn't know how to ask directly for what I really wanted.

Smart parenting would have addressed the feeling of a little boy not just solve his whining by making his sibling yield the bottle.

"No, I gave this bottle to your sister. Let's find another one for you---or something special just for you." Or offer my sister her choice of something else special so that she could give me the little bottle, and have us both feel good. Many win-win strategies were available.

As a two year old, I let my feelings get me into stupid trouble, but my feelings weren't stupid, nor was my desire for something special

with my mother. I didn't know how to ask for it directly, and she didn't hear it indirectly. So much pain came from so little a thing, and so little effort and sensitivity could have prevented so much.
****

(My comments:

Connectedness in feeling brings an innate sensitivity, an empathy which reflects an emotional intelligence that yields big-picture thinking---- or more global approaches to problems and challenges---a smart thing! Feeling is a smart thing!

Defenses against feeling often do more damage or hurt than the feelings themselves---that's stupid!)

Eva: No More Punishment

I am a beautiful woman and I know it. I'm also very cultured. I speak four languages, and I know my theater and opera. I've been the president of my own international antique business, and frequently travel to Europe. Men swoon over me, and many have proposed marriage to me. I find myself attracted to older, very secure men, who would die to have me as their own. Once I know just how much they value and desire me, I dump them. I seem to get pleasure out of it. I'm still waiting for the man who can take me away from all this.

My sophistication and competence has hidden an inner loneliness, and the magical thinking of a wounded child. In therapy I uncovered it. My father had left the family when I was still an infant, and my strong, independent mother pushed me to succeed and "not need a man". Every time I found an older man who was attracted to me, my child-circuitry kicked in to heighten his desire. Dumping him at the apex of that was my message of anger and revenge to my father. "See what you are missing by not having me? See how it hurts when I leave you?"

Only by reconnecting with my deep pain and sense of loss did I come to neutralize this pattern in my life. I no longer had to punish bad-Daddy, and wait for the good-Daddy to show up. Before therapy, I didn't have a clue about this behavior, and only immediately before therapy did I begin to feel inner emptiness and futility beneath my accomplished sense of self.

Three Stories About My Daughter, Kaia

Behaviorist, B.F. Skinner supposedly raised his daughter with the help of one of his animal conditioning "boxes" to apply his psychological theories of reinforcement to her upbringing. I, being of a different psychological persuasion, took my daughter, Kaia, to inner-work workshops to facilitate her development. She breathed her way through Holotropic Breathwork™ workshops and screamed her way through the sustained acupressure-point holding sessions by the age of eleven--- by her own choice, of course. Through her I've gotten to behold very intimately the reality and depth of emotional imprinting and memory storage. How do I know it was real? Because I had played an active role in the original moments that made up those retrieved memories. Here's three vignettes that stand out:

Kaia--1

"I wanna come! I don't want to have scoliosis!" whined eleven-year old Kaia on hearing I was heading off to a workshop on spinal healing without her. She had just been screened for spinal curvature at school, and the nurse had recommended her for medical follow-up.

"I'm not going for treatment," I reasonably explained to her. "I'm going to learn how to help others."

"I wanna come! Let them help me," she insisted.

"You're too young. And I've already made baby-sitting arrangements for you for the weekend. You'll have fun."

"That's not a good reason. Don't you want what's best for me?" she challenged.

I hesitated.

"Then fuck you if you don't!"

("Fuck you?" She said "fuck you" to me?)

"OK, OK, I'll call and see if they'll let you come." (She said "fuck you" to me?) I wasn't sure if I was upset or proud.

"Thanks, Dad!" And she gave me a big hug.

I called the workshop people and explained Kaia's situation and strong desire. They were open to it.

"Kaia, guess what?" I said, hanging up the phone, with my mouth hanging open. "They said you could come, and they'd treat you."

"Yay!"

So we drove to North Carolina from Atlanta to attend a Body Electronics weekend, where the focus centered on acupressure points along the spine, and the emotional/psychological "issues" related to spinal problems.

A chiropractor in the group confirmed Kaia's scoliosis, and clearly pointed out the lateral curvature of her spine to the rest of us. When it was Kaia's turn for treatment, she lay face down on a massage table, and our instructor positioned four other workshop participants to hold points on her back for an extended time.

As they applied some pressure with fingertips, Kaia flinched and said, "That hurts!"

As time passed, the points, located right in the convex and concave areas of her "faulty" curve, became more painful, and Kaia started crying.

"Why are you hurting me?" she wailed.

"What else hurts you?" asked the facilitator.

"Nothing else hurts me, you jerk!"

"You sound angry".

"Duh!"

"Kaia, what does this pain feel like?"

"It feels like you're pulling me apart!"

"Say that again!"

"It feels like you're pulling me apart!" Her voice quivered.

"Again!"

"It feels like you're pulling me apart!" she sobbed. "Why can't you just live together?" Suddenly she switched into talking about me and her mother, separated and living in different states, both wanting Kaia.

"What about that, Kaia?" asks the facilitator kneeling by her head.

"When I'm with my Mom, I miss my Dad, and he wants me to be with him, and when I'm with him I miss my Mom who wants me too. It's not fair!"

Kaia rolled and squirmed as if to loosen the hold at the contact points. She fumed and shouted. "It's not fair! Get off my back!"

"What do you want?" interrupted the facilitator.

"I want to be supported wherever I am! I want to feel good wherever I am!" she sobbed even deeper.

Her agony continued for almost two hours. Pointholders reported major heat in their fingertips. Sweat saturated Kaia's clothes.

"I deserve to be supported wherever I am, without you two pulling on me. I love you both. I can't decide between you. It's not fair!" She vacillated between tears and anger, often including the pointholders in her complaints. After some silence, her tone softened, with both resignation and acceptance.

"I can't make my parents stop fighting over me. I hate it when they do, even though I know they do it 'cause they each love me." Long silence, and it seemed Kaia had drifted off to sleep.

She roused enough to continue her inner ramblings, more gently, like thinking outloud.

"I do get to live in different parts of the country---on a farm and in the city. I guess I'm lucky in a way. It's not like I don't have both my parents....."

Her points cooled down. Kaia had made peace with an unworkable situation. After lots of hugging and rubbing, she rolled up off the table. Teary-eyed, I embraced her.

"I'm so sorry, Kaia. I didn't know what I was doing to you. Of course I want you to live with me, but I won't put this kind of pressure on you any more."

She went limp, sobbing in my arms. "I won't choose between you and my Mom. I won't!"

"You don't have to. I'm going to have a talk with her, and we'll work something out. It's not up to you. You don't have to choose." Kaia seemed more present somehow. "You know, Kaia, you seem more 'grown up' to me right now.....Actually, you seem taller."

Sure enough, Kaia's spine had straightened, and she stood an inch taller than before! When her highly charged feelings of being pulled apart along with her confusion and anger erupted out of the depths of her spine where she had somehow posited them, her spine straightened. Our resident chiropractor confirmed by exam what our eyes could clearly see.

Four hours later, while Kaia was napping, and the workshop

was taking a break, I got a call from Kaia's mother. She'd tracked us down in North Carolina via some friends.

"Andy, sorry to disturb you, but I felt compelled to call you. I've been doing some serious thinking all day about our situation with Kaia. You know, it's not fair to her, both of us putting pressure on her to live with us. I feel bad about it, and I just can't do it any more. I'm telling you, even if it means she lives with you....I just want to be more supportive. What do you say? Andy? You there?"

I closed my open mouth. "Ah, yes, I'm here. Funny you should bring that up now. I think you're right. We need to take the pressure off of her, whatever we decide."

"Wow, that's very understanding of you. We're not fighting about this?"

"No, we're not. I'll tell you the whole story later."

Kaia--2

When Kaia was thirteen years old, she returned from a year with her mother in New Mexico to live with me. Because of her "miraculous" experience with her scoliosis, she continued her interest in my work, and often chose to come along to workshops. On one such occasion, she joined in with our therapy group of adults as we took turns "working". To my surprise, Kaia volunteered to take her turn in the "hot seat".

"I'm doing this because sometimes I get this funny nervous feeling, and it's uncomfortable and weird."

"Are you noticing it now?"

"A little. Twittery in my head."

"Close you eyes, and be with the feeling. Let it happen..."

She closed her eyes. "I feel like I'm disappearing. I'm scared!"

"We'll keep you safe. Let it happen".

Our body-oriented approach encouraged nonverbal inner exploration along with the verbal, so when Kaia lay down on the carpet, closed her eyes, and began a rapid breathing, I wasn't too alarmed. When she curled up, and started arching and thrusting her head back, I perked up and got concerned. "What's going on here?" I wondered. The group gathered closer to Kaia, who continued writhing and twisting unabashedly, and seemingly uncontrollably. Kaia's neck stiffened and tensed. I felt deep stirrings within myself, and even though I'd facilitated all sorts of intense sessions before, I felt afraid for her safety.

"This looks like birth," I ruminated silently to myself. I had been present at her birth thirteen years ago. Although her mother and I had planned a wonderful Leboyer-style gentle delivery, Kaia's head had gotten stuck in the birth canal---sideways. No amount of pushing or contractions freed her. I remembered my panic when the doctor announced, "the baby's stuck", and called in the anesthesiologist. I remember trembling, and feeling I had to be "strong" for my wife.

Suddenly, in the present, contorted on the floor, as if she'd read my mind, Kaia said, "Don't be scared, Daddy. Don't be scared," and I started balling. I was transported back, remembering just how afraid I had been that day thirteen years ago, that my baby would die. I was crying, my daughter was crying, everyone else was crying.

"My baby," I mumbled outloud. Kaia's head quirked and twitched a few times, and suddenly, there in front of us all, bright red indentations about one to two inches long raised themselves along both her temples--- forcep marks!"

"Don't be afraid, Daddy. I'll be OK," she said, and I was totally balling now, caught up in the deep connectedness of the moment, and in awe over the forces of memory and unrepression before our eyes. Kaia and I were feeling the feelings of a mutually unfinished scene in our lives. Her newborn body/mind system, had registered both my fear and the physical forcep trauma at the same time, and both were now emerging.

Along with repressing my dread over the possible loss of my daughter at her birth, I had also shut down my capacity to fully bond with her. My fears had dissipated and spread out over the years, and had settled in like a thin veil between us. Somehow baby Kaia had carried "Don't be afraid for me, Daddy", unspoken all those years. We embraced and snuggled together, and wept with all the joy and mystery of the original Day One of her life---a scene we relived and integrated together thirteen years later! My baby had been delivered to me safely. By finally feeling the fear this time, I didn't need to be afraid any more. And she didn't need to carry it for me any more, either.

Kaia--3

Kaia, at age 15, visited me in Florida for the summer. After a full, hectic year in high school, she was ready to hit the beaches and blob out for a time. She also wanted to "do a session", to further explore any inner connections about her recurrent bouts with psoriasis. .

We set up a massage table in the center of our living room, and Lynne and I and our son, Eli gathered around her as she lay on her back . We each "plugged" into an acupressure point, and I cranked up some earthy music to help set the mood. Kaia let herself sink into deep feeling. Nothing dramatic, in fact, nothing at all happened for about thirty minutes. In the silence after the tape quit, we continued focusing on Kaia's breathing and expression.

"I'm getting a horrible feeling. I've felt it before, and it scares me. It's taking me way down."

"Go with it, honey. We'll keep you safe. What's the feeling?" we ask, concerned and curious.

"It's in my stomach, and it's making me nauseous."

"Stay with it."

"It's horrible. It sounds weird to say it, but it's like somehow God doesn't want me to be to be born," Kaia cried. "How can I be here if God doesn't want me here?" She moaned gently and started gagging.

I'm stunned. My brain races and I start sweating. "What's going on here? What's she talking about? This is no conscious belief she's ever expressed to me before. What can she possibly mean by this?"

Kaia too broke into a sweat, with wrinkles of dismay quilting her brow.

Then it hit me! "It's me she's talking about!" Unbeknownst to Kaia, before her birth, upon learning of her mother's pregnancy, (we weren't married), I was not pleased. I loved my bachelor's ways, and did not want a child. On my insistence, her mother made an appointment at the local abortion clinic, and only there, in the waiting room, did she burst into tears with, "I can't do this! I'm having this baby!" I reluctantly agreed. But for months before, I actively hadn't wanted the child, and little fetus-Kaia, somehow had picked up on it, and was currently experiencing that memory. For her own healing, and for mine.

"I'm so sorry," I blubbered outloud. "Kaia, that's not God. That's me before you were born. I wanted your mother to have an abortion. I'm so sorry, sweetie."

Little vulnerable tears spilled out of Kaia's eyes.

"I've been carrying this awful feeling my whole life!"

"I was young and stupid. I'm so sorry. I do want you here, and God has always wanted you here. It was just me who didn't want you for a short while---and that was before I met you. I've wanted you ever since."

The deepest nagging doubt about her existence had today come undone, uprooted from the recesses of her fetal imprinted mind. Kaia cried and cried.

"I'm so sorry," I kept stammering.

After a long silence, Kaia sighed. "So God wants me here after all. I'm glad to know that." She sighed again, sat upright on the edge of the table, and blew her nose into a tissue. "I'm glad that's over!" and we hooted with laughter through our tears!

Heinrich: Too Much Pain

I can only begin to tell you the many levels of insight reliving this one scene from my infancy has brought me. I'm not talking "insight" as in intellectual savvy, either. Not only do I now know what's made me feel bad much of my life, I no longer feel driven to ever go there again. It even feels strange to talk about the whole thing now, because it's finally where it belongs--my past!

After many therapy sessions of crying, it finally seemed like I was cried out. I lay on the carpet feeling empty, but not in the good sense. I've learned in therapy to go with my feelings, and sink into them, but this one felt so vague, very much body-sensation-oriented. So I just breathed into it, and before long I entered what's like a 3-D movie. I felt the presence of big people, and feelings of excitement, somehow shrouded with religiousness. It reminded me of the vibe in the Temple where I was Bar-Mitzvahed.

I felt myself very little, cradled in large hands. I felt the total-body relaxed sense of trust as my arms and thighs were strapped to the table top. I heard the deep chanting of a man's voice, and felt swells of pride and tears from my mother sitting nearby. And then the horrible pain! The bearded man had grabbed my penis, swabbed it with something very cold, and then cut into me! I tightened every muscle and strained as my penis burned with agonizing hurt. I couldn't cry or scream hard enough to keep the throbbing ache away. My system went into shock, physically, emotionally, and spiritually, if you will. Waves of pain washed over me. Thoughts like: "I can never feel good again" and "Nobody knows my pain" crashed through my little brain, and my heart contracted to remove me from this horrible place. How could I ever relax in the presence of others again?

"Human contact means unpredictable senseless pain" has been my unspoken motto my whole life, with numerous reinforcements along the way.

I experienced something in that moment of reliving, that I've noticed in other therapy sessions too: inner connections. Other scenes throughout my life, even up to adult life, that I knew were directly connected to this single original scene flashed into my consciousness. I recognized them as not related, but the same as. You could call it "making sense" if you wanted to. I got it, because my body got it.

For me, I flashed on numerous times right after sex with my girlfriends, I'd have that same horrible empty feeling along with "nobody knows my pain". I always thought I was weird like that. I flashed on times people I was close with had gotten angry at me, and how I always seemed to go into "mini-shock" over it, and frequently would say: "That came out of nowhere". Any little shocks resonated that big shock response still locked within me.

I've reflected on my circumcision experience many times since that session. How tragic that we humans can inflict pain so unconsciously that we even celebrate it with feelings like pride or patriotism. How can we be so oblivious to the pain of others? I think about how we wage war, and rationalize all the misery that comes with it. I have a whole different view about senseless pain now that I've felt what it's like to be the innocent object of it.

"For this is the journey that men (and women) make; to find them-selves. If they fail in this, it doesn't matter much else what they find."
---James A. Michener

7

Post Script

Exercises to Help You Lose Your Mind and Come to Your Senses

Stuck in a rut? Can't see your way out of your problems? You could be suffering from Status Quo. A fresh sense of novelty might be what you need to set your mind and heart free. The best solutions arise out of a new perspective outside the boundaries of familiar ways of thinking and perceiving. Remember, if you do the same old thing, expect the same old result. Therefore, do something radically different to help access a new world. Because our brain is wired to keep things "stable" and familiar, it may take some effort to rediscover a new sense of self and possibilities. Try these exercises to explore untested aspects of yourself, which may turn into new inner resources to help you navigate through tough times more successfully.

Children follow their impulses to satisfy their curiosity and experience joy. All it takes for them is parental spoken or unspoken permission. So give yourself permission.

Some of my favorites:

**When I was in college, I wore a blindfold for an entire day without giving anyone an explanation. I maneuvered all around campus using my other senses, and to my delight, friends and even professors helped me get around, and engaged me with both respect and playfulness. I was touched and hugged, and even kissed more than usual!

　　**Once I bought a crate of apples, and distributed them as I proceeded through my appointments. At first I restricted my giving to my friends, but later expanded it to sharing with strangers. Before long, my heart connected with a universal joy of unconditional giving. What a gift for me!

　　**One Spring day, two friends and I set up an open canopy over a central area where two footpaths crossed in a local public park. We decorated it with balloons and crepe paper, and a sign which read: "HUG PAVILION". Our plan: to offer free hugs to passersby. The result: some people purposely went off the path to avoid us, but most came for the hugs. Some cried openly. After about an hour I felt completely intoxicated!

Here are some other suggestions:

* Practice leaving the world: close your eyes and meditate on what it would be like if you could never open them again. Spend several minutes imagining leaving everyone and everything.

* Unplug yourself from your machines for a day, including computer, TV, phone, and if you're bold, lights! Get back to basics--and candlelight.

* Go silent for a day. Wear a sign that says: "In Silence Today". Resist the temptation to explain your actions or make an exception.

* Fast one day a week. Free your energy from the food chain, and rediscover it the next day! Anything you've used food to distract yourself from will naturally surface, and so prepare yourself for an inner encounter. You'll probably be surprised at the energy increase that comes with fasting! How nice to rekindle a simple appreciation of food!

* Locate Yourself: When you're alone, see how it feels to say these things

out loud: "I am what I want," "I am what I think", "I am what I need", "I am what I perceive", "I am what I control", "I am what I feel". Tune into each expression and feel how you resonate with it. With which one do you identify most?

Now say the opposite of each of those statements: "I am not what I want", "I am not what I think", etc. to get a sense of how you are more than any one of those things. Feel how you resonate with each declaration. Add your own. Explore the sense of "I", and challenge it every step of the way.

* Lose Your Mind and Come to Your Senses: spend an hour doing something that would ordinarily take you minutes, such as the act of eating a single piece of fruit, or shampooing a friend's hair, or walking somewhere you would normally drive to.

* Find Your Mind. This is the opposite of the above exercise. Sit quietly and discover the thoughts and images in your mind. Notice them floating through (some at great speed!) like clouds in the sky. Become the observer of the Mind. This practice helps to disengage from your thoughts, so that you have them, and they don't have you.

* Find Your Heart. Sit quietly by yourself and pay attention to your heart, whatever that means to you. Some people actually do this by focusing on the sensations and feelings in their chest area. Let any feelings or images surface and breathe into them. You may find yourself crying, or smiling. Can finding your heart really be that simple? Why not? It's there.

* Plan your own funeral and write your own memorial service. Do you want tears or laughter? What stories would you tell about yourself that highlighted your life?

* Declare a "service-to-others" day. If you're a professional, do pro bono work. Volunteer for a service project, or do one with your kids.

* With a friend or relative, take turns telling each other what makes the other unique, special, and great. Use phrases like: "What's great about

you is......" Do it for two minutes each. Notice, and afterwards share how it feels to be in either the giving or receiving role.

* With a friend or relative, pretend you are meeting at a reunion after a decade of doing exactly what you wanted, and share in the present tense where you are in that future time. Notice the excitement that comes from fulfilling dreams!

* Laugh out loud. I've picked certain "laugh zones" for myself. One is elevators. It started spontaneously one day as I entered a lawyer's office building elevator that was enclosed in mirrors. I was so struck by the multiple images of myself looking so serious that I laughed out loud. Since then elevators have become "laugh zones" for me. The bathroom mirror is another good zone.

* Laugh inside. Cultivate an inner smile, and practice it. Just because.

For ideas on fun breakthroughs, look to Random Acts of Kindness by the Editors of Conari Press, Something Good For a Change by Wavy Gravy, and Gesundheit by Dr. Patch Adams. Enjoy!

Nursing Tales

Along with the many wonderful serious lessons I learned working as a hospital nurse, I have also collected some amusing anecdotes about some of my patients. Below are a few of my favorite stories:

Kid's Perspective

One evening, when I was in nursing school, I was assigned to the med/surg pediatric unit. I went from bed to bed tucking in the little ones for the night. I tiptoed into 3-year-old Beth's darkened room, only to find her on top of the covers, turned at 180 degrees, feet on her pillow. She stared at me silently as I quietly approached. I knelt down, putting my face close to her ear, pointed to the proper place for her head, and whispered, "You need to put your head at that end." Beth looked where I was pointing, wiggled her feet, then turned to me with a little shrug of her shoulders, and whispered back, "I can't. No room."

Nice Try

An outstanding vascular surgeon, Dr. Winchester, was notorious for his lousy bedside manner. He referred to his patients as "The Carotid in 117" or "The Aneurysm in 121." He breezed through his rounds as though he were timing himself. One morning he came to the Peripheral Vascular floor, determined to dispel the rumors about his inhumane behavior. He made a point of spending quality time with a patient by actually sitting on her bed, holding her hand, and talking loudly to her in endearing terms about how she was in good hands and could put her complete faith in him . Occasionally he glanced through the open door to the nurses' station, making sure we were all watching and listening as he demonstrated his sensitivity. As he paraded out of the patient's room with a hearty "Take care now!" he turned to face the group of us who were guffawing as quietly as we could. He looked surprised at our obviously misplaced mirth, and indignantly bellowed, "What's wrong?"

"Nothing is wrong, Doctor," his PA giggled. "It's just that she isn't your patient!"

Oops!

Whenever I worked the night shift in the ICU I made a point of keeping the lights off in order for the patients' circadian rhythms to remain as undisturbed as possible. One midnight I was scheduled to give a rectal suppository to an especially obese woman. I entered her darkened room quietly, whispered what I was going to do, turned her on her side, proceeded to put my gloves on, lubricate the suppository with K-Y jelly, and then began groping my way through many rolling, fatty folds of tissue to insert the medicine. As I was quietly tiptoeing out, my patient whispered to me: "I'm sure you're a good nurse, and I appreciate your being so gentle, considerate, and quiet, but I think you put that suppository in the wrong place."

After many profuse and awkward apologies, I rectified (oops!) the situation by preparing another suppository and inserting it properly. I next wrote up the incident report as matter-of-factly as possible: "Rectal suppository administered vaginally."

As our unit had a policy of posting incident reports for all colleagues to read, I was met for weeks on end in all areas of the hospital by stifled laughs, and comments like: "Don't let Andy deliver that, you never know where he'll put it!"

Mae West is Best

During a brief stint as a home health nurse, I encountered a 93-year-old patient who informed me that he had worked in Vaudeville and in the Ziegfield Follies, and knew greats like Jack Benny and Mae West. I asked him about his most memorable moment from those days.

"Well," he said, perking up, "It was with Mae West. What a woman! She was being coy with me one evening and said something with her sultry voice that I'll never forget:

"My right thigh is Christmas, and my left thigh is New Year's Eve. Why don't you come visit me between the holidays?" I almost died right then and there!

The Venerable Loof Lirpa

To celebrate a certain holiday, my ICU co-workers and I played a trick on a fellow RN, Pamela, who was to take my patients at shift change. While preparing our group report, our unit manager added the make-believe existence of a patient in room 205. His name was Loof Lirpa, venerated Tibetan monk, who had suffered a heart attack in our town while on a world tour. Our unit manager stressed the importance of adhering to Tibetan customs as part of our astute multi-cultural nursing practice. In my private report to Pamela, I not only detailed Mr. Lirpa's made-up drips and EKG strips, but also let her in on the rituals Mr. Lirpa was accustomed to: "The nurse is to enter the monk's room in a respectful manner, chanting his name while carrying a lit candle and wearing a towel draped over her head to cover her hair."

My colleagues and I ceremoniously lit the candle for Pamela, which she placed prayerfully between her hands, then we helped her fold the towel just right over her head, after which she proceeded solemnly to march into the dimly lit room 205, chanting "Loof Lirpa, Loof Lirpa"-- only to be met by a colleague with a flash camera! "Loof Lirpa," of course, is April Fool spelled backwards!

True Blue and Red in the Face

My new patient was a true anomaly--a 35-year-old survivor of a congenital heart defect that had gone undetected in his infancy. So much of his blood had been recirculated without being oxygenated that not only did he suffer from chronic and extreme thrombocytopenia, but he was also very blue. Yes, blue. Not blue-ish, but blue.

I entered his room for the first time, determined to be nonchalant about his coloration, and not mention it. I had to stifle my impulse to stare. He was so--blue! He was watching cartoons on TV as I put the blood pressure cuff on his arm. I peripherally glanced up at the screen to make small talk, and in my nervousness, before I could stop myself, said the very last thing I wanted to come from my lips: "So, do you like the Smurfs?"

I Do, I Do

Grandpa had just died, and his wife of 35 years was in a wheelchair after suffering a stroke. Their two grown children sat in the family-style lounge outside his Hospice room, waiting for the funeral home to come for the body. They cried and laughed together as they reminisced about him, and consoled each other through much kissing and hugging. Grandma said all she had to say with the only two words left her after her stroke: "I do." She communicated mainly with her very expressive voice inflections and hand gestures. How odd for me, as Hospice counselor, to witness such a loving interaction repeatedly punctuated with the words "I do, I do."

The ten-year-old granddaughter, Minerva, returned from the childrens' room carrying a cutout gold leaf bearing the word "grandpa." Her parents and Grandma hugged her. Minerva held up the leaf to show Grandma, who proudly said, "I do, I do."

"Come with me, everybody!" Minerva announced, tugging at her mother's sleeve. Without questioning, all of us, except Grandma, stood up and followed Minerva into the central part of the Hospice entrance way. I helped Grandma along in her wheelchair, which I parked facing the bronze Hospice Tree of Life embossed on the wall. Minerva reached up as high as she could and taped Grandpa's leaf onto one of the branches. She turned to the family with a sense of success, and her parents hugged and thanked her. Grandma said, "I do, I do" with a tear in her eye, and caressed Minerva's hair with gratitude. Grandma then reached up to the leaf, as if to bid a final farewell through a final touch. The leaf, however, was well out of her reach. She said, "I do, I do" as she stretched up. Her son stepped forward to help her connect, but she waved him back with an "I do, I do."

We watched Grandma scoot herself to the edge of her wheelchair, place her left foot on the floor, and make the herculean effort to stand up, all the while saying, "I do, I do." With her right hand stabilizing her weight against the chair, her left foot planted, and her left arm reaching up at a 45-degree angle, Grandma strained upwards. Minerva looked on, holding her breath, until Grandma's fingertip touched the leaf, and her voice cooed "I do, I do," the words drenched with love. We all cried and then laughed out loud as Minerva clapped her hands and cheered, "I do, too!"

Laughter is the Best Medicine

The cardiac alarm bleeped raucously right as I stood next to my patient sleeping on a special air bed in his ICU room. I quickly glanced up at the monitor screen and saw the rapid out-of-control rhythm of ventricular tachycardia, and did what I was trained to do: I thumped my fist once on his chest to stun his vibrating heart into regular rhythm, and when this failed, proceeded to climb onto the bed and initiate chest compressions.

Unfortunately, in my excitement, I had forgotten to flip the emergency CPR rapid-deflation switch on the air mattress, so my chest compressions only served to bounce both me and the patient up and down on the buoyant air-filled surface. He woke up startled by the shock of being pounded, and then broke out into laughter over being bounced up and down by me perched over him in CPR position. I, too, burst into laughter, and in the next moment his heart converted to normal sinus rhythm. Laughter really is the best medicine!

Nursery School Notes:
Out of the Mouths of Babes

Besides the serious, often catastrophic conclusions kids arrive at through their primitive processing of information, they also use their unique and uncluttered view of reality to come up with chucklers. Years ago when I worked as a daycare teacher of two-year-olds, I often posted on the bulletin board near my classroom door a funny anecdote about the day for parents to read. Here are some of the gems:

1.   "Can I have another cookie?" Beth pleaded after snack.
        "No, Beth, it has too much sugar," I reasonably replied.
        "But that's OK," Beth said, "I like too much sugar."

2.   This morning when Beth discovered that one of our fish died over the weekend, her first response was: "Who shot it?" Later she asked me if I was going to take it to the doctor.

3.   When I announced it was time to put books away and climb onto their cots for naptime, Beth reluctantly slammed her book shut, and loudly said, "Damn!"

4.   The children came up with two new words today: "caterpus" for caterpillar, and "greencumber" for cucumber. I like their words better.

5.   "Andy, Thomas called me "B.J.," whined B.J.
        "But that's your name," I replied.
        "Oh."

6.   Chrissie cried when Mark and Beth said they were going to turn her into a donkey. "I want to be a person!" she wailed.

7.   When B.J. hit Beth and made her cry, I stooped down in front of him, placed my hands on his shoulders, and said, "Hey, what did you do that for?" and he said:
        "For Beth."

8.   At naptime one Spring day, while I was rubbing his back, Brian looked up at me and whispered, "Santa Claus is watching us right now."

9.   Today, while we were getting ready to go out, Brian exclaimed: "Teachers don't go to the bathroom, do they?"

10.   After I got Courtney started on the swing, she turned to me and said, "Thanks, Andy. You push decent."

11.   In the course of playing house in grown-up sized high heels, Whitney stumbled, bumped her head, and promptly got a cold towel to put on it. She was still holding it to her forehead when some other kids, all dressed up as her children, approached her chattering loudly.
    "Be quiet, Mama has a headache," Whitney said.

12.   "Look, Jessica. It's pouring outside!" I pointed out.
    "It's raining too," she replied.
13.   "What are some things we need to do to take care of our new books?" I asked in group time today.
    "Don't fight over them," someone offered.
    "Don't step on them," suggested someone else. A long pause ensued.
    "Don't throw up on them," Donna added.

14.   "Hey, Andy! Guess what!? My mother's almost pregnant!"

15.   Jay was working with the Donald Duck puzzle, and looking down at the white of Donald's lower torso and legs under the sailor shirt. He exclaimed: "Panty hose!"

16.   After the toilet was flushed once, Matthew tried it again and found it didn't work no matter how much he jiggled the handle. He turned to me and said, "No batteries?"

17.   This morning we were playing "riddles," and I said, "I am tall and strong. I live outside and I have leaves on me. What am I?"
    With no hesitation Eric said, "The Jolly Green Giant!"

18.   Out of the clear blue, just before naptime, Brian asked me, "How do giraffes take a bath?"

"They just jump in a lake, I guess," I said.

After a pause he said, "Won't the sharks get 'em?" And then later, "Do dinosaurs take a bath in the lake too?"

"Sure," I said.

"Why don't their Mommies give them a bath?"

19.   The other morning when I went to wake Kaia up, I said, "Brrr, it's still Winter outside, Kaia," and she replied, snuggling and half-sleepily, "Well, it's still Spring under these blankets."

20.   Today while we were at the table, one of the kids suddenly came out with this: "My Mommy was in a race car with her old man."

21.   Somehow at the lunch table we started talking about our Mommies and Daddies' names. When it was Bart's turn he said his Mommy's name was Barbara.

"What's your Daddy's name?" I asked.

He thought a bit and then said, "Coach."

22.   Just before naptime Brian said, "Andy, do you know what I wish?"

"What?"

"I wish we had a lot of bathrooms so we didn't have to learn how to share."

23.   "Dena, would you please tuck all the chairs in?" I requested after lunch cleanup.

"But they're not wearing any shirts!"

24.   "How old are you, David?" I asked him today, his birthday.

"I'll be three in a minute."

25.   "That's a pretty dress, Kaia," Eric said when he first saw her in it this morning. He paused a while, and then said very seriously, "Are you married?"

26.   We talked about Halloween today, and Chrissie said, "I'm gonna' be a 'dancerina'!"

27.   "You don't know where I live," mocked Susan.
"Well, where do you live?"
"I live where there's a dog and a cat."

28.   Just as we got out the door on our way to the playground, I heard Brian say out loud, "Hey, it's a little bit cold and a little bit warm out here!"

29.   I saw Chrissie crying and rubbing her knee and asked her, "Did you fall over?" and she said through her tears, "No, I fell down!"

30.   "Brian, when you rinse the toothpaste out of your mouth, don't swallow the water," I said.
"If I do, am I out of the game?"

31.   Today at lunch Beth picked up on today's grouptime theme of emotions, by going from person to person and declaring "happy face" or "sad face."
"Sarah has a happy face. Seth has a happy face. Jason has a sad face." When she came to B.J. who was well into his tomato soup, she said, "You have a dirty face!"

32.   At naptime I told Beth not to hang her hand over the edge of her cot, and she said, "It will get lost?"

33.   "When my Daddy spanks me," Beth declared, "he makes my fanny come on fire."

34.   "We're going outside. Go get your shoes," I told B.J. In dashing to his cubby across the room, he tripped over his flapping sock, rolled over twice, and landed right on top of his shoes. After a long pause, his eyes moistened with tears, he looked up at me, and started laughing!

35.   In her full Halloween outfit, and carrying her pumpkin candy

container, Beth looked into the mirror and said, "The mirror has a jack-o-lantern too!"

36.   Working on the theme of temperature, I asked the kids at grouptime, "What do you feel like when the sun is shining and you have a sweater on?"

"HOT!" everyone chorused.

"OK, what about if you were out in the rain with no clothes on? What would you feel like?" I asked.

"Like singing!" shouted Matthew.

Suggested Reading:
Book Reviews

In no particular order:

1. <u>The Power of the Mind to Heal</u>, by Joan Borysenko, PhD & Miroslav Borysenko, PhD. Hay House, Inc., Carson, California, 1994.

Two powerhouse medical scientists pull together a very humanistic documentation of the healing power of the mind from such diverse areas as medical case studies, near death experiences, and ancient Buddhist scriptures. They intersperse their book with little "exercises" to make the didactic material real in the moment. The Borysenko's, although very highly professionally credentialed, are far from "stuffy intellectuals", and serve up a very palatable fare in this eclectic work.

2. <u>Anatomy of an Illness</u>, by Normin Cousins. Bantam Books. New York, New York, 1979.

This is the classic work of the Father of the modern Mind/Body movement, and remains as inspiring and valid as ever. Norman Cousins healed himself of a degenerative autoimmune condition through the power of laughter, and formulated a viable mind/body paradigm in the process.

3. <u>Bodymind</u>, by Ken Dychtwald. GP Putnam's Sons, New York, New York. 1977.

Presents a conceptual "map" of the body areas and what aspects of personality or emotion can be read in them. Synthesizes the work of Reich, Feldenkrais, and Fritz Perls to suggest body-oriented ways of facilitating therapy and personal development. The feel of this book is dated to the Human Potential Movement of the Sixties and Seventies.

4. <u>Mind /Body Medicine: How to Use Your Mind for Better Health</u>, edited by Daniel Goleman, PhD and Joel Gurin. Consumer Reports Books, Yonkers, New York, 1993.

Only Consumer Reports could come up with such a factual non-woo-woo approach to the mind/body connection, and still include a topic like: "Mindfulness Meditation: Health Benefits of an Ancient Buddhist Practice"! The more I look through this volume of diverse articles, the more I like its solid presentation and comprehensive introduction to a potentially difficult topic. I also appreciate the Resources section in the back, which helps a person network with groups and organizations, provides professional references for researchers or serious students of the mind/body connection, as well as publication referrals for the lay reader. Good job, Consumer Reports!

5. <u>Your Body Speaks Its Mind</u>, by Stanley Keleman. Center Press, Berkeley, California, 1975.

What is the body's perspective on itself, the existence of others, its being in the world? This is not only the goal of Keleman's book, it is also its style: a stream-of-consciousness, on-going body metaphor that reads like the diary of an aboriginal native in downtown Manhattan. Kelemen's point, made from within his Reichian/bioenergetics background, is that the body is in fact aboriginal, meaning it was there first. He speaks of the human being as primarily "embodied", yet in a way that stands far afield from Skinner's behavioristic view as well as from the Romantic perspective of the body as "Primitive Child". The body, says Keleman, is a matter of "embodied consciousness", which speaks of an innate intelligence, sensitivity, and even relatedness----a natural "mind", if you will, that is more unity-oriented than divisive, more connected than separate. Thus the way to "read" or reach the mind is through the embodied messages of the body. Keleman, primarily a psychotherapist rather than a bodyworker, focuses on soma to reach psyche.

This book follows an unrelenting course in its body-as-metaphor style, but basically it's a good trip.

6. <u>The Healing Brain: Breakthrough Discoveries About How the Brain Keeps Us Healthy,</u> by Robert Ornstein and David Sobel. Simon and Schuster, New York, New York, 1987.

I'm not sure why this isn't an exciting book. The authors present the basic psychoneuroimmunology information in a very readable fashion, and even have funny chapter titles like, "Pressure: Social and Blood", or "Great Expectations: On the Reduction of Warts and the Enlargement of Breasts", or "Friends Can Be Good Medicine". Brain research studies described from firsthand experience along with all the other science presented in the book are flawless and plentiful. All the right ingredients are present. The book is decently organized, notated, and indexed. It's just not inspiring. I give it a "B-".

7. The Healer Within: the New Medicine of Mind and Body, by Steven Locke, MD, and Douglas Colligan. New American Library, New York, New York, 1986.

I continue to tap the vast resources of this book, chock full of great "hard science" about the mind-body connection and fanciful story-telling. The depths of linkage between physical science at the level of cellular activity and the experiential level of experience makes for a noble effort indeed! Like looking at the vast array of stars at night with text-book in hand, we are still primarily left with a sense of mystery and awe. Dr. Locke's explanations of immune function and its response to various emotional stimuli, seem to speak the language of science, but remain rooted in this heartland of wonder. Also contains a full 50 pages of appendices, networking resources, glossary, and index.

8. Living Beyond Limits: New Hope and Help for Facing Life-Threatening Illness, by David Spiegel, M.D. Times Books, New York, New York, 1993.

Dr. Spiegel is responsible for the definitive study which showed that social connectedness has a statistically significant, positive influence on health, and conversely, how social isolation contributes to medical deterioration.

He followed a group of women with recurrent breast cancer for years, dividing them into two groups, one which received "normal" cancer treatment, and the other which in addition to such treatment, participated in on-going support meetings. The women who engaged in support groups did dramatically better in every single measurement criterium, not only in subjectively reporting a sense of better adjustment, coping, and self-satisfaction, but in the medical areas as well. For starters, they lived an average of twice as long as those in the control group!

Interestingly, and perhaps surprisingly, Dr. Spiegel takes scathing issue with the imagery work of the Simontons, and the mind-body work of Dr. Bernie Siegel. He maintains that the health-yielding benefits of mind-body interventions have to do with the social connected-ness they bring, and nothing else. He refers to the Simonton's imagery work as misdirected "wish-it-away" therapy, and chides Dr. Siegel for fostering a notion that cancer patients have somehow caused their dis-ease by having the wrong attitude. He also refers to the dangers of what he calls the "prison of positive thinking", in which a subtle form of isolationism gets implanted with the ideas that ill people need to keep their spirits up and think only good thoughts, or that they can some-how control the disease by maintaining the right mental outlook. In a period of facing a serious illness which is isolating enough in itself, "the last thing you need is to feel bad about feeling bad," he says.

Living Beyond Limits also covers important strategies for pain control, dealing with doctors, and fortifying family ties.

9. Heart of the Mind: Engaging Your Inner Power to Change with Neuro-Linguistic Programming, by Connirae Andreas, PhD, and Steve Andreas, MA. Real People Press, Moab, Utah. 1989.

When you interact with a child who is "misbehaving", first stop the dangerous aspects of the behavior, and then tune in to the positive intentions of the unwanted behavior with phrases like: "What is it you want?" or "What are you trying to do?". Then agree with the positive intention of the behavior, and pursue "How else could you accomplish that?" All that instead of just saying "no" and bumming the kid out. In other words, it's possible to get the same outcome with a positively worded approach that makes the child feel good.

Same thing is true, say the authors, about approaching hot top-ics like weight loss, healing shame and guilt, making decisions, and engaging the body's natural ability to heal.

10-14. The Primal Revolution; Simon & Shuster; New York, New York; 1972.
Primal Man: the New Consciousness; Thomas Y. Crowell Co.;New York, New York;1975.
Imprints: the Lifelong Effects of the Birth Experience; Coward-McCann, Inc.; New York, New York, 1983.
The New Primal Scream: Primal Therapy 20 Years On; Enterprise Pub-lishing, Inc.; Wilmington, Delaware; 1991.

<u>Why You Get Sick; How You Get Well</u>; Dove Books; West Hollywood, California; 1996. All by Dr. Arthur Janov.

Let me sing the praises of Dr. Janov and the significance of his work in bringing deep feeling therapy to the forefront of psychological inquiry. I've been following his career for over 25 years now. He single-handedly spearheaded the movement in therapy in the early Seventies away from the prevalent strict rational and behavioral approaches, and into the depths of the Unconscious, and has since systematically worked to quantify his findings with rigorous scientific research. Janov has done more to justify and verify the humanistic, feeling approach to wellness than even Carl Rogers, the creator of Client-Centered Therapy, who also insisted on studious research and follow-through in his work.

Janov has taken the brilliance of the Freudian notion that illness results from suppressed childhood trauma, and married it with the latest in neurobiological discovery, to develope a practical methodology (Primal Therapy) for not only understanding the underlying causes of diseases, but also for getting well.

Janov is the only one of merit in the field of psychology who has had the balls to speak of cure when it comes to mental illness. His approach and results are convincing and compelling.

15 & 16. <u>Super Immunity;</u> by Dr. Paul Pearsall; Ballentine Books; New York, New York; 1987. and <u>The Heart's Code: Tapping the Wisdom and Power of Our Heart Energy;</u> by Paul Pearsall; Broadway Books; New York, New York; 1998.

Dr. Pearsall bases his definition of super immunity ("the capacity to think and feel in ways that can protect us from disease,") on the Rational-Emotive Therapy (RET) premise that thought precedes behavior determines feelings. He then makes an elaborate case that this chain of command, with thought at its front, influences health. "Immune cells behave as confidently and effectively as the thinker in which the cells circulate," he states.

He goes on to introduce the concept of Hot and Cold personality traits (loosely drawn from Oriental Medicine) to provide a structure within which to facilitate the inner harmony of opposites necessary to bring about health. The restoration of immune function can be brought about through a peaceful focus on balance, and does not require more aggressively-based Pacman-type imagery work a la the Simontons, he maintains.

Hot and Cold aside, the importance of this book, in my opinion, lies in its recognition of happiness as central to wellness, and unhappiness as a prelude to disease---hinting at the central role of the heart in the disease and healing process.

A great seguay to Dr. Pearsall's latest book, <u>The Heart's Code</u>, in which he finally makes the leap beyond his brain's desperate attempts to make way for the heart, and steps into the realm of the heart itself. Enough of Hot and Cold already!

In <u>The Heart's Code</u>, Dr. Pearsall continues his eloquent infusion of good science into matters of heart and mind. This book reads like a revelation, in which Dr. Pearsall orchestrates the latest findings in the cellular world of neurotransmitters, peptides, and receptors to harmonize with his own inner vision and experience of the energy and importance of the heart in healing. His personal growth from Super Immunity days shows dramatically, like the difference between a stock market report and a poetry reading.

17. <u>The Relaxation Response</u>; by Dr. Herbert Benson; William Morrow; New York, New York; 1975.

A classic from 1975 in which Dr. Benson makes a compelling case for meditation as an antidote to stress. He shows evidence via oxygen consumption tests, brainwave activity, and blood lactate levels (associated with anxiety) that meditation is more beneficial than sleep.

His book marks the first time, I believe, that the term "altered states of consciousness" is presented in medical literature, as something not only innate to human capacity, but also something beneficial. I like how Dr. Benson presents this healthy alteration of consciousness as an outcropping from what is primarily a body response. Which makes Dr. Benson an important cohort in the mind-body movement.

18. <u>The Transparent Self</u>; by Sidney Jourard; Divan Nostrand Co., Inc.; Princeton, New Jersey; 1964.

I met Sidney Jourard at a meeting of the American Ontoanalytic Association in Miami when I was nineteen, about five years after <u>The</u>

<u>Transpersonal Self</u> came out. I found his openness, down-to-earth style, and personal availability to embody the themes of this book: That people who are healthy are those who have found ways of life that permit them to be and express their selves with purpose, meaning, hope, and interest; that it is necessary for health to let oneself be known through full disclosure to another; that healthy people pay attention to the "all is not well" signals, and then change what they are doing, including their ways of behaving with others; that inauthentic being lies not only at the root of mental illness, but also at the root of the susceptibility to physical illness; that self-disclosure is a potent antidote to repression and self-isolation, which are killers. "Man can attain to healthy and fuller functioning only insofar as he gain courage to be himself among others...."

He talks about physical illness in terms of an "altruistic suicide" or bodily destruction for the preservation of unhealthy roles and social systems, and goes so far as to call psychiatric illness only one step up from that: as rebelling against inauthenticity without courage or effectiveness. Radical.

The <u>Transparent Self</u> also includes interesting research on self-disclosure, which may or may not be dated. It concludes that men do not disclose as much about themselves as women do. That women disclose more to mother and female friend than they do to father or boyfriend. That white males disclose minimally to both parents and male friend, and even less to female friend. That Black men disclose most to mother, and almost nothing to father, male friend, or woman friend. That men basically go relatively unknown till they marry. Hence, men's higher and earlier mortality rates, no doubt.

19. <u>The Joy of Feeling: Bodymind Acupressure</u>; by Iona M. Teeguarden; Japan Publications, Inc.; New York, New York; 1984.

Seeing as how I also incorporate acupressure into my psychotherapy work, how could I not buy a book with a title like this? I'm curious whenever I discover a therapist who blends bodywork with inner work.

Teeguarden's premise of: "unblock the body, unlock the psyche" goes hand in hand with her faith in a natural unfolding of health from the inside out, lifting any external restrictions or impositions on the feeling life, such as "should's" or "have-to's" or "nice". She deals with the psychological and physical armoring of the person by focusing on un-blocking emotions.

Most of this book intricately weaves an Oriental Medicine ap-proach with all its yin-yang, hot-cold, energy-flow terminology into a neo-Reichian approach to psychotherapy via many case studies. The mythological style with which she relates organ systems to feelings, high-lights, in my opinion, the right-brain way body-mind reality really works. Unless you're interested in the specific mappings of Oriental medicine, though, this book is not for you.

20. <u>Space, Time, and Medicine</u>; by Dr. Larry Dossey; New Science Li-brary; Boston, Massachusetts; 1982.

Dr. Dossey maintains that the crisis in healthcare today prima-rily reflects the crisis of perception we are collectively encountering. He elucidates how Medicine too, needs to break through the restrictive Newtonian assumptions, and is just beginning to embrace newer para-digms of healing which draw on reality as viewed through Relativity Theory and Quantum Physics. He talks about the paradox of holo-grams in which the part contains the whole, and of non-local mind, and of how the human factors of social support play into a new model for medicine. This is a great "heady" piece which challenges and dis-mantles the baseline suppositions of space and time rooted in Cartesian thinking. Very philosophical, and yet somehow strangely inspiring.

21. <u>Depression and the Body: the Biological Basis of Faith and Reality</u>; by Alexander Lowen; Penguin Books; New York, New York; 1972.

This book presents a view and treatment of depression via Bioen-ergetics, Lowen's body-oriented psychotherapy offshoot of Wilhelm Reich's work. Because depression stands as a symptom of a severance with reality, the aim of treatment is to reconnect with reality. But which beliefs or perceptions are "real"? The only common and abiding reality is bodily reality. Therefore mental illness as distinct from bodily reality is an illusion. The marriage of body and mind happen through emo-tion. Emotional illness (rather than "mental" illness) results when emo-tions don't move, and remain frozen within the body. Therefore, recon-necting with reality means getting in touch with and moving emotion.

A depressed person is someone unable to respond to life, like a violin with flaccid strings. Tighten the strings and the instrument comes alive with a renewed ability to respond. Help a person reconnect with emotion at a bodily level, and he's no longer depressed.

Lowen grounds his treatments in the body, using bioenergetic techniques to focus on the movement of emotion. This might involve pressing the feet into the handle of a tennis racket until they hurt as a way of re-awakening feeling in a numbed-out area. It might involve swinging arms and pounding pillows till anger flows. Or reaching with arms outstretched for love and pleasure until grief flows forth in tears and sobs. Only when the past gets mechanically unlocked from the body can the entire system become un-depressed and return to the naturally joyous reality of engaging the world with biological pleasure. Lowen defines "faith" as that quality of experience that associates contact with the world with pleasure and satisfaction, and makes reaching out for it an act of positive expectation.

The premise of Bioenergetics that the body is the person, absolutely radicalizes the treatment, and makes this book fascinating.

22. Man's Search for Meaning; by Viktor Frankl; Washington Square Press; New York, New York; 1959.

> *"He who has a why to live can bear almost any how."*
> ---Frederick Nietsche

The first half of this book presents an autobiographical glimpse into the horrific world of Nazi deathcamps, and provides a bridge to Frankl's development of his existential approach to therapy. A personal account alone of how he survived his concentration camp ordeals would have sufficed as an invaluable contribution to the annals of psychological survivorship, but Logotherapy, a distillation out of personal suffering, a systematic approach to facilitating wellness for others, truly leaves to humanity a psychotherapeutic treasure.

Frankl coined the phrase "the will to meaning" to refer to the guiding force in a human life that supersedes defense mechanisms or even traumas in determining personal and inner outcomes. Mental health, more than a system of homeostasis which decries discharge of tension at any cost, is imbibed with "noodynamics": "a polar field of tension when one pole is represented by a meaning that is to be fulfilled, and the other pole by the man who has to fulfill it." Just as an architect who wants to strengthen a weak arch will increase the load which is laid upon it to firm the parts together, "so if therapists wish to foster their patients' mental health, they should not be afraid to create a sound amount of tension through a reorientation toward the meaning of life." Grappling with and finding a personal meaning in life fosters mental health. And conversely, an existential vacuum of meaninglessness lies at the root of most problems.

Logotherapy is not so retrospective and introspective as therapy is wont to be, but rather looks to the meaning yet to be fulfilled--a future-oriented approach. Although the "meaning of life" sounds abstract, Frankl uses it more to denote the situational "best move". As in: there's no universal, single "best move" in chess, but there is one in each moment in each particular game. Frankl keeps his work grounded with moving personal stories. His writing brims over with great dignity and indelible authority.

23. The Path of Least Resistance; by Robert Fritz; Fawcett Columbine; New York, New York; 1984.

Although this book purports to have more to do with the process of creativity than with therapy, I have found it and Fritz' Technologies for Creating™ valuable therapeutic tools.

Fritz brilliantly makes the distinction between psychological or physiological tension, which debilitate a person, and structural tension, which empowers him. His model of the creative orientation makes for a forward-moving system fueled by meaningful desire and clever choices. Funny, how a paradigm of creativity, so un-therapy-like, so closely mirrors Victor Frankl's Logotherapy and his idea of will-to-meaning!

Therapy is not, after all, only about going backwards to heal the past. It must also address the course of life and the choices made to direct that course.

24. Frogs Into Princes; by Richard Bandler and John Grinder; Real People Press; Moab, Utah; 1985.

Using the fact that the subconscious mind makes no distinction between inner and outer realities and is thereby open to suggestions,

Neurolinguistic Programming (NLP) sets about facilitating life changes directly and quickly. Bandler and Grinder distilled out of their astute evaluation and analysis of the interactive work of great therapists such as Fritz Perls, Milton Erickson, and Virginia Satir, an elegant methodology for accessing and effecting the inner world of the subconscious. This book introduces the notion of adjusting to the client's communication style via accessing cues, anchoring and reframing techniques. Although I value their work and intent, and agree that transformation doesn't have to take a long time, I believe they shortchange the role of emotions in the process.

25. <u>The Psychobiology of Mind Body Healing</u>: <u>New Concepts of Therapeutic Hypnosis</u>; by Ernest L. Rossi, Ph.D.; W.W. Norton & Co., Inc.; New York, New York; 1986.

Talk about scholarly and sophisticated! Listen to this: *"Wondering absentmindedly about a personal problem during the comfort of a psycho-biological ultradian rest period is a natural way of accessing and spontaneously reframing and resolving the state-bound encoding of the problem."* So many new concepts! Such consciousness about the smallest of cues from the client! Such subtle interventions!

Rossi not only outlines his own hypnotherapeutic approach to therapy, giving rationale in the most sophisticated of scientific understandings, he also includes for the reader a comprehensive history of the development of neurobiology that lead up to his understanding and use of it.

Rossi played right-hand man to master practitioner, Milton Erickson, for years, and in this work proves himself masterful in his own right. If you don't mind tackling sentences like the italicized one above, and are willing to learn the specific lingo involved, this book is supreme in its field.

26. <u>Intoxicated By My Illness, and Other Writings on Life and Death</u>; by Anatole Broyard; Clarkston Potter Publishers; New York, New York; 1992.

Listen to this: *"A critical illness is like a great permission, an authorization or absolving. It's all right for a threatened man to be romantic, even crazy, if he feels like it. All your life you think you have to hold back your craziness, but when you're sick you can let it out in all its garish colors.*"

Or this: "*When my friends heard I had cancer, they found me surprisingly cheerful and talked about my courage. But it has nothing to do with courage, at least not for me. As far as I can tell, it's a question of desire. I'm filled with desire--to live, to write, to do everything. Desire itself is a kind of immortality. While I've always had trouble concentrating, I now feel as concentrated as a diamond or a microchip.*"

I loved reading this work, and sighed a deep sigh of satisfaction upon turning the last page. Highly recommended.

27. <u>Facing the Wolf: Inside the Process of Deep Feeling Therapy</u>; by Theresa Sheppard Alexander; Plume Books; New York, New York; 1996.

I cried my way through this account of Alexander's own therapy, especially about two things. Firstly, over the pain she experienced as a little girl at the hand of her viciously cruel father, and secondly, over the kind, right-on, helpful, and conscious treatment of her therapist. Covering eight sessions of a Primal Therapy Intensive from both the client's and therapist's point of view, in narrative form, Alexander does more to convey the essence and even technique of deep feeling therapy than any didactic material on the topic. I frequently share this book with my clients.

28. <u>Molecules of Emotion: Why You Feel the Way You Feel</u>; by Candace Pert, Ph.D.; Scribner; New York, New York; 1997.

Candace Pert wins the MVP award in her league of mind/body inquiry. In this book she not only outlines in easy lay terminology, the latest scientific understanding of the neuropeptide system as carrier of emotional messages throughout the body, but also provides a very personal history of key discoveries in the field. Lord knows, she was there! She also paints a macabre picture of scientific politics involved in the development of her Peptide T treatment for AIDS.

Meeting Ms. Pert in 1996 absolutely confirmed my status as her fan. If you get to hear her lecture, go for it.

29. <u>Trances People Live: Healing Approaches in Quantum Psychology</u>; by Stephen Wolinsky, Ph.D., with Margaret O. Ryan; The Bramble Company; Falls Village, Connecticut; 1991.

This book is both scholarly in weaving theoretical structures with which to understand the idea of trance, and practical in providing many examples and guided instructions for moving beyond the trance state.

Wolinsky devotes at least a chapter to each of his identified trance states, including age regression, time distortion, sensory distortion, and hypnotic dreaming. He introduces the idea of hypnotic identity formation (a sense of self formed out of early-life suggestions), and how these inevitably develope into conflicting polar opposites.

Wolinsky "treats" the trance state, not by overlaying it with a "therapeutic" trance, as in classical hypnotherapy, but rather by exposing the roots of a trance state to the light of awareness, and thereby diminishing its unconscious hold. He encourages the client to "do" the trance as she becomes aware of it, thus rendering it an act of will. He teaches a subtle approach of nonresistance.

I especially enjoyed the creativity of Wolinsky's techniques like: stripping gears, zigzagging, and using archetypes---as outlined in his Appendices.

30. Primal Connections: How Our Experiences From Conception to Birth Influence Our Emotions, Behavior, and Health; by Elizabeth Noble; Fireside Book; New York, New York; 1993.

This book actually focuses on accessing and making conscious, imprints from prenatal times. Noble believes that problems in the present remain rooted in the system as long as they lay shrouded in a cloud of amnesia surrounding original trauma. Bodily sensations from conception to birth build the foundation of feelings, relationship styles, and sense of self, and therefore have a primary unconscious effect on our present lives.

Noble highlights the mythological, almost cosmic, nature of perinatal imagery and thought, and spells out the sort of open-ended therapeutic environment required to facilitate inner access at these levels of awareness. Expect anything! The prebirth world has its own reality and rules! Primal Connections brims over with case studies and enough actual therapy scenarios to paint a credible picture of an incredible reality.

31. Kids Learn From the Inside Out: How to Enhance the Human Matrix; by Shirley L. Randolph, MA, PT, and Margot C. Heiniger, MA, OTR; Legendary Publishing Company; Boise, Idaho; 1994.

All problems stem from missed or thwarted stages of development. Therefore, treatment for conditions like ADD, emotional disturbance, and, well, just about everything, relies on methods to redo those retarded elements of nervous system functioning.

The authors elucidate normal human development in the formative years of childhood, showing how growth truly begins from inner impulses, and progresses outward into contact functions. They point out the key areas where this process can be derailed, and offer the basic tools to remedy and facilitate the nervous system getting back on track. It comes down to three basic treatments: skin brushing, cross-crawl repatterning, and corrective re-parenting. Too simple? Maybe that basic.

32. At the Speed of Life: A New Approach to Personal Change Through Body-Centered Therapy; by Gay Hendricks, Ph.D, and Kathlyn Hendricks, Ph.D.; Bantam Books; New York, New York; 1993.

"Essence seeks to get us to the light, but persona seeks only to get us through the night." Thus do the authors make the distinction between the authentic and less-than-authentic identities we embody at different times. They say body-centered therapy solves the central split between thinking and feeling by facilitating a direct reconnection with bodily reality.

They offer the five fundamental principles behind body-centered therapy: Presencing ("be with it"), Magnification ("feel it more"), Breathing ("breathe into it"), Moving ("let your body express itself"), and Communication ("tell the truth"), and numerous techniques to facilitate them.

I love the Hendricks' working definitions of the truth ("something you can't argue about") and love ("being happy in the same space as someone or something else"). Kudos to the Hendricks' for making their art so reachable and teachable.

33. Beliefs: Pathways to Health & Well-being; by Robert Dilts, Tim Hallbom, and Suzi Smith; Metamorphous Press; Portland, Oregon;

1990.

Some beliefs set the stage for a desired outcome to show up without effort. Limiting beliefs interfere with what we want. Therefore, changing our belief structure can make a significant difference to our reality.

The authors present a Neurolinguistic Programming (NLP) methodology for reworking the sequencing of inner pictures and voices that go into approaching desired results, from those "strategies" which derail the process to those that bring it to fruition. NLP provides the tools for successfully reframing our inner reality in a way to elicit positive body-responses and neutralize negative beliefs.

Robert Dilts believes his intensive NLP/belief-work with his mother after her grim diagnosis of metastasized cancer, helped her get well. Very hopeful for someone looking for tools. This book demonstrates why people use the word "magic" to describe NLP.

34. The Healthy Mind, Healthy Body Handbook; by David S. Sobel, M.D., & Robert Ornstein, Ph.D.; Los Altos, California; 1996.

Very much a handbook and not a text book, and therefore somewhat "fluff and puff" in terms of depth, it still contains helpful, practical ways to improve the mental and emotional quality of life. Includes strategies for improved time management, sleeping better, surviving trauma, dealing with chronic pain, and features an excellent section on coping with doctors, medical testing, medications, and surgery.

35. Cure By Crying; How to Cure Your Own Depression, Nervousness, Headaches, Violent Temper, Insomnia, Marital Problems, Addictions by Uncovering Your Repressed Memories; by Thomas A. Stone; Cure By Crying Incorporated, Des Moines, Iowa; 1995.

Although I find this work to be simplistic, I like it. Stone's basic premise is "the more you cry, the more you get well". Of course that doesn't seem to hold true for some depressives who need more than the act of crying to integrate feelings and move forward in life, but still stands up well as a working principle for deep-feeling therapy. I like Stone's strong sense that it doesn't really require professional intervention to get going on the path of feeling and healing. This puts the responsibility and possibility of inner processing and getting well square in the lap of the average person.

Stone calls his work "The Therapy", and makes a strong case for do-it-yourself. His raw enthusiasm and confidence in the process, along with an easy writing style made for a book I was glad to engage and sorry to finish.

36. Any book by Dr. Bernie Siegel, M.D.

I have a client who'd been to see Bernie Siegel. She said, "Bernie gave me his home phone number and told me to call him any time". That's the kind of humanism and availability that comes through Dr. Siegel's writing.

He gets an A+ on bedside manner. Reading his books is like having him hold your hand as he tells you inspiring stories, helps you find humor in seemingly bleak times, and helps you kickstart a healthy rebellious attitude. He is a serious reminder of spirit's innate ability to claim healing no matter what the medical outcome.

37. A General Theory of Love; by Thomas Lewis, M.D., Fari Amini, M.D., and Richard Lannon, M.D.; Random House; New York; 2000.

Reading A General Theory of Love is like watching a Discovery Channel special on animal intelligence while sipping champagne in a hot tub: soothing and sensual, insightful and affirming--all the while maintaining a strong scientific edge.

The authors, three psychiatrists, wax poetic in their earnest investigation into the origin, function, and even the future of love. Taking our current understanding of the brain to its zenith, they espouse a unifying theory to explain how love truly sits at the center of what it means to be a human.

Beginning with a novel concept they call limbic resonance to explain our innate capacity as mammals to perceive the inner reality of others, they proceed to solidify their case for the evolutionary triumph of feelings, and ultimately of love itself.

This book overflows with magic, both in fluency of style and in its mixture of hard fact and poetic vision. To receive scientific verification of the heart's pivotal place in nature's design, validates our humanness in a way that relaxes and energizes, and fills the reader with, OK, I'll say it: divinity.

38. Provocative Therapy; by Frank Farrelly and Jeff Brandsma; Meta Publications; Capitola, CA; 1974.

Provocative Therapy carries on in the tradition of Carl Whitaker and Fritz Perls, two therapists who used challenging encounters and thwarting the expectations of their clients as their main therapeutic tools. The authors present a manual to teach therapists how to use an irreverent, provocative attitude as a means of establishing a therapeutic rapport and to promote positive change. With this approach, the therapist establishes himself as your loving brother who can insult you and get away with it because you know he's on your side and is just telling it like it is.

Although the authors describe developing their approach as if it would revolutionize therapy itself, the truth is it never caught on at all, and the book remains no more than an obscure gem from the Seventies. Too bad--it makes sense and has heart.

Two Other Resources:

1. For the definitive word on meditation/getting in touch inside, contact Elan Vital at PO Box 6130, Malibu, CA 90264-6130, or call: (818) 889-1193, or visit http://ElanVital.org, on the web, or e-mail to info@elanvital.org

2. For the definitive word on raw food cuisine, alternative healing, and healthy spa living, contact The Hippocrates Health Institute at 1443 Palmdale Court, West Palm Beach, Florida 33411, or call (561) 471-8876, or visit http://www.hippocratesinst.com on the web.

Post Script
True to the Core: Way to Be!

Returning to the Heart

Returning to the heart stands as the omega point of all human endeavors. Heart, with its innate love and wisdom, is where our home is, and where we yearn to be. Knowing and feeling the heart is what makes us happy. Living outside the heart's domain is what keeps us confused and unhappy. How blessed are the things that stir the heart to wake up and live. How special are the people and events that initiate or quicken our journey. This is what therapy is all about, and what makes it a sacred event when it succeeds.

My Quickening

When I was seventeen, living the life of an ordinary high school kid, the shutters to my heart unexpectedly fluttered open allowing new light and fresh air to stream in. At first it hurt. I sputtered around, gasping and blinking, as I adjusted to a whole new atmosphere.

Her name was Joyce--tall, slender, with porcelain skin and long blond hair parted in the middle. She gazed with quiet melancholy eyes, and spoke with a deep yearning in her voice.

"I imagine myself sitting under a large shade tree in the summer, with the man I love, resting his head in my lap," she cooed to our marathon encounter group in the woods of West Virginia, and I sighed with longing. Ten of us shared many hours sitting in a circle, spilling our adolescent guts out to each other for an entire weekend. We struggled, squirmed, complained and confronted. We held up mirrors, and pushed each other to new horizons of self-revealing. During a break, as I wearily stumbled outside into the autumn day, to regroup and commune with the crisp cool air and bright sunlight, I saw Joyce sitting about twenty yards away on the sloping lawn in front of the conference house. The breeze tousled her hair as her lithe figure rested tranquilly against the patchwork of reds, yellows, and browns. What a goddess! My cells burst with poetry and desire at the sight of her! Suddenly a pure white kitten ambled from behind the rustic lodge, and through the tall grass over to Joyce, climbing onto her lap. Too timid to approach, I just watched, entranced. The perfection and sweet torture of that moment burned themselves into my nervous system. I was a teenager in love--and more.

During that weekend I confessed to the group that I was feeling sad and isolated. I cried unabashedly in Joyce's arms, and she held me gently and lovingly. Later when we were alone, I lay frozen in my bed as she sat at my side. I didn't have a clue about what to do with all my new feelings. I didn't know how to continue reaching out. I wish my heart could have done its own talking, because in my inept hands, my voice became mute.

"Do you have a crush on me?" she asked me, and I mumbled a reply, "Yes, I guess I do".

"Do you want to kiss me?" she asked, and I said, "Yes, I do". When our lips touched, my soul danced and my mind froze. "You have a cold nose", I stammered. Then awkward silence. Why didn't I add, "I love your cold nose!"? Why didn't I shout: "Joyce, I adore you. I love your sad ways, and feel so moved by you!" Why didn't I say, "I've never wanted to be close to someone the way I want to be close with you now"? Why didn't I swear, "Joyce, I'd give anything to have your nose touch my cheek every day for the rest of my life!"? That weekend my heart jump-started into motion a lifelong quest to feel forever what I felt with Joyce those days in Harper's Ferry. And, of course, to get it right. To drink deeply from the cup of life's nectar without choking.

Reading this you might think: "Dumbass, why didn't you just love her?" or "Hey, all teenagers are awkward. Don't be so hard on yourself". But that's exactly my point: by the time I was seventeen I was so emotionally clogged, out of touch, and lost, that I missed out on the greatest treasure of life! As much as I remember my Harper's Ferry experience as an awakening, I also tag it as a reminder of how emotionally absent I've been in my life; something I've been healing personally and advocating professionally ever since. I am claiming that treasure now not only because it makes life more rewarding and fulfilling, but because life without it makes no sense.

I know now that what I want is within me. Despite my foolish teenage wistfulness, I know it isn't or wasn't Joyce. When I met her years later, she had grown more cynical and jaded about finding true love in the world. What I had witnessed in her during the earlier days was the yearning of my own heart for recovery and salvation. I still crave that. I want the heart's passion that sits beyond the appearances and duality of the world. I want the truth of enduring beauty. And I still want to rest in its arms.

We're All Double Agents

I've learned that I myself am a double-agent, sincerely striving for truth and heart, and yet constantly coping with a strong tendency to get lost. I've learned that even my own mind distorts the brand-new-ness of the present moment, and thereby betrays me. I've learned to face the degree to which I inhibit self-expression for the sake of "safety" and the status quo.

I hate to admit it, but I am a liar, weaving all sorts of stories, rationalizations, and excuses to restrain my innate freedom to love deeply. In my fear, I even believe that those tales I think of as my "history", somehow preordain what can and cannot happen in the present. Unchecked and unchallenged, I perpetuate the lie of history. So I need help. I need a love that reaches past my stories, through my history, to touch my core. I need the courage and wisdom to challenge and destroy my unreal system. This is where therapy comes in. This is why I do therapy. They say: "Put the wettest logs closest to the fire", and that's me. I do therapy because it's my way of participating in liberation. It helps me stay conscious and focused on what is real. Besides, when I give help I get help. It's a good system. I recommend it. I'm grateful for it.

History Is a Lie

History as memory or story may be a lie, but to deny the effects of history on the moment, to presume a purely anti-historical stance in therapy perpetuates an even greater lie: that freedom from limitation can somehow be attained by intellect or will alone. Not so. Freedom, as an experience (and not a circumstance), emerges in the wake of the heart's awakening, and springs forth out of our innate capacity to feel deeply. Feeling remains securely anchored as the cornerstone of loving and being loved, and therefore exists at the core of freedom itself.

Only feeling has the power to overthrow the dominance of past imprints, present restrictions and future imaginings--- thereby saving us from dissipating our lives into unreal virtual worlds. Congruence with the heart serves to overthrow the stranglehold of false appearances and our built-in capacity to lie and be fooled. Only the heart has the ability to navigate us through the dualistic, paradoxical human condition, keeping us both fully engaged and totally detached simultaneously, and loving throughout. Jesus' edict to "be in the world but not of it" points the way to the heart's true code of being.

Commitment to a true-to-the-core life, calls for relentless truth-telling, on-going risk-taking, a deliberate confrontation of self-righteous moralism, a willingness to confess our lies, and a healthy tolerance for chaos, the absurd, and the unknown. That's the brave new world I crave and choose to inhabit. I hereby relegate everything I already know to take a back seat to that which I can discover anew, and for that I need to hold onto my heart for dear life. My heart---compass, guide, signpost, frontier, and destination all in one.

> ## "Thank God for the heart! Without it what would my life be? Where would my sanity be?"
> -------Maharaji

Every day, I'm given a second chance to be real, to heal woundedness, to confess my untruths, to pursue whatever stirs the depths within me, and ultimately to enjoy my life as both co-creator and creature. Beyond the therapy setting, true-to-the-core is a way of being. It compels me to extend my need to be and know what's real, to being real with you. Please help me by being real with me. Help me by being true to the core in your own life, in your own way. I need you to be feeling and conscious, not in the unequal way I needed my parents when I was a child, but rather as an equal, walking beside you.

As double-agents in life, both conscious and unconscious, we have the capacity to both advance and distract each other from the central process of being in touch. Entranced within our mind's virtual reality, we cast forth limiting assumptions and judgements like fishing nets, binding each other by our concepts. Only our love and depth of feeling can cut us free. In the most challenging times when neither of us is in touch with anything transcendent, wise, or kind, our raw pledge to true-to-the-core living may be all we have to pull us through. When each of us alone might falter and sink, our combined commitment to, and faith in, the process of becoming, builds a life raft for us all. I love Maharaji's comment: "The power to touch a heart--never underestimate that!" I find this salvation in my marriage, in therapy, in groups.

I do therapy to help me stay in touch, and to fill my world with feeling people. People who have integrated their pain, thus fully aware of the healing power of deep feeling, provide deeply satisfying company. They become part of the real world that honors the original human impetus to trust and love. Their world is governed by ease, positive effort, and natural optimism-- a place that's safe and exciting, and never boring.

Heart is the Alpha and Omega

Heart is the alpha and omega of the human journey. Body-oriented deep feeling therapy lends a helping hand to set the heart back on the grand track of life. When the veil of pain is lifted, the heart in all its strength and vulnerability, finds its own rhythm, and comes into its own innate power to know and convey light, and to enjoy life. One by one, day by day, we inch closer to the core, touching our realness with a growing depth of feeling and understanding. We need each other to get real and get well. When we touch each other with honest feeling beyond all pain, we make a perfect life even better, and do humanity proud. Let's do humanity proud.

Index

A

B

C

O

Obsessive Compulsive Disorder 96
orgasm 135, 136, 141
 sleep and 136
overdrive pacing 252

P

pain 15, 19, 33, 37, 99–101, 101, 103, 109, 129, 132
 mind-grids and 111
pedophilia 139
Perls, Fritz 41, 96, 120, 163, 291, 301
personal mythology 146
personality types 23, 60
Pert, Candace 39, 60, 302
Piaget, Jean 108
placebo 59
polar reconciliation system 199
pornography 137, 247
positive thinking 26, 34, 257
premature ejaculation 141
prenatal life 303
Primal Therapy 12, 148
projection 67
psychoneuroimmunology 14, 36, 73–75, 185, 187
psychosemantics 21
psychosomatic 60
puberty 118

Q

quantum physics 158

R

reaction formation 67
receptor sites 26
 opiate 99
recovery 97, 153, 200–201
regression 12, 31, 108–117, 114
Reich, Wilhelm 39, 291
relationship 55
 money and 218
relaxation response 296
repression 18, 28, 31, 33, 76, 80, 132, 264
resistance 96, 190

About Andy Bernay-Roman

Andy Bernay-Roman, LMHC, NCC, MS, RN, LMT works in his private psychotherapy practice in South Florida and lives with his therapist/artist wife, Lynne, and their Golden Retriever, Daisy, and two cats, Luce´ and Spunky.

Andy was a 1995 nominee for the Norman Cousins Award and the Rosalyn Carter Caregiver Award.

Andy has also served since 1990 as Head of the Psychological Support Department of the world-renowned Hippocrates Health Institute in West Palm Beach, Florida, where he treats individuals, couples, and families, and also facilitates the on-going support group.

Feedback and Contact

Deep Feeling, Deep Healing is Andy's first book, and he welcomes your feedback. You can contact him by e-mail at deepfeeling1@aol.com, and visit his website at:
http://members.aol.com/deepfeeling1.

Ordering More Books

If you would like to order more copies of Deep Feeling, Deep Healing, call Bookmasters, Inc. at: 1-800-247-6553 twenty-four hours a day, or order online at: http://www.atlasbooks.com/marktplc/00572.htm

1-800-247-6553